SCANDAL AND AFTEREFFECT

SCANDAL AND AFTEREFFECT

Blanchot and France since 1930

STEVEN UNGAR

UNIVERSITY OF MINNESOTA PRESS

Minneapolis / London

Copyright 1995 by the Regents of the University of Minnesota

Parts of chapter 1 were previously published in "The Appeal of History: Reading Gi-
rard on Camus," *Helios* 17 (1990): 45–55, reprinted by permission of *Helios* and Texas
Tech University Press; and in "Against Forgetting: Notes on Revision and the Writing of
History," *Diacritics* 22, no. 2 (Summer 1992): 62–69, reprinted by permission of The
Johns Hopkins University Press. Parts of chapter 2 were previously published in "Scan-
dal and Aftereffect: Martin Heidegger in France," *South Central Review* 13, no. 2 (Sum-
mer 1989): 19–31, reprinted with permission of *South Central Review*. Parts of chapter
3 were previously published in "Drôle d'histoire, drôle de récit: lire *L'Arrêt de mort*,"
Seminari Pasquali di analisi testuale 6. "L'Arrêt de mort" (Pisa: ETS Editrice, 1991).
Parts of chapters 5 and 6 were previously published in "Paulhan before Blanchot: From
Terror to Letters between the Wars," *Studies in Twentieth Century Literature* 10, no. 1
(Fall 1985): 69–80, reprinted with permission of *Studies in Twentieth Century Litera-
ture;* and in "Review of Jean-Paul Aron, *Les Modernes*," *MLN* 102 (1987): 948–53,
reprinted by permission of The Johns Hopkins University Press. Parts of chapter 7
have been previously published in "Gray Zones: Vichy, Maurice Blanchot, and the
Problem of Aftereffect," in Nancy Harrowitz, ed., *Tainted Greatness: Anti-Semitism,
Prejudice, and Cultural Heroes* (Philadelphia: Temple University Press, 1994), reprinted
by permission of Temple University Press.

Published by the University of Minnesota Press
111 Third Avenue South, Suite 290, Minneapolis, MN 55401–2520
Printed in the United States of America on acid-free paper

Library of Congress Cataloging-in-Publication Data
Ungar, Steven, 1945–
    Scandal and aftereffect : Blanchot and France since 1930 / Steven Ungar.
        p.   cm.
    Includes bibliographical references and indexes.
    ISBN 0-8166-2526-3. — ISBN 0-8166-2527-1 (pbk.)
    1. France—Intellectual life—20th century.   2. Scandals—Political aspects—
France.   3. Literature and history—France.   4. Politics and literature—France.
5. France—Politics and government—1914–1940—Philosophy.   6. Vichy
(France)—Politics and government—Philosophy.   I. Title.
DC33.7.U49   1995
944.08—dc20   94-22019

The University of Minnesota is an equal-opportunity educator and employer.

I dedicate this book to the past and for the future: to the memory of my father's mother, Anna Löwy Ungar (1893–1944), who died at Auschwitz, and to my daughters, Anna and Shira.

There is an unavoidable necessity for the reader, who naturally comes to the essay from without, to refrain at first and for a long time from perceiving and interpreting the facts of the case in terms of the reticent domain that is the source of what has to be thought. For the author himself, however, there remains the pressing need of speaking each time in the language most opportune for each of the various stations on his way.

Martin Heidegger,
"The Origin of the Work of Art"

One must in the end speak dangerously and dangerously remain silent in the very act of breaking this silence.

Maurice Blanchot
(from a letter to Emmanuel Lévinas,
February 11, 1980)

Contents

~

Acknowledgments

One never ends with the book one starts to write because one never writes alone. Friends and colleagues have challenged me through their efforts and words to see things I never foresaw when this project first took shape. At the University of Iowa, I thank my colleagues (past and present) Dudley Andrew, Paul Greenough, Allan Megill, Kathleen Newman, Herman Rapaport, Rosemarie Scullion, Alan Spitzer, and Abby Zanger for dialogue and critique. Since 1985, Jay Semel and Lorna Olson have provided me with space at the University of Iowa Center for Advanced Studies in an environment uniquely conducive to long-term research. Out on the road from Los Angeles to New Haven and from Urbino to Warwick, I had the good fortune to be invited by Dana Polan, Gayatri Spivak, Lynn Higgins, Hugh Silverman, Francesco Casetti, Shuhsi Kao, Geoffrey Waite, Philip Lewis, Ora Avni, Sydney Lévy, Carolyn Gill, Mary Lydon, and Christopher Thompson to present sections of this work in progress. The readings of my manuscript that Denis Hollier, Ann Smock, and Réda Bensmaïa provided to the University of Minnesota Press were incisive and illuminating. In Paris, conversations with Margaret and Daniel Wronecki kept things in a French perspective. Closer to home, I recall with gratitude the participation of Ben Attias, Joanna Klink, Laura Rozen, and Elliott Van Skike in my 1990 seminar on Bataille and Blanchot. Thanks also to David Eick for help under pressure with the index.

Finally, I am grateful for the support that Walter Strauss, Michael Holland, and Tom Conley provided at critical stages along the way. As with so much else that I value in my life, Robin Ungar has accompanied this project from start to finish.

This book contains revisions of previously published materials. Sections of chapter 1 appeared in *Helios* 17 (1990) and *Diacritics* 22, no. 2 (Summer 1992). A shorter version of chapter 2 appeared in *South Central Review* 13, no. 2 (1989) and in Richard J. Golsan, ed., *Fascism, Aesthetics, and Culture: Commitments and Controversies* (Hanover: University of New England Press, 1992). A section of chapter 3 appeared under the title "Drôle d'histoire, drôle de récit: lire *L'Arrêt de mort*," in *Seminari Pasquali di analisi testuale, no. 6 "L'Arrêt de mort"* (Pisa: ETS Editrice, 1991). Chapters 5 and 6 contain passages from articles published in *Studies in Twentieth-Century Literature* 10, no. 1 (Fall 1985) and *MLN* 102 (1987). A section of chapter 7 is taken from "Gray Zones: Vichy, Maurice Blanchot, and the Problem of Aftereffect," in Nancy Harrowitz, ed., *Tainted Greatness: Anti-Semitism, Prejudice, and Cultural Heroes* (Philadelphia: Temple University Press, 1994). I thank the editors of these journals and presses for permission to reprint. The introduction, most of chapters 1, 3, 5, and 7 and all of chapter 4 appear here in print for the first time.

~

Introduction

Out of the Past

Every presentation of history must begin with awakening; in
fact, it should deal with nothing else.
Walter Benjamin, *Konvolut N*

This book explores a convergence over the past twenty years of shared concerns among literary scholars and historians studying France since 1930. It is
organized around a series of questions about the recent past and the assumptions on which inquiry into it is grounded. In what ways—how, when,
and where—does historical understanding evolve when the memory of a
specific period is contested among those who lived it and those whose access
to it depends on the accounts of others? How, in particular, has it come to
pass that received accounts of interwar and wartime France have been increasingly open to question? Does this belated questioning always pertain?
Or is it peculiar to the period under study and, by extension, to a genealogy
of contemporary historical experience? These questions do not amount to
an argument, nor do they set forth on their own anything like a working hypothesis. In listing them, I mean to identify a range of issues and problems
related to the study of France since 1930 as debated by a growing minority of
critics, theorists, and interdisciplinary types from the déclassé historian to
the historically minded litterateur.[1]

This convergence is discernible first in a change of object that has cast the 1930s as a Janus-like decade, both conclusion of the Third Republic and prologue to the 1940–44 Etat Français at Vichy. This model of concurrent decline and renewal remains contested. Some have trivialized it as contingent and relative, a result of passing time rather than anything more marked and meaningful. Others have seen instead the consequence of a turn (return?) to history associated with "new historicisms" and poststructuralist theorizings of culture. Yet others have linked it to counterhistories that revise received accounts with a polemical intent.[2] My sense when I began this project about ten years ago was that the convergence of literary and historical concerns I had identified was more than a surface effect, that it was directed less toward the data on which historical understanding was produced than toward assumptions of method, object, and ambition on which this production was grounded. To state this somewhat differently, the change in question was less a matter of adjusting or correcting details than something more emphatic on the order of what historians of science have referred to as epistemological breaks (Gaston Bachelard) and paradigm shifts (Thomas S. Kuhn).

Scandal and Aftereffect grew from my overlapping interests in literary theory, France between 1930 and 1945, and the writing of history. The project took a decidedly critical turn once I realized the extent to which issues of writing history—invariably also issues of writing in history—entered fully into the encounter between post-Enlightenment reason and the emergent technologies of communication analyzed by Jean-François Lyotard in conjunction with a postmodern condition of knowledge.[3] Yet postmodernity should not be equated with a specific moment, doctrine, or set of practices. Following Lyotard, I take it less as a finite duration than as a condition—a *pre*condition, really—imposed by a shift from understanding measured as a concern for achieving adequate representation toward a looser appreciation of how signs circulate as images and simulacra. What, then, are the implications of this shift for inquiry into the recent past that it supplements? If modernity is inevitably no longer what it was twenty, thirty, or fifty years ago, what might it mean to think (rethink?) a determinate duration within it at a moment when the concerns of literary critics and theorists of culture converge increasingly with those of historians? What, finally, might this rethinking mean if and when it undermined received understanding by disclosing modernity as something other than what it had been taken to be?

Anton Kaes began *From Hitler to Heimat: The Return of History as Film* by asserting that the further the past receded, the closer it became because images "fixed on celluloid, stored in archives, and reproduced thousands of times" kept the past ever present.[4] Focusing on Hans Jürgen Syberberg's *Hitler, ein Film aus Deutschland* (distributed in the United States as *Our Hitler*) and Edgar Reitz's *Heimat, Eine Chronik in Elf Teilen* (Heimat, a chronicle in eleven parts), Kaes linked words and images associated with National Socialism and the figure of Adolf Hitler to structures of affective response that, during the 1970s, kept Germany's wartime past highly charged and present. Like Kaes, Saul Friedländer discerned in a slippage between discourse about Nazism and Nazism itself the strong ambivalence surrounding desire and its exorcism in an overlaying of past and present that bordered on the pathological: "Nazism has disappeared, but the obsession it represents for the contemporary imagination—as well as the birth of a new discourse that ceaselessly elaborates and reinterprets it—necessarily confronts us with this ultimate question: Is such attention fixed on the past a gratuitous reverie, the attraction of spectacle, exorcism, or the result of a need to understand; or is it, again, and still, an expression of profound fears and, on the part of some, mute yearnings as well?"[5]

Concerning France since 1930, the memory of Vichy has haunted those who have sought to explore it from the perspective of national identity and inscribed within longer durations from the Dreyfus affair to the present. The persistence of debate in the press and mass media also illustrates the extent to which irresolution has maintained words and images surrounding Vichy visible within a public sphere, as an object of scandal all the more forceful in light of efforts to suppress it. This effect of scandal is enhanced by an untimeliness that projects back onto the 1930s and 1940s what Régine Robin has called "the phantasms and anxiety of today."[6] As I have come to see them, these phantasms and anxiety are, in turn, tied to attitudes of normalized difference such as ethnicity, race, and religion, and through them to deep-seated prejudices that these attitudes sustain. Exploring specific instances of normalized difference illuminates the evolving forms of prejudice that are all too often neglected when prejudice is reduced to a dehistoricized constant. It is no coincidence that debate surrounding Vichy has come to focus increasingly on figures of scandal (Klaus Barbie, René Bousquet, Paul Touvier) allegedly linked to racist policies of the Etat Français that only a fraction of the current French population witnessed firsthand. One reason that debate remains unresolved is that many surviving witnesses (as well as others intent on keeping the past "forgotten" and out of the present) refuse to admit that acts of exclusion and violence perpetrated under Vichy toward internal minorities brought home to France practices that had been insti-tuted abroad through colonial rule.

Frantz Fanon asserted more than thirty years ago in *The Wretched of the Earth* that Nazism had transformed the whole of Europe into a veritable colony.[7] More recently, Kwame Anthony Appiah has written that the lesson the Africans drew from the Nazis and from World War II as a whole was the apparent ease with which white people destroyed one another using the same murderous tools of modernity that European colonialism had em-ployed to lay waste to African lives.[8] The myth of a direct transition from colonial to postcolonial as marker of collective identity elides a slippage from the explicit territorial nature of the colonial to the subtler economic and cultural domination fostered in the postcolonial by illusions of inde-pendence and self-determination. Unless it is questioned, the category of the postcolonial can all too easily operate as a decoy allowing new orientalisms and new prejudices to go unchallenged.[9] Contending with the risk of neo-colonial backlash means recognizing the ploy of the postcolonial as it can be used to raise thresholds of intolerance where one might expect instead to find them lowered.[10] It also means adjusting critically to the revised sign-systems that have allowed the neocolonial in the guise of the postcolonial to extend some of the very practices from which the latter had seemingly broken.

A corollary of the transition from colonial to postcolonial can be traced in the case of France through the evolving interplay of social structures and cultural practices since Vichy. Robert Young has argued that if the prehistory of "so-called 'so-called' poststructuralism" were related to a single historical moment, that moment would not be the uprising of students and workers in France associated with May 1968, but the 1954–62 Algerian war of indepen-dence.[11] Determining an exact moment of origin is, I believe, less important than understanding how ongoing irresolution surrounding Vichy supple-ments France's longer-term amnesia concerning its colonial past. Young's thesis is provocative not merely because it asserts that France's postwar iden-tity as a nation remains bound to the fate of its former colonies, but also be-cause it suggests that the demographic presence of former colonies as do-mestic minorities is still perceived as a threat to social and national stability.

Racist assumptions are more than a holdover of colonial mentalities when they sustain forms of exclusion first institutionalized by the juridical structure of the French state in the context of managing colonies abroad and immigrants at home.[12] "La France aux Français" ("France for the French") was an infamous rallying cry of the French right during the 1930s. Its revival over the past decade among supporters of the Front National party (National Front) under Jean-Marie Le Pen is all the more chilling because it suggests that, for some, the appeal of prejudices concerning ethnic and national identity that it asserts remains as forceful today as some fifty to sixty years ago. For Tahar Ben Jelloun, the tradition of "La France aux Français" goes back even further in time to the Ligue Antisémite founded in 1889 by Edouard Drumont:

> It is almost natural: with each serious economic crisis, voices are raised to identify the foreigner as the responsible one: a threatening shadow, a body unseen because it is not acknowledged, and yet a body present and guilty in advance. Guilty of exactly what? Of being there, of working, of moving about with the native village written all over the face, with these few tatters of life that pass for the outward signs of a culture.[13]

Back through the 1930s and toward the early decades of the Third Republic, it is almost as though an established paradigm of racist attitudes and practices had preinscribed current debate surrounding Vichy within a longer genealogy of the national question in France and a passage from colonial to postcolonial identities that, as Young's remarks suggest, remains problematic and contested.

Scandal and Aftereffect began as a study of articles on politics and literature written by Maurice Blanchot between 1932 and 1937. It soon became something else. For as Blanchot's early writings opened onto the complex relations between literature and politics in France between 1930 and 1945, I recognized the degree to which my previous understanding of the period was skewed and incomplete. My first reaction was to determine the extent of this incompletion; what I found was well over one hundred articles under Blanchot's signature between 1931 and 1940 and close to as many again between 1941 and 1944. To my knowledge, only a small minority of these texts had been analyzed or even referred to in detail.[14] Had the early writings been "forgotten" or suppressed? If so, what might be at stake in remembering them?

My inquiry broadened once I realized the extent to which Blanchot's texts of the 1930s had remained more or less invisible among his readers. To a large extent, this invisibility prevails. In September 1990, the French journal *Lignes* devoted a special issue to Blanchot's postwar fiction and criticism as well as to articles written by him during the 1958–59 debate in France over the fate of Algeria. The journal also contained an extensive dossier documenting Blanchot's efforts on behalf of the failed *Revue Internationale* of the early 1960s. No mention was made of his articles from the 1930s. The journal's editor, Michel Surya, was presumably unaware of this oversight when he wrote without qualification of Blanchot's commitment to an "intense *public* presence."[15] Yet by the time the *Lignes* issue appeared, I had determined that what Surya called Blanchot's "intense *public* presence" extended back to the 1930s and that the gaps and silences I had encountered in exploring Blanchot's interwar writings resulted less from a failure on my part to consult available materials than from denial by omission on the part of others. Whether this denial was the result of concerted effort I could not at the time determine with certainty.

The three chapters of this book devoted to what I have come to call "The Blanchot File" analyze articles on politics and culture written between 1932 and 1937 by a major literary figure associated after the 1944 liberation of France almost exclusively with fiction, criticism, and theory. These chapters also explore the exclusion of these interwar writings from almost all discussions of Blanchot's place in literary modernity. My analyses seek to determine the extent to which issues raised related to the memory of Vichy extend to a critical reassessment of France in the 1930s for which Blanchot's early articles serve as a test case. I had been working on this book for several years when the appearance of Victor Farías's *Heidegger et le nazisme* (*Heidegger and Nazism*) in October 1987 precipitated a major scandal in France surrounding National Socialism and ongoing debate on the memory of Vichy. When allegations concerning articles written by Paul de Man in wartime Belgium surfaced within weeks of the furor over *Heidegger and Nazism*, it was hard not to suspect a common principle or logic of disclosure above and beyond the specificity of Blanchot's interwar involvement with a militant French right.

My ambition to inscribe the 1930s in the genealogy of the more recent "post-age" no longer allowed me to dissociate issues of how the past was written and rewritten from my sense that clarity on what had been left unsaid about Blanchot might help to account for the dynamics of scandal that had erupted around the figures of Heidegger and de Man. Adopting a self-critical perspective also meant recognizing the extent to which the resistances I had discovered belatedly in regard to Blanchot's writings of the 1930s bore on my inquiry some fifty to sixty years after the fact. Transference, as Dominick LaCapra has noted, is often integral to the procedures by which we arrive at objective knowledge of the past: "The problems we investigate find their displaced analogues in our account of them."[16] As I address such transference in chapter 2 of this book, debate in the wake of Farías's work resulted less from simple convergence—"Why Heidegger and National

Socialism?"—than from a more meaningful temporal displacement that recast the question as "Why Heidegger and National Socialism . . . now?"

Yet once the controversies over Heidegger and de Man had cooled, something scandalous remained. In retrospect, I am able to identify that something as an irruption (after*affect?*) of confusion and anger. Even if the allegations against Heidegger and de Man were never proved, they had forced
readers to contend with the implications of dubious acts allegedly committed forty-five to fifty-five years earlier by two major figures of postwar
modernity. Whatever the long-term outcome of debate, the change in perception fostered by scandal marked a break with received opinions.

A second aftereffect is more personal. Whenever I speak on Blanchot or
on France in the 1930s, older members of the audience tell me—usually af-
terward and on a one-to-one basis—that I could not possibly understand
interwar and wartime France because my relative youth (I was born in 1945)
meant that I could approach the periods only indirectly. Though I accept
that my perspective could never be that of an eyewitness, the belatedness
imposed by circumstance allows me to see and to say things that many eyewitnesses have found themselves unable (unwilling?) to see and to say.

The historian Eugen Weber has confessed that, like many of his generation, he knew "little or nothing about the right, except as bogeys, let alone
about monarchism" before noting that once he looked beyond stereotypes
he came to see a "more complex, nuanced, interesting picture" in which the
politics of the Action Française were no more a bloc than the French Revolution.[17] Weber added that his work on fascism had taught him that the
point was not merely to be wholly in the right, but also "to draw attention to
aspects of past reality that we had ignored."[18] Weber's remarks identify a
taboo concerning the extreme right among a generation of scholars of
France—both French and non-French—who lived the events of 1930–45 as
adolescents and young adults. Included in this generation, born for the most
part between 1915 and 1930, are those who chide me for my belatedness, as
well as those who were the teachers from whom I learned about twentieth-
century French literature and history.

As my work on Blanchot disclosed aspects of an interwar France about
which I knew less than I had once thought, I wondered why my teachers had
seldom ventured beyond major figures such as André Gide, Paul Valéry,
François Mauriac, Colette, Jean Giraudoux, and André Malraux. Louis-Fer-
dinand Céline was already part of the modernist canon when I first read
Voyage au bout de la nuit (*Journey to the End of the Night*) as an undergradu-
ate at the University of Wisconsin in 1964. Even then, however, Céline was

cast as a "dangerous" exception: a brilliant stylist whose political diatribes promoted a virulent anti-Semitism. The literary merits of *Voyage* were praised, while Céline's hateful pamphlets remained taboo. At the time, I did not know enough to question my teachers' reluctance to contend with Céline's pamphlets, although I have often pondered since then the extent to which a failure to address them was complicit with a self-censorship that anticipated the gaps and silences I have identified surrounding Blanchot, Heidegger, and de Man. As Alice Kaplan has put it, Céline remains a figure of deep contradiction whose "elegies to society's marginal characters, to foreignness and the common path toward death, came under the grip of a mad anti-Semitism in the 1930s, claiming his writing style was the expression of his pure French blood, his 'native rhythm.'"[19] At least now, thanks to the efforts of Kaplan and others, the contradiction is being engaged rather than suppressed.

My belated doubts concerning interwar and wartime France extended as well toward the Gaullist myth of Vichy that pitted a unified popular resistance against a weak minority regime. The progressive collapse of this myth over the past twenty-five years has recast the occupation as a more complex and unstable phenomenon. A first change involved how the period was to be broken down into phases and moments. Within weeks after Germany occupied France in June 1940, the initial choice of armistice that led to collaboration had evolved. Pétain's politics were not those of Pierre Laval, nor were the Vichy traditionalists and technocrats to be equated with the pro-Nazi ideologues of Paris, or the Militia State of 1944 with the whimpering regime of 1940.[20] Recent inquiry has also lifted taboos surrounding officials of the Vichy government who had avoided prosecution for alleged wartime activities. Yet instead of merely naming names, the challenge at present for those who seek both understanding and justice is to make the historical case as irrefutable as possible. As Tony Judt argues in his study of intellectuals in postwar France, the historian who seeks to explain something that is intrinsically unattractive and to which his or her reader would normally respond with distaste is not for that reason excused from an obligation to be accurate.[21]

As received accounts of Vichy are increasingly questioned and broken with, a more informed and nuanced historical sense holds the promise—some see it more as a threat—of a substantially revised understanding of the period. Revision of this kind encounters resistance because it signals what Gayatri Spivak has called the failures of received accounts in relation to which revision promotes violence and crisis:

> A functional change in a sign-system is a violent event. . . . Yet, if the space
> for a change (necessarily also an addition) had not been there in the prior
> function of the sign-system, the crisis could not have made the change hap-
> pen. The change in signification-function supplements the previous func-
> tion.[22]

Sign-systems construct claims to knowledge linked to institutions and practices. In the words of Joan Wallach Scott, any ordering of the world asserts a
claim to knowledge that invariably exercises power: "Knowledge is not prior
to social organization; it is inseparable from social organization."[23] Recasting racist violence in terms of power and knowledge guarantees neither an
immediate nor a lasting solution to problems of social formation within
which such violence is deep-seated. It does, however, suggest that this violence and its persistence cannot be set apart from inquiry into how determinate institutions and practices form and evolve. For Foucault, the purpose of
history guided by genealogy was neither to solidify identity nor to discover a
unique threshold of origin. History was instead what made visible the dis-
continuities that crossed this threshold and that precluded the promise of a
return to the past as to a homeland.[24]

Despite attempts to go on as if nothing had changed, it is unlikely that the
writings of Heidegger and de Man will ever again be read as they were read
before 1987. Difference here results both from passing time and from a
break with received opinion imposed by new questions for which there may
be no satisfactory answers. Following the irresolution hanging over Heidegger and de Man, then, what might be at stake in analyzing Maurice Blanchot's journalism of the 1930s? How might Blanchot's early texts articulate
with the postwar writings more readily identified with the abstract temporality of literary space? The volume of Blanchot's entire corpus is such that
no single statement is likely to serve as anything more than a point of entry
within a corpus that spans more than sixty years. Recalling such caveats, it is
necessary to start somewhere in order to convey a preliminary sense of these
questions and the kind of inquiry they make possible.

In "Les Intellectuels en question" (Intellectuals in question), an article
published in 1984 (three years before the scandals touched off by *Heidegger
and Nazism* and de Man's wartime journalism), Blanchot commented in a
lengthy footnote on the issue of Heidegger's links to the National Socialist
party. Rereading his words in the wake of Farías's book demonstrates the
prophecy and irony out of which a particular instance of aftereffect has
emerged.

The more importance given to Heidegger's thought, the more necessary it becomes to seek to elucidate the meaning of the political engagement of 1933–34. It is, in a strict sense, understandable that Heidegger agreed to become rector in order to serve the University. It is even possible to go further and not attach too much importance to his membership in Hitler's party, a purely formal membership meant to facilitate the administrative duties of his new office. But unexplainable and indefensible are the political proclamations in which Heidegger agrees with Hitler, either to exalt National Socialism and its myths by exalting the "hero" Schlageter, in calling out to others to vote for the Führer and his referendum (in view of leaving the League of Nations), in encouraging his students to respond favorably to the Work Service—and to do so in his own philosophical language, which he puts, as though without reservation, in the service of pure causes and which is thus discredited by the use to which he puts it. There, in my opinion, lies the most serious responsibility: there has occurred a corruption of writing, abuse, travesty, and a misuse of language. On [Heidegger] will henceforth weigh a suspicion.[25]

Blanchot first asserted the integral role of political engagement within a "thought" that Heidegger and those around him had kept at a remove from the political history of the Third Reich. He also considered the degree to which Heidegger may have acted out of expediency to uphold a superficial commitment to the National Socialist movement. Yet in his concluding remarks, Blanchot just as clearly marked the limit of a more personal tolerance when he specified actions he found reprehensible and for which, presumably, he considered Heidegger accountable. When Blanchot invoked "the most serious responsibility," he did so without detaching ethical from aesthetic or philosophical concerns. Nor did he claim to distinguish what Heidegger may have said or done in the name of National Socialism from his writings of the period that were ostensibly removed from partisan engagement. Although Blanchot referred openly to a "most serious responsibility," the ethical ring of the expression neither displaced nor dissipated a grounding in historical agency that recent apologists for Heidegger have tried to deny. Because the passage just cited operates as an instance of projection and transference, what Blanchot wrote in 1984 concerning Heidegger provides an initial clue on how to approach his own corpus along similar lines.

An unanticipated aftereffect within this project involved the degree to which I came to understand standard accounts of the 1930s and wartime France as gestures of denial and displacement that allowed past violences to remain "forgotten." According to a temporality I have come to associate with the postmodern, the occurrence of violence was followed by a period of denial that, in turn, enhanced the force of belatedness I analyze here in chapter

1 as aftereffect and in chapter 2 as scandal. As a preliminary example of such denial, the French term *déportation* flattens the strong affect associated with acts under Vichy that produced what might be referred to with bitter irony as a minor genocide. Understatement once again marks the deep ambivalence within a French nation and society so divided over the recent past; as recently as July 1992, President François Mitterrand still refused to admit that the roundup and transportation of Jews to camps outside France had resulted from policies promulgated by the Vichy government.[26] Mitterrand asserted that refusal of the Etat Français had already served as the basis of the underground resistance movements, the de Gaulle government in exile, and the postwar Fourth Republic. Relying on a Gaullist refrain that rang increasingly hollow, Mitterrand concluded that Vichy (l'Etat Français) was not France (la République Française). Seemingly, the matter was closed. As Mitterrand tried to state with Cartesian presumption, "Il faut être clair" (One must be clear).[27]

The character of Alvy Singer portrayed by Woody Allen refused at the start of *Annie Hall* to enter a movie theater once the film had begun because he could not stand to miss anything. Singer suggested that he and Annie go to see *The Sorrow and the Pity* instead. He said that he had seen the Ophuls film before, so presumably he knew the story it told. Why, then, would he want to see it again?

Extending this question to my discussion of Vichy, I might ask why viewers would see *The Sorrow and the Pity* (or *Hôtel Terminus*) more than once when they, like Alvy Singer, already knew the story. Much depends on what is meant by the terms "knowing" and "story." For even if one claimed to know in advance the outcome of events narrated in the Ophuls film—especially events in a real as opposed to an invented past—this kind of knowledge would not be the same as watching an account of acts whose reality remained (at least for some) contested. The understatement with which Allen staged this moment of minor resistance was all the more meaningful in light of the moral discomfort that was a common response to the accounts of Vichy provided by Ophuls.

Singer's preference for *The Sorrow and the Pity* over the Ingmar Bergman film he and Annie had planned to see expressed his desire to see again a vision of the past that he still considered painful and unresolved. Seeing *The Sorrow and the Pity* or *Hôtel Terminus* a first or second time could never be equated with witnessing the event itself. Nor could watching the films undo the real violence they portrayed, each in its own way. Yet it was as though for Alvy Singer and others like him, forcing oneself to see the painful event narrated over and over again was the only way to preserve a vision of its violence strong enough to prevent recurrence of the real acts portrayed. Frequent evocation of this sort was far from pleasurable, but it did, in the words of Primo Levi, work against the slow degradation of memory over time by keeping memories fresh and alive "in the same manner in which a muscle often used remains efficient."[28]

It is no small irony that the very gestures of recall and repetition that are said to keep memory alive can also turn it against itself and collapse it from within. Thus, as has been surmised concerning the desensitizing that results from repeated exposure to graphic depictions of violence, a memory evoked too often in the form of a story can become fixed as a stereotype at the expense of the raw memory that it replaces. The point here for Levi was not merely to sharpen the paradox surrounding recall and accounts of the past, but to assert that because the consequences of trauma remained whether the trauma was recalled or repressed, the most one might hope for would be that recalling past traumas might prevent the recurrence of similar traumas in the future.

How the passage of time mediates the fact of past violence also bears on the writing of history, especially when subsequent accounts feign blindness to this violence by contesting, misrepresenting, or denying it. I have already suggested the extent to which debates surrounding recent inquiry into France since 1930 have been fueled by disclosures of racist acts under Vichy. As in the case of the police files used in the July 1942 roundups of Jews in Paris, documents that were long claimed to have been destroyed or even nonexistent suddenly turned up, either "misplaced" in other archives or without any explanation whatsoever. Debate over the memory of Vichy has been complicated by the fact that it has been staged in large part among historians born after the war (Pascal Ory, Henry Rousso) and others who lived it as children (Pierre Vidal-Naquet, Serge Klarsfeld, André Kaspi). For some, this belatedness was advantageous because it freed inquiry from the strong affect that burdened eyewitnesses of the Vichy period. For others, belatedness was insurmountable, an obstacle that undermined any claim to authentic understanding.

Between eyewitnesses who invoke the authority of lived experience and those who come to Vichy belatedly, a prime danger is that because the former have yet to resolve differences among themselves, succeeding generations will rely by default on accounts that are partial and inconclusive. From the perspective of the latter, the very belatedness invoked by eyewitnesses to discredit indirect access allows for informed understanding grounded on new as well as retrieved documentation. Belated disclosures of "lost" and "nonexistent" documents make it possible to see in detail the complexity that made Vichy both plural and singular, a monolithic bloc and a varied microcosm.[29] As the 1940–44 occupation period is reconstructed in terms that account more fully for acts and episodes that have remained suppressed and "forgotten," the decade of the 1930s also emerges as a formative moment from which the so-called National Revolution under Vichy drew force and inspiration. Among those who look more closely at the memory of Vichy, the 1930s are no longer merely a prologue in a narrow sense of chronology, but a determinate period of intense conflict in politics and culture whose full complexity has yet to be understood. A prime objective of *Scandal and Aftereffect* is to inscribe the 1930s more fully within current debates surrounding the memory of Vichy and French national identity as it has evolved over the past fifty years.

Iowa City, Iowa
October 1993

CHAPTER ONE

Vichy as Paradigm of Contested Memory

We invariably find that a memory is repressed which has only
become a trauma by *deferred action.*
Sigmund Freud, *Project for a Scientific Psychology*

We, the survivors, are not the true witnesses. . . . We are those who by their
prevarications or abilities or good luck did not touch bottom. Those who
did so . . . have not returned to tell about it or have returned mute,
but they are the "Muslims," the submerged, the complete witnesses,
the ones whose deposition would have a general significance.
They are the rule, we are the exception.
Primo Levi, *The Drowned and the Saved*

Scandal I

Just as Sigmund Freud believed in the return of what consciousness tries to
repress, so an uneasy awareness haunts a current generation of literary critics, theorists, and historians at work on France since 1930. One source of
this uneasiness involves a crisis of authority related to scholarly disciplines
and differing—often rival—claims to knowledge. We may agree in principle
with Geoffrey Hartman that historians should become better readers and
literary scholars better historians, but ingrained habits of profession and
discipline often force a closing of ranks to a point where such agreement is

nothing more than wishful thinking.[1] A more substantial source of uneasiness derives from the belated disclosure of suppressed elements in accounts of the recent past increasingly open to question. Concerning France, it is only over the past twenty years that disclosures surrounding the 1940–44 occupation and the Etat Français at Vichy have promoted critical revision of the interwar and wartime periods in the face of resistance from those for whom the equation of revision with denial has itself generated controversy.

My opening reference to the concept of repression is intended as figurative. It redirects a clinical usage toward effects of ambivalence, denial, and resistance in recent debates surrounding literary theory and the writing of history. Freud saw the effects of repression as both immediate and long term, with many of the latter intelligible as instances of what he termed aftereffect (*Nachträglichkeit*).[2] As in a narrow sense of the verb *tragen* contained in the German noun, something is carried along as addendum or supplement. (Curiously, a secondary meaning of the German verb denotes resentment or the bearing of a grudge.)

Three qualifications are in order. First, it is important to note that what Freud took for repression in the case of the individual is closer in terms of collective identity to suppression. To transpose repression from individual to collective behavior diffuses the specificity of actions and the kinds of accountability to which their perpetrators are subject. In so doing, the particular is reduced by way of the symptom to categories of the general and the pathological.

A second reduction promoted by the use of psychoanalytic terms concerns ambivalence and what James E. Young has analyzed in terms of memory-conflict and strategies of denial: "If memory of an event is repressed by an individual who lacks the context—either emotional or epistemological—to assimilate it, that is one thing. But to suggest that a society "represses" memory because it is not in its interest to remember, or because it is ashamed of this memory, is to lose sight of the many other social and political forces underpinning national memory."[3]

Finally, because Freud associated aftereffect with other unconscious processes, he did not conceive of it apart from related mechanisms such as suppression (*Unterdrückung*), displacement (*Verschiebung*), and repression (*Verdrängung*). These, in turn, lent themselves to metaphors ranging from echo, ricochet, and reverberation to the seismic figure of aftershock. Aftereffect also occurs as a flashback phenomenon whose force takes figurative expression in tropes such as analepsis and prolepsis.

Gregory Ulmer has coined the expression "post-age" to characterize the

1980s as a decade dominated by communications technologies ranging from satellite networks to holograms.[4] To Ulmer's ear, the "post-" particle resonates as a bilingual pun and homonym of the French word, *poste*, for radio or television receiver. The prefix also denotes a sense of temporal difference and spacing such as that at work in the aftereffect I have invoked. Yet this temporality is not synonymous with a heightened sense of context linked to recent turns in literary studies toward new historicisms and cultural poetics.[5] What many literary scholars take for a turn to history is closer to the repetition Freud associated with the return of the repressed. A third (and admittedly skewed) sense of the "post-" prefix points to what Jean-François Lyotard has termed a temporal paradox of the future perfect. Because the prefix precedes the signifier in normal syntax, a work could be said to be modern only after having been postmodern.[6] The effect is subversive and close to parody. The precedence of what will have been over what could or might have been undermines the determination of probable truth toward which a certain conception of historical inquiry points.[7]

More in line with aftereffect in its Freudian resonance, Lyotard has invoked a concept of originary shock (*refoulé d'origine* in French, *Urverdrängung* in German) to describe a condition he sees removed from representation and yet all the more present by force of its absence:

> A "past" that has not passed, that does not haunt the present in the sense that it would abandon it, be missed by it, would presently point to itself like a specter, an absence, that does not inhabit it in the status of a beautiful and good reality, that is not the object of memory like something forgotten that should be recalled (with a view toward "proper end" or proper knowledge). That is not therefore there as a blank, absence, *terra incognita*, but that is however there.[8]

Because he recognized the extent to which the past was not just an objective reality that could be grasped and contained, Lyotard avoided the pitfalls of historicist practices that transposed context into a stable entity. It is also the case that disclosing the originary trauma did not guarantee release from symptoms that were for all intents and purposes chronic.

The past is not just "out there" as an entity accessible at any moment. It will not suffice simply to recall it without considering how and to what end this recall occurs. Whenever history is invoked to remedy or correct what are taken for the limitations of literary study, it is also necessary to determine the claim to understanding asserted on behalf of history and seemingly denied to literature. At stake in such distinctions is not only the priority of one discipline over another, but the social formations that this priority and exclusion imply. Blind spots and slippage are certainly not exclusive to literary studies. This pertains not merely because explanation varies from one discipline or discourse to another, but because claims to literary and/or historical understanding are increasingly under scrutiny. The historian confronted with a document can no longer take it as a transparent medium, an "open window" providing direct access to a past reality (Ginzburg, 83). Instead, the document as a historical entity is subject to mediations that often preclude direct access. As a result, it becomes difficult to maintain the opposition between historical inquiry conceived as systematic analysis grounded on indisputable ("hard") documentary evidence and ("softer") literary approaches that focus on discourse, rhetoric, and interpretation. What, then, might be the meaningful distinctions between the historical and the literary at a "post-" moment (poststructuralist, postmodern, postcolonial) characterized by new historicisms and self-reflexive historiography?

Maurice Blanchot seems at first an unlikely figure to examine in the context of a postmodernity whose signs are encountered on an everyday basis in recycled "period" pieces of architecture, fashion, film, and design. Yet the untimeliness integral to such recycling expresses exactly the kind of doubling conveyed by the aftereffect I have described. Untimeliness is also integral to the increased frequency with which the interwar and wartime periods have appeared in Blanchot's texts of the past twenty years, often in ways surprisingly at odds with the more ahistorical tone of his earlier postwar fiction and criticism of the 1950s and 1960s. From *Le pas au-delà* (1973) (*The Step Not Beyond*) to *L'écriture du désastre* (1980) (*The Writing of the Disaster*), *Après coup* (1983) (*Vicious Circles*), and *La Communauté inavouable* (1983) (*The Unavowable Community*), acute sensibilities of doubling—between past and present, high and low, visible and invisible—characterize Blanchot's singular place within the postmodern.

Two preliminary examples articulate the convergence of Blanchot, the postmodern, and aftereffect. Both involve an interplay between word and image. The first example is "Blanchot et ses voisins" (Blanchot and his neighbors), an article that appeared in the March 20–26, 1987, issue of the mass-circulation French weekly *Le Nouvel Observateur*, in a dossier on three writers who made up an "Académie des muets" (Academy of silent ones; the other writers, besides Blanchot, were Julien Gracq and the late René Char). The author of the piece on Blanchot, identified as Jean-Marc Parisis, organized his account around an inability to make direct contact with his subject. Perhaps to compensate for this frustration, Parisis used wordplay and allusions to set the figure of the notoriously private writer against the sterility of a fresh-air ("aerobic") suburb outside Paris. The result was a strange mix of reportage and satire:

> The town of T   is a tinsel knot at the lace-ends of the valley of the Chevreuse. Opposite the bell tower, a post office in modern brick and wood forwards letters and book parcels toward a very French name that is nevertheless taught in universities throughout the world. Maurice Blanchot lives—writes—in T
>
> He gets out from the front passenger's seat ["la 'place du mort'"] of the harmless Renault and it can be said that this man of tall stature—all bones and angles, with fine white hair flowing down the back of his neck—has chosen an extraordinary seclusion. Kidnapped in the 1960s by the builders of Levittown tract houses, T   has developed its residential transformation in colors of white, blue, yellow, burgundy, and dark green shutters that open more readily onto Canal-Plus than onto literary space. This is perhaps what Blanchot was looking for when he moved in, it is said, some twenty years ago: a paradoxical hole, an anonymity that flatters his abstractions among the petty and middle bourgeoisie. . . .
>
> Access to the house is strictly regulated: if you are not on call to repair a leak or to have a registered letter signed, you're better off not pushing the matter. After ten steps along a walkway, the sound of the doorbell only makes the curtains tremble. No one opens, no one gets in. A woman's voice wafts through the intercom and sends you off curtly. Maurice Blanchot maintains communication with the 1980s by publishing books, by bestowing some papers to the left-leaning press—fully in keeping with his signature on the 1960 "Manifesto of the 121" and his place on the Committee of Writers and Students eight years later, in the midst of May. Maurice Blanchot, double agent on the essay and novel front, *will not speak*. Graded a perfect score ["noté vingt sur vingt"] for the effectiveness of his self-effacement: not a single photo in the files of his publishers . . .
>
> Convinced that the writer is fundamentally misunderstood, [Blanchot] has chosen the extremism of a silence rarely broken . . . Sublime detachment beneath the empty suburban winds, amid the scent of mowed lawns and aerobic incense. Do not disturb the remarkably silent seventy-eight-year-old man who is forever drilling in the secret pockets of writing. Long ago Madame Blanchot confessed that as for worldly things, her brother-in-law had already known them all and that these matters no longer interested him; at least that's what a neighbor was led to believe. Of course there is something else that he protects from suspicion with a fierceness that might make one take him for someone who is damned. An accursed share ["une part maudite"], unable to behave affectedly, that the taxi that stops occasionally at the Place des Pensées (yes, des Pensées) carries off perhaps to the rue Sébastien-Bottin, Bernard-Palissy, or surely elsewhere.[9]

This minimalist portrait of the literary recluse trapped in the suburban sprawl of greater Paris was striking. Parisis deflated the myth of the respected writer often called "Blanchot l'obscur" (Blanchot the obscure) by setting references to a text such as *L'Espace littéraire* (*The Space of Literature*)—a 1955 collection of Blanchot's critical essays on literature—alongside another to the privatized French pay-channel, Canal-Plus. Such mixing of high and low registers of culture through puns and allusions enhanced a critical portrayal of postmodern commodification worthy of Jean Baudrillard or Fredric Jameson. *La Part maudite* (*The Accursed Share*), for example, was the title of a book by Blanchot's late friend Georges Bataille. The Place des Pensées (presumably a real address, but one that translates literally as "The Square of Thoughts") evoked the title of Claude Lévi-Strauss's 1961 book, *La Pensée sauvage* (*The Savage Mind*) with the wordplay of *pensée* as the French term for both "thought" and "pansy" retained in full force! This collage of literary and popular cultures enhanced the ironies inherent in approaching an esoteric and demanding writer such as Blanchot on anything like a personal basis. In an aerobic suburb, any such approach bordered on the ludicrous. Shuttered windows and high-tech security precluded the possibility of a meaningful encounter while extending the myth of obscurity surrounding Blanchot. The result—close to allegorical—recalled the plights of K. in *The Castle* by Kafka. On a lighter note, the article concluded by suggesting the difficult itinerary to be traveled by the taxi called to Place des Pensées from the anonymous suburb toward the more *literary* space of Left Bank Paris. Rue Sébastien-Bottin and rue Bernard-Palissy are the streets in Paris on which the editorial offices of Blanchot's major publishers, Editions Gallimard and Editions de Minuit, are located.

From word to image. The *Nouvel Observateur* article was accompanied by a photograph of an elderly man next to a Renault 4 in a parking lot. My first reaction was one of disbelief. Was this finally the elusive Blanchot caught on film? A caption indicated that it was. Blanchot was notoriously obscure and unforthcoming, responding to letters in a measured writing but providing few details of biography and, above all, refusing all interviews, public appearances, and—to the best of my knowledge—photographs. What, then, was to be made of the *Nouvel Observateur* photograph? Was it the real thing or was it only a hoax, a red—or perhaps white (*blanc*, Blanchot)—herring? Giddiness led me to improvise outrageous captions—"Portrait of the Artist at the Shopping Mall," "Orpheus in the Parking Lot," "Mr. Blanchot's Neighborhood"—to account for a photographic image that extended the myth of Blanchot's obscurity in a gesture that seemingly broke it! Unable to verify through comparison, I could grant to this image neither the authority of evidence I desired nor even the pleasure of seeing for the first time what so few had seen before.

A second image (a set of two, really) appeared in a recent book on Emmanuel Lévinas.[10] Two photo portraits showed a young but recognizable Lévinas in the company of a tall gaunt man with high cheekbones and an intense gaze. Captions on the photos read Strasbourg, 1929, and identified the young man as Maurice Blanchot. I was drawn to the intense expression on the man's face. Could it be the gaze of Orpheus to which Blanchot alluded in *Le Livre à venir*? If so, who was the woman who appeared in the two photos? Was she a classmate, possibly Blanchot's or someone else's Eurydice? If every picture told a story, then something in the stories *these* pictures told framed the story of Blanchot's early writings as I propose to explore it at length in chapters 3, 4, and 5 of this book.

Even if irony corrected adulation, the *Nouvel Observateur* portrait of Blanchot would still be disturbing. Turning Blanchot's own vocabulary against the received figure of the respected writer, the author of the short piece flattened the myth of Blanchot's obscurity into just another cultural commodity. Even in the mode of parody often associated with the postmodern, mock reverence was a suitable remedy for the august silence that continued to surround Blanchot's writings. As with the 1990 issue of *Lignes* devoted to Blanchot, a clear partition kept the interwar writings more or less invisible. Taboo is a strong term. In a Freudian resonance, it determines what may and what may not be said. As I have come to identify it, the taboo at work in the ongoing silence surrounding Blanchot's early writings is reducible neither to politics nor to fascism. Nor can it be equated with a sustained anti-Semitism, despite clear traces in a number of texts devoted to the Popular Front government headed by Léon Blum between 1936 and 1938.

One starting point for my exploration was a suspicion that Blanchot's place in interwar French modernity was not what it had been thought to be. Although it was tempting to personalize this hypothesis and project accountability onto Blanchot as others had done in debate on de Man's wartime articles in *Le Soir*, I saw that the issues raised surrounding Blanchot were better understood in terms of censorship and displacement. Rather than attribute accountability to a single historical agent, it was necessary to identify what was at stake in the desire to attribute accountability. As Diane Rubenstein has noted in her incisive study of the Ecole Normale Supérieure and the French right, mechanisms of exclusion such as taboo erase "the insistence of the literary signature within political/legal authority" that marks the inextricable tie between writing and politics.[11] Working against the grain of conventional biography, I have sought instead to identify the social and political formations within which Blanchot's interwar writings elucidated the authority of what Rubenstein calls the literary signature. As I have come to see it, the internal difference of the literary signature associated with Blanchot's writings points to the issues and problems to be addressed in the wider study of interwar and wartime France I will discuss.

Finally, the *Nouvel Observateur* photo of the elderly man in black was especially disturbing because the ghostlike figure (Nosferatu as critic/theorist?) might have been anyone or no one in particular. Was this really a photo of Blanchot, a long-awaited image of the great writer snapped . . . in a suburban parking lot? At first I took uneasiness as a sign of my ambivalence concerning a literary figure about whom my thoughts were becoming more conflicted. Only later did I understand that my response was not just something I had imposed on a neutral object, but an integral element of the portrait function whose referent was nothing more or other than a name or a signature.

Before and After

Far from an isolated instance of projection, the meaning I attributed to the *Nouvel Observateur* portrait of Blanchot was a symptom of the complex responses to the recent past that Henry Rousso has analyzed in terms of a Vichy syndrome consisting of four phases.[12] The first of the four, from 1944 to roughly 1954, was a period of unfinished mourning without any serious attempt to contend with the contradictions unresolved in the wake of the Liberation. Despite the deep conflicts related to purge and amnesty, many in France preferred to believe that the passage of time would eventually reunite a divided country. The years 1954 to 1971 marked a second phase of extended repression that recast memories of Vichy as a mythic struggle between collaborators and resistance militants. For Rousso, this "resistancialist" myth minimized the importance of the regime under Pétain and Laval while it equated a widespread and unified resistance movement with the interests of the French nation as a whole. In retrospect, the illusion of a unified resistance further displaced the real extent of collaboration among the French.

Pierre Sorlin has described the postwar memory of Vichy somewhat differently as an initial period (1945–50) of testimonies followed by a twenty-year hiatus. Over the interim, the occupation was almost exclusively displaced onto the resistance, as though the latter served as a French equivalent of a mythic American West: "There were the goodies and the baddies, the past and the future, totalitarianism and democracy, the unity of the well-intentioned."[13] When *The Sorrow and the Pity* appeared as a counterimage to this Gaullist myth of heroic resistance, it did so as a nonfilm made originally for French television. For Sorlin, the shift from large to small screen affected not only the visual format but also the referential status of historical representation. Unlike films whose verisimilitude conformed to visual models (color, lines, texture) of painting and engraving, television often built its representation of the past around media documents ranging from the daily press and periodicals to newsreels and film clips. The effect of this shift in visual and referential models brought the past out of the past with an immediacy that films seldom conveyed. Cinematic history looked like school history, but televisual history had the flavor of ever-present memory (Sorlin, 174).

As Rousso saw it, the collapse of the resistancialist myth in the late 1960s coincided with the decline of Gaullism. In this sense, demonstrators during the "Red spring" (*le printemps rouge*) of 1968 who protested against the de Gaulle government's educational and economic policies were also responding to the deep contradictions their elders continued to carry, unresolved, two decades after the fact. Following 1968, the force of this irresolution exploded when the repressed memory of Vichy returned to shatter the past like a "broken mirror." Rousso's third phase started in 1971 with the release of *The Sorrow and the Pity* as cornerstone of a forties revival (*une mode rétro*) that seemed to "reoccupy" France in the guise of books, records, scholarly articles, and front page newspaper coverage. To his credit, Rousso refused to dismiss the *mode rétro* as a passing fad; to the contrary, he saw it as a prerequisite for a long fourth phase (ongoing since 1974) of obsession with Vichy. In the spectacular forms of film, music, and fashion that evoked irresolution over the interwar and wartime periods, the *mode rétro* measured the continual force of aftereffect at a remove of some thirty to forty years from its object. Aftereffect also accounted for the force with which the memory of Vichy that irrupted in film and television (notably in *The Sorrow and the Pity* and the miniseries *The Holocaust*, but later as well in *Lacombe Lucien, The Last Metro, Au Revoir les enfants, Hôtel Terminus,* and *Uranus*) has persisted in the political and social spheres of post-1968 France.

Rousso's thesis of a Vichy syndrome helped to account for the continued eruptions of scandal and debate surrounding wartime France. Responses to *The Sorrow and the Pity* in the early 1970s left little doubt that the upsurge of fresh memories, new questions, and a rekindled fascination with the recent past shattered the Gaullist accounts of Vichy that had dominated the previous twenty years: "The change first became apparent between 1971 and 1974 in the cultural sphere, from which emanated the most significant and visible signs of a new outlook on the past. But these changes were as much revelation as catalyst: the forties revival became a social fact only because the ground was already prepared and a demand for the new cultural product already existed" (Rousso, 127). Among historians, the "broken mirror" phase was further heightened by Robert Paxton's controversial *Vichy France: Old Guard and New Order, 1940–44,* published in English in 1972 and in French one year later.

As much revelation as catalyst. The *mode rétro* bordered on obsession because it disclosed the unresolved contradictions related to a past that some preferred to forget and that others were constructed—by gender, age, class, religion—never even to see or hear. Predictably, such disclosures were challenged or dismissed until they became too numerous to be ignored. If, as Rousso argued, neither resistance veterans nor the Jewish community needed Marcel Ophuls or Patrick Modiano to jog their memories of Vichy, the force of aftereffect spread among a wider public whose desire to learn more about a contested past clashed with the more conflicted attitudes of its elders.

Debate has not yet resolved the problem of Vichy's place in France's national memory. Ongoing disclosures have often served as flash points around which debate has been fueled by controversy and scandal. Since 1990, these disclosures have ranged from the arrest and trial of Paul Touvier, an alleged accomplice of Klaus Barbie who was hidden in monasteries in France for more than forty years, to the discovery of an allegedly nonexistent file of names and addresses used by the Paris police in conjunction with roundups of Jews. The file, compiled during the occupation and said to contain close to one hundred fifty thousand names, turned up in 1991 at the Ministry of Veterans' Affairs. One can only wonder why it was not destroyed outright, or why whoever failed to do so did not realize that it would eventually be found. Even more scandalous was the murder in June 1993 of René Bousquet, who oversaw the July 1942 roundup and incarceration of Jews at the Vélodrome d'Hiver. The projected trial of Bousquet for crimes against humanity had been considered by many as a major show trial to try the Etat Français for acts committed toward Jews and other minorities. The heightened stakes of debate were also apparent among those who denounced the visibility afforded to the occupation period as an attempt to rehabilitate fascism. Along these lines, many in France denounced further disclosures surrounding Vichy because they feared that ensuing debate ran the risk of being appropriated by the "wrong" people and/or for the "wrong" reasons. Although the premise equating visibility with legitimation on which these denunciations were grounded was questionable, the fears of appropriation that they expressed were hard to ignore.

Whether or not one accepted Rousso's argument in its entirety, the thesis of a Vichy syndrome pointed to the strong affect that continued to emanate surrounding memory of the period. Rousso seemed to sense the delicacy of a position that engaged him personally and professionally when he cast his opening remarks with a self-consciousness rare among historians:

> What surprised me the most was not the passionate reactions—even among historians—to everything written about the "dark years" of the war but the *immediacy* of the period, its astonishing presentness, which at times rose to the level of obsession: witness the constant scandals, the endless invective and insult, the libel suits, and the many affairs that attracted the attention of all of France, such as the trial of Klaus Barbie and the arrest of Paul Touvier. The cultural sphere, moreover, was inundated by images of a troubled yet fascinating past. (1; emphasis in the original)

The passage marked Rousso's conception of Vichy as an object of "history as memory" (*l'histoire-mémoire*) to be studied in the form and content of social practices that perpetuated the memory of the past within a particular group or society. What made *The Vichy Syndrome* especially compelling was Rousso's refusal to dismiss from his own treatment the gaps and silences that gave presence and immediacy (*actualité*) to the memory of Vichy. The persistence of these gaps and silences imposed its own meaning. It implied that memory was always incomplete because it was doubled by a structure of forgetting that the historian internalized as the condition of his or her historicity: "Whether professional or amateur, the historian is always a product of his own time and place. He stands at a crossroads in the byways of collective memory" (Rousso, 4).

If, as Rousso argued, the historian always contended with the force imposed by a dominant memory, he or she was also a privileged agent whose account of the past might also inflect future representations. The variable position of the historian as an agent in and of time extended as well toward his or her capacity to carry the past as witness, citizen, or scholar. Because any individual could carry the past in a number of possible capacities at any one time, specific practices were often complex and problematic. The perspective of a lycée professor who, for example, taught modern history and had been born in Germany could be expected to differ from that of her teenage students in Paris whose first sense of the occupation period might have come from having watched the *Holocaust* miniseries on television. Such obvious differences point to the complexity of what is often referred to as collective or popular memory. The lycée professor might also happen to be a Jewish woman whose parents fled to France from Germany in the 1930s. Many of her students might have been born in Paris of Algerian parents who came to France following the 1962 Evian agreements that legitimized an independent Algeria. Some of these students might be Jewish, but most would be Muslim and thus in either case neither Catholic nor even Christian. On what basis, then, might Vichy be approached in a hypothetical discussion involving the lycée professor and her students? What would it mean if, for example, the parents of certain students protested to school officials that the professor's attitude toward Vichy was affected prejudicially by her religion and by her status as a first-generation offspring of foreign Jews? What might motivate such allegations? And what if the professor responded that her successful defense of a doctoral thesis on German Jews in wartime Paris qualified her among historians as having specialized knowledge of the period? What would be the grounds for negotiating differences among the professor, her students, and their parents?

Rousso reiterated a commonplace when he wrote that the lines of division surrounding the memory of Vichy continued to move and change "following the period and what was at stake at a specific moment."[14] Yes, the lines do continue to change. The more visible a period such as Vichy becomes, the greater the discrepancies between conflicting claims made in the name of a diffuse memory that develops in opposition to facts, opinions, and other carriers of the past grounded on a sense of wrongdoing for which there is often no reliable measurement. Where Rousso referred to zones of obscurity and individual difference, I think instead of my hypothetical lycée class and especially of the students whose sense of Vichy is shaped as much by what they are told by family, friends, and peers as by the institutions and media to which they are exposed. The point here is that because memory is constructed out of conflicting accounts, subsequent understanding must contend with multiple and contested sources as they evolve through time. The force of memory is also determined in part by invisibility and relative absence, as when the historical realities of the Holocaust and deportation are challenged to the point of dismissal. Throughout the duration of the Vichy syndrome, attitudes in France toward Vietnam, Algeria, Israel, and the Intifada were seen as variants of evolving racist assumptions. The object of these assumptions varied and attenuated practices aimed at a specific group, but the underlying identification of an object of otherness and difference remained constant.

There is little doubt that the "broken mirror" phase of the early 1970s has inflected the memory of Vichy toward higher visibility. Because this phase coincided with the decline of Gaullism, it has served increasingly as a test case for French national identity. A brief comparison with Germany is instructive. Debate in France has yet to rival the "historians' struggle" (*Historikerstreit*) where differences over the impact of the National Socialist regime on postwar German identity have been waged in public over the past fifteen years. Debate in Germany turned in large part on the issue of the exceptionality of excesses under Hitler. Questions raised were on the order of whether the deeds of a Stalin or a Mussolini were not the products of a generic European phenomenon that tended by definition to produce the same excesses. Such parallels exculpated excesses committed under the Third Reich from the charge of exceptional and unique criminality. By comparison, the issue of memory was much less pronounced because Germany was forced to face its guilt as soon as the Second World War ended in 1945.

The force of the Vichy syndrome was often dispersed and variable within each of Rousso's four phases. As early as 1955 and thus at the start of what Rousso called the "repressions phase," a young François Truffaut wrote that what overwhelmed him about Alain Resnais's *Nuit et brouillard* (*Night and Fog*) was the understatement with which the film treated the deportation. For Truffaut, this understatement resulted in a sublime work that one could barely criticize or discuss: "For a few hours *Nuit et brouillard* wipes out the memory of all other films. . . . When the lights go on at the end, no one dares applaud. We stand speechless before such a work, struck dumb by the importance and necessity of these thousand meters of film" (Rousso, 229).[15] In 1955, Resnais's film was an anomaly and all the more powerful because it seemed to erupt from nowhere to break the taboo of silence surrounding the death camps. At a moment when many of the French preferred not to talk about certain aspects of Vichy, Resnais was among the first to record it (at least in part) in moving images so that it would not disappear, so that no one who saw it could claim later to have seen nothing.

Denying denial was a first phase of reconstructing memory. Truffaut's response measured the force of belated recognition with which the image of a repressed ("forgotten") past was imposed on those who saw the film. Still, it was one thing to portray the deportation and quite another to bear full witness to the extent of involvement that allowed the deportation to occur, not just in film images projected onto a screen, but in a lived past that many of the film's viewers had witnessed. Nor did the attempt to contend with memory of the past go unchallenged. Hostile critics questioned the existence of the death camps while some survivors were divided by desires both to recall a painful past and to preserve the authenticity of its memory through silence. The opposition between memory and forgetting—between recall and silence—is symptomatic of the originary shock (*refoulé d'origine* or *Urverdrängung*) that, for Lyotard, has come to transpose the question of what to say concerning the recent past into interrelated questions of how to say what words may not be able to convey or transmit but that is nonetheless likely to encounter resistance.

Rousso's sense of Vichy as a *refoulé d'origine* haunting France did far more than simply review ongoing debate over the occupation years. Well beyond a review, his analyses showed the extent to which the evolving memory of the period continued to shape conflicting representations of national identity. In such terms, Rousso argued, Vichy symbolized a Franco-French war whose memory remained a source of division between those for whom it fouled Republican France and those for whom it purged France of enemies—both foreign and native—who threatened its national identity. Where the former saw the occupation as a period of shame and repression, the latter recalled it as holding the promise of return to a strong and orderly nation. As the temporal distance between Vichy and the present increased, debates were waged less by those who had lived the period and who had sought a final opportunity to bear witness to their experience than by others whose access to it was indirect. Rousso, for example, admitted that he belonged to the latter group and that he grew up "in the rather burdensome shadow of remembrance and mimicry of May '68" (Rousso, 1). This difference of age and generation bore directly on the access that determined how the past was remembered in words, images, sounds, and forms.

The passage of time has also led to a change in the nature of debate. Vichy remains a crucial point of reference, but the divergent responses that it elicits among those who lived the occupation are tempered for a postwar generation for whom this struggle over the past is waged with concrete political implications for the present. In France, struggle over the memory of Vichy has pointed increasingly to allegations of crimes against humanity involving the deportation of thousands of French and foreign Jews.[16] Debate among those born after the war has often been transposed from politics to ethics, that is, from issues of national identity to those of collective memory in various expressions. Alain Finkielkraut seemed to recognize the consequences of this transposition and the risks that it entailed when he wrote in 1982 that memory wanted both "to know the genocide and to recognize it as un-known; it wants to guarantee its presence so that it may not be forgotten, yet hold it at a distance so as to prevent reductive explanations; it wants to make the event contemporary and yet maintain it beyond our grasp" (cited in Rousso, 162).

For Finkielkraut as for others, the memory of Vichy was highly charged with ambivalence because it was linked to a grounding principle of genocide whose recognition remained complex and painful. Where some survivors of Vichy maintained silence, others of the same generation broke this silence when they felt that the memory of the pain they had lived was compromised by denial. Debate following the "broken mirror" phase of the early 1970s has inscribed the memory of Vichy within an equivalent in France of what Jür-gen Habermas had called the attempt to master the past (*Vergangenheitsbe-wältigung*) in relation to more recent issues of national identity in Ger-many.[17] In such terms, the issue was not merely one of proving what had happened in the face of denials, but also how the "revealed" past was to be understood at a moment when the last among those who lived it were rapidly disappearing. In Germany, debate over an unmasterable past has fo-cused on efforts to think through in full "problematic issues about the lan-guage and the use of history."[18] The point is well taken, even though I prefer to pluralize the objects of debate into languages and uses in order to assert that these issues remain so contested that debates are more likely to divide than bring together those who participate in them.

The specificity of debate in France over Vichy does not negate the extent to which it recasts an earlier struggle among Germans over the postwar past. In 1959, Theodor Adorno anticipated a prime issue of recent debate when he asked, "What does coming to terms with the past mean?" Adorno's ques-tion—also the title of an essay—can be understood in a number of ways. Its syntax and tone recall Immanuel Kant's 1784 tract "Response to the Ques-tion: What Is Enlightenment?" and point to considerations of the ends of Enlightenment reason that Habermas and Lyotard have made into a prime concern of the postmodern. The concept of "coming to terms" (*Aufar-beitung*) also connotes the operations of working up or working through that the English term "reprocessing" does not fully transmit. The proximity of psychoanalytic and political codes is noteworthy, because Adorno raised his question concerning the past in order to deny attempts on the part of some to attain precipitous closure: "'Coming to terms' [as understood by Adorno in 1959] implied neither a serious working through of the past nor a conscious attempt to break of its spell."[19] The desire to "forget"—that is, to be done with—National Socialism and to turn the page of Germany's recent past was symptomatic of a social condition that made coming to terms with the past an exercise in collective self-delusion: "In this forgetting of what is scarcely past, one senses the fury of the one who has to talk himself out of what everyone else knows, before he can talk them out of it" (Adorno, 117–18). The equation of "coming to terms with the past" and forgetting seemingly repaired a damaged national identity by simulating a return to normalcy. Yet it also connoted the internal division within operations of re-covery that both salvaged the past and covered it over again. For Adorno as for many others, such recovery was anything but innocent.

Against Forgetting

Ernest Renan stated in a lecture at the Sorbonne in 1882 that error was so crucial to a sense of nation that its correction through "progress in historical studies" was often seen as a threat to the principle of nationality.[20] We may question today the faith Renan placed in historical understanding, but there is little doubt that the issues he raised more than a century ago anticipated the extent to which the memories of Vichy and the Holocaust have engaged similar concerns with national identity in postwar France and Germany. De-bate at present remains variable and mobile; its site is just as likely to be Lon-don or Los Angeles as Paris, Jerusalem, or Frankfurt. As a result, nation space is no longer reducible to determinate borders, or to anything permanent, sta-ble, and thus immune to change. The paradox of geography and what Renan called the principle of nationality is nowhere as evident as in the expression "La Plus Grande France" ("Larger [Greater? Greatest?] France") used as late as the 1960s in reference to colonial regimes imposed by the French in North and sub-Saharan Africa, the Far East, the Pacific, and the Caribbean.

More than thirty years ago, Adorno already saw the illusion of *Aufar-beitung* as a convenience that invoked healing (*Wiedergutmachung*) in order to reprocess and close off painful disclosure of Germany's National Socialist past. The *Historikerstreit* of the 1980s suggested that at least some Germans continued to explore the recent past in terms of a memorial work (*Denkmal-Arbeit*) that deflected debate away from mastery and toward a clearer sense of how the relationship to past events lived on in the present.[21] Tendentious memory—and the orientation toward a specific goal or objective—under-mines any innocence we project onto it with a view toward consolation. This tendentiousness is all the stronger when memory is nonredemptive and when it is taken instead for what Lawrence L. Langer has described as an "intense form of uncompensating recall."[22] Dropping expectations that memory can "make things good" again changes the nature of debate that otherwise set witnesses and nonwitnesses against each other. What, then, becomes of memory when we consider it against—that is, both alongside and in opposition to—forgetting? And what are the implications of this proximity in terms of the principles of nation and nationality invoked by Renan?

My answer to these questions begins with an excursus in the form of two intertexts: one from a novel, the other from a feature-length film. The first is a passage in Milan Kundera's *The Book of Laughter and Forgetting* in which the narrator describes efforts by Gustáv Husak to erase signs of the recent past following the 1968 Soviet overthrow of Czechoslovakia's reformist government headed by Alexander Dubček. These efforts included dismissing 145 historians from their posts at universities and research institutes. One of those dismissed, Milan Hubl, later told Kundera that the first step in liquidating a people was to erase its memory through a program of *organized forgetting:* "Destroy its books, its culture, its history. Then have someone write new books, manufacture a new culture, invent a new history. Before long the nation will begin to forget what it is and what it was. The world around it will forget even faster."[23]

My second intertext comes from *The Nasty Girl* (*Das schreckliche Mädchen*), a 1989 film by the German director Michael Verhoeven about a teenager who enters a national essay contest by writing on the history of her hometown in Bavaria during the Third Reich. The girl, whom Verhoeven names Sonja, is repeatedly denied access to certain files on the period in the municipal archives. Ever earnest, she begins to suspect that the discrepancies among accounts of the wartime point to deeds that some would prefer to keep forgotten. Over several years and as she senses the extent of the deception perpetrated by her elders, Sonja increases her efforts to determine exactly what happened. After suing the city to obtain the "missing" files, she finds herself in the role of an outcast (*schrecklich* in the primary sense of an unruly child, *ein schreckliches Kind*) who is made to bear the hatred of her neighbors and even her family. At one point, Sonja is roughed up by young thugs and her apartment bombed. At another, her husband leaves her and their children. Unexpectedly, scorn turns to praise. Those who had ostracized the "nasty girl" suddenly eulogize her when she receives honorary degrees from the universities of Vienna and Paris. The film ends as Sonja makes a scene at a city hall reception when she realizes that a new statue commissioned in her honor is yet another attempt to discourage her from disclosing any more of her hometown's "forgotten" past.

Both intertexts show the extent to which forgetting promotes practices that seek to legitimize social and political orders as well as those that invoke the past for aesthetic ends.[24] By calling Husak the "president of forgetting," Kundera was suggesting that Husak needed to ground a certain political present in a symbolic past retrieved in the guise of a "new" memory. This retrieval was possible only by forgetting—that is, by erasing, omitting, or silencing—what had served previously to legitimize origin. No longer even a matter of choosing between rival accounts, it was as if each regime irrupted with its own past fully formed. Of course, this invented past was neither natural nor neutral, but rather revised by each regime according to the ambitions on which it grounded its claim to legitimacy.

The Nasty Girl inscribed elements of a determinate nonfictional past within fiction. Parts of the film simulated a documentary, and Verhoeven played on the likelihood that viewers were aware of the real incidents in the Bavarian city of Passau and the story of Anja Elisabeth Rosmus, on whom Sonja's character was based.[25] In addition, Verhoeven occasionally had Sonja address her viewers directly as though to remind them that the events narrated in voice-over derived from personal remembrance retrieved in the form of an object lesson. Images of Sonja as a teenager set against rear projections of the municipal archive and others of her romance with and marriage to her former teacher promoted the merging of lived and recounted pasts. The effect showed the extent to which the aesthetic treatment of a lived past was invariably partial and incomplete. But though the film portrayed Sonja's attempts to retrieve a forgotten past in the name of accountability in the present, its uncertain ending did little to clarify the consequences of these attempts either for her or for those around her.

The aftereffects at work in *The Book of Laughter and Forgetting* and *The Nasty Girl* resist stable resolution and closure of a reopened past. I welcome this openness because it counters the narrower understanding resulting from precipitous closure. Nonclosure should not, however, be mistaken for aporetics and for a silence imposed by extreme uncertainty. There must be limits of both the sayable and the unsayable. If we transpose Sonja's unruliness onto the writing of history, a major issue becomes that of determining, as in the case of *The Nasty Girl,* just how far one can and should go. What are the limits—"reasonable" and other—of inquiry into the past? What is at stake in determining—and in possibly transgressing—these limits? Before considering such matters, it might be helpful to admit that, like Verhoeven's narrator, few of us know in advance how far we need to go when we encounter a "forgotten" past and the revelations it brings to light. Invariably, we know only after the fact—and often too late—that we have gone either too far or not yet far enough.[26]

Saul Friedländer has noted that it is unrealistic to expect the scholar working today to treat the 1930s like a decade in the fifteenth century: "It may be that historians who work on their own past, on the past of their own party or people—and under the shadow of the most chilling events of the century—are more hampered than outsiders are."[27] Friedländer's remarks appeared in a review of Zeev Sternhell's Neither Right nor Left, a book he described as the latest in a series of studies on fascism in France written by foreigners (others named included Eugen Weber and Robert Soucy), who did not display the timidity and self-restraint of most French historians at work on the period. Sternhell's book promoted controversy because it reopened unhealed wounds concerning the extent to which fascist ideology had penetrated French society. Moreover, it did so at a moment when few surviving witnesses remained to contest the claims of those whose knowledge of the period in question was textual rather than firsthand. Controversy surrounding Neither Right nor Left derived in large part from a tension between claims set forth in the name of scholarship and those growing out of personal experience. As with the Historikerstreit in Germany, Neither Right nor Left transposed what some had dismissed as an academic matter into a wider sphere that was decidedly public.

Involvement as Friedländer addressed it in relation to Sternhell should not be misconstrued as overly abstract or theoretical. Nor should it be equated with commitment in the Sartrean sense, as it emphasizes the primacy of affect within what might otherwise be taken for action in the name of morally principled inquiry. Involvement here is also the counterpart of a concern for objectivity. I do not mean to suggest that emotion and objectivity are incompatible when it comes to historical understanding; to the contrary, they seem instead bound together in various configurations along a continuum ranging from the encounter with historical time that Sartre called embarquement to the various practices of remembrance associated with ethnicity, religion, gender, and nation. Objectivity in this sense turns out to be less a matter of principled reason than the awareness that claims to understanding devolve as much from the multiple and often contradictory concerns the historian brings to his or her inquiry as from some transcendental truth fixed ("out there") in space and time.

It might be useful at this point to follow Lynn Hunt's lead in considering history as an "ethical and political practice rather than as an epistemology with a clear ontological status."[28] What Hunt refers to as the ongoing tension within history between stories that have been told and others that might be told is akin to what Friedländer has described as an aesthetic frisson—"the presence of a desire, the workings of an exorcism"—resulting from the emergence of profound contradictions relating to the ways Nazism is represented in word and image.[29] This frisson falls somewhere between an individual response to a collective memory that subsumes discrete events within unchanging models of immobile (so-called timeless) history and a more conventional consciousness of the past based on a perception of change, with a corresponding need to interpret diverse events in the specific temporal setting: "When historical consciousness tends toward a static, monumental representation of the past, we stand at the gates of collective memory."[30]

We probably do not need Foucault or Kundera to know that certain discourses prevail because they succeed in displacing—and often silencing—other discourses they deem threatening. But reading Foucault reminds us that what we may already have known about governments and regimes also holds true for the practices of representation he refers to as the order of discourse. Among the various terms used to designate such displacement, revision is of special relevance. Revision extends aftereffect in and through time. Yet the term remains complex and overdetermined. I use it here with misgivings and despite its current associations with attempts to claim that the murder of millions of European Jews and others under the Third Reich never took place. Revision is not identical to revisionism, but setting the two terms alongside each other begs the question of what is at stake in current debates over the writing of history. Intense affect alone should not, however, prevent us from engaging revision and its consequences in view of what they may hold for our understanding of interwar modernity and its belated return as scandal.

Current usage links revision to the derived terms "revisionism" and "revisionist" associated with concerted attempts to negate the Final Solution. Pierre Vidal-Naquet has distinguished between revisionist practices and absolute revisionism as a doctrine claiming that the genocide practiced by Nazi Germany against Jews, Gypsies, and others did not happen, that it is "a myth, a fable, a hoax."[31] The phenomenon of revisionism is anything but recent, but Vidal-Naquet cautioned that revisionist practices since the late 1970s should not be dismissed as merely another version, account, or explanation of wartime atrocities because their ambition—shades of Kundera and Verhoeven—was to invent a fictitious world ("a myth, a fable, a hoax") by erasing an immense event from history. The binding of invention and erasure reflected what Vidal-Naquet called the serious threat posed by attempts to relativize the Final Solution to a point where the administrative massacre of millions lost its specificity. The risk was that the proliferation of "new" accounts would transpose the reality of the genocide into discourse; that is, reduce it to words and images: "Revisionism is not new, but the revisionist crisis did not appear in the West until the massive airing of the television film *Holocaust*. That is, it appeared after the spectacularization of genocide, its transformation into pure language and into an object of mass consumption" (Vidal-Naquet, 319).

Such remarks engaged the complexity of revisionism as a doctrine at the crossroads of diverse, sometimes contradictory ideologies. The threat raised by absolute revisionism lay in the potential trap it represented for historical understanding. Vidal-Naquet recognized the extent to which the logic of reversal at work in revisionism appealed to historians. At the same time, he resisted its consequences: "By definition, historians see things relatively. This is what makes the understanding of revisionist discourse so difficult. The word in itself contains nothing that shocks the historian" (318). This appeal of the relative seemingly endowed revisionism with an initial legitimacy its proponents built into a counterdiscourse. Ironically, those who resisted this counterdiscourse could not help but endow it with a degree of legitimacy in the sense that they could be seen by others as contending with it on its terms and presumably against a more affective response of silent resistance. Thus Vidal-Naquet conceded that two revisionist books, *The Hoax of the Twentieth Century* by Arthur Butz and *Der Auschwitz Mythos* by Wilhelm Stäglich, represented a remarkable achievement because they were cast as historical narratives: "Moreover, they seem to be critical inquiries with all the exterior traits that define the history book, except the one that precisely defines its value: the truth" (318).

The occurrence of revision as a reversal or inversion of orthodoxy also pointed to the fragility of consensus, whether such consensus be understood as idea and opinion or, in more pragmatic terms, as doctrine and policy. Because revisionism held that the historian interpreted a past from which he or she could not stand apart, a prime issue became that of determining how past and present were articulated. We may believe in what is called an objective past, but the questions we ask imply that we often approach it in terms that are subjective and personal. Whether we applaud or bristle at the claims set forth in the cause of revisionism and its proponents, our reactions reveal that what is at stake in debate often exceeds what is implied by a conception associated with objective ("scientific") understanding of the past. What, then, is the pertinence of revision to historical understanding? What is the

nature of the historian's engagement with revisionist debate? These questions are large—perhaps too large for anyone to answer all at once. It is likely
that the absence of closure concerning these matters will be disquieting to
some and unacceptable to others. Neither a critic nor a theorist of literature,
Vidal-Naquet is my point of reference here because the questions he raises
in conjunction with revisionist debate over the Final Solution engage the inevitable controversy resulting from the collision between a historiography
"that insists on a full study of specifics and one that tries to integrate the
great massacre into the currents of world history, where it will not easily go"
(Vidal-Naquet, 317).

Adorno's 1959 critique of *Aufarbeitung* anticipated by a full decade the
more critical coming to terms with the past that Rousso has explored as the
third phase of the Vichy syndrome. But where the displacement at work in
Aufarbeitung was willful and tendentious, more recent commentators have
looked increasingly at varieties of collective memory. Along these lines,
Pierre Nora has described a sense of the increasingly rapid slippage of the
present into a "historical past that is gone for good."[32] This acceleration has
eradicated a conception of memory as the evolving set of lived practices on
which societies found common identities. In addition, this eradication has
occurred in the name of a self-reflexive historiographic consciousness expressed as an emergent history of history. For Nora, because what we call
memory today is already history, the quest for memory is identified increasingly with a search for history. This conflation of memory and history re-
sponds to the sense of temporal slippage extending from a lost past to an
ephemeral present and an uncertain future.

The urge to preserve anything and everything borders on obsession.
Nora has noted that even as traditional memory disappears, an obligation to
collect "remains, testimonies, documents, images, speeches, any visible sign
of what has been" disinclined one from destroying anything that might rein-
force the institutions of memory. Driven by a fear of unrecoverable loss, historicized memory preserved every artifact perceived as an indicator of the
past, while it recorded the present in the name of a future archive whose status was by definition open and undetermined. Because the archive memory
never coincided fully with lived experience, there was always at least a hint
that the turn to historical awareness Nora associated with historicized memory was only a sophisticated simulation. Digital recording and high-defini-
tion images may have dazzled us for a moment of illusory redemption, but
they could not bridge the gap separating us from the lived past. Nora con-

cluded that what we seek is no longer genesis, but instead "the decipherment of what we are in the light of what we are no longer" (18).

From Event to Narration

If every fully realized story, however we define that familiar but conceptually elusive entity, is a kind of allegory, points to a moral, or endows events, whether real or imaginary, with a significance that they do not possess as a mere sequence, then it seems possible to conclude that every historical narrative has as its latent or manifest purpose the desire to moralize the events of which it treats.
Hayden White, *The Content of the Form*

Are you ashamed because you are alive in place of another? And in particular, of a man more generous, more sensitive, more useful, wiser, worthier of living than you?
Primo Levi, *The Drowned and the Saved*

How does narration elaborate past experience as memory? What happens to this elaboration when, in the terms used by Pierre Nora, standard distinctions between memory and history break down? These questions test the extent to which accounts composed after the fact invariably mediate the experiences to which they refer. This mediation is not by necessity either abstract or artificial. Nor is it always the result of intentional actions. To the contrary, it often occurs in the minor omissions and distortions by which we negotiate everyday life. Few of us are unaware that even casual accounts alter our sense of experience in terms of what we say, to whom we say it, and in what tone. If slippage between experience and narration is unavoidable, to what extent is it controllable? Even the anecdote (*fait divers* or *historiette*) told in passing is an act of narration whose completion carries meaning and finality. As with longer and less trivial acts of narration, anecdotes fashion their ends by endowing experience with the coherence and closure associated with literary form. Anecdotes often achieve closure through the grace of a suitable term (*bon mot*) or by a turn of phrase whose rhetorical force displaces ("swallows up") the event to which they refer as well as the irresolution often contained within them.[33] This displacement of the event increases with the passage of time until it becomes more and more difficult to detach the originary experience from the account or accounts by which we refer to it. The philosopher Edmund Husserl held that such displacement posited an intuition of time as a determinate phenomenon against a continuous flux of appearances that shaded originary experience with subsequent moments of reverberation (*Nachmalmomenten*).[34] Where Husserl understood that flux as absolutely subjective, the narrator of Marcel Proust's *Recherche* approached it instead as a series of sensations—the taste of *petites madeleines* dipped in tea, the clinking of silverware or chiming of church bells—out of which the work of art constructed a meaningful order whose eloquence was enhanced as the temporal gap between experience and recall widened.

Displacement is further heightened whenever challenges to narration as invalid or unreliable extend to the experience that narration purports to convey. The anecdote may be considered a trivial form of narration, but it is all the more meaningful when its understatement masks the finality toward which it is invariably directed. The force animating a desire to have the last word can be rhetorical, as when a joke or witticism is used proleptically to control response, displace judgment, and seemingly resolve (Lyotard's "swallow up") conflict. Alternatively, the move to closure bears on cognitive and even moral claims when finality is associated with an account that is taken to be true and full. When narration functions as a historical account referring to real events in a real past, coherence and the demand for closure transpose those events into elements of what Hayden White has called "moral drama."[35] This transposition asserts common traits of language, form, and rhetoric over and against assumed distinctions between fiction and nonfiction, yet it remains imprecise until one specifies among types of historical narrative such as annal, chronicle, and historical discourse proper. It is also possible to see the anecdote as a minimal unit of narrative whose insertion within a longer sequence occurs in practices ranging from fiction, autobiography, and essay to the varieties of historical narration analyzed by White.

The anecdote brings concerns with form, style, and rhetoric into line with issues of reference and closure bearing on specific accounts of experience as we encounter them in everyday life. In such terms, memory is inscribed in the forms, techniques, and assumptions of authority related to narration. A second, and considerably less trivial, example is in order. In his preface to *The Drowned and the Saved*, Primo Levi commented on a passage from Simon Wiesenthal's *The Murderers Are among Us* in which Wiesenthal recounted how SS militiamen were alleged to have taunted their death camp prisoners by boasting that the truth about the camps would never be known:

> However this war may end, we have won the war against you; none of you will be left to bear witness, but even if someone were to survive, the world would not believe him. There will perhaps be suspicions, discussions, re-

search by historians, but there will be no certainties, because we will destroy the evidence together with you. And even if some proof should remain and some of you survive, people will say that the events you describe are too monstrous to be believed; they will say that they are the exaggerations of Allied propaganda and will believe us, who will deny everything, and not you. We will be the ones to dictate the history of the Lagers.[36]

The challenge that the SS militiamen would dictate the history of the Lagers added an even more horrific threat to the imminence of physical annihilation. Directing this challenge against the prisoners whom they could kill at any moment, the guards stated that any prisoners who managed to survive the war were likely to find their accounts dismissed as unbelievable. The intent of this taunting was arrogant and its effect nothing less than what Levi had referred to in an earlier book as an assault on the truth.

Denial of the past as Levi found it in Wiesenthal's account was a variant of the tendentious selection identified by Pierre Nora as an offshoot of historicized memory. Levi's remarks also suggested that by stating in advance their intention to deny the Holocaust even as they perpetrated it, the SS militiamen were already revising the war before it had ended. In this sense, the threat contained in the militiamen's taunt was not only the crime itself, but, in words used elsewhere by Vidal-Naquet, "the negation of the crime within the crime itself."[37]

Working from materials at Yale University's Fortunoff Video Archive for Holocaust testimonies, Lawrence L. Langer has analyzed a number of interviews as disrupted narratives cast against the very threat embodied by Wiesenthal in his portrayal of the SS militiamen. Although a prime objective of the taped accounts was to negate ("undo") a negation, their reliability was often undermined by discontinuity and suffering. Dividing the narratives into variations of memory described as deep, anguished, humiliated, tainted, and unheroic, Langer linked each variation to identity as a buried, divided, besieged, impromptu, and diminished self. His organizing principle was less one of typology than of movement toward a fuller sense of the diminished self associated with unheroic memory. Each variation of memory and self pointed to the implications for a post-Holocaust present to assess accounts of a painful past beyond the redemptive celebrations of a resourceful human spirit of which Langer had become suspicious.

It was possible to read Langer's *Holocaust Testimonies* as a simple progression from deep to unheroic memory and from buried to diminished self. Yet Langer argued forcefully that these variations were copresent in the symptoms and acts we tended to perceive in part or by selection. Of particular relevance was his attempt to explore the Holocaust testimonies as narratives disrupted not only by the uncertainties of personal recall, but also by the nature of the experiences they recorded. The losses recorded by these testimonies raised "few expectations of renewal or hopes of reconciliation" (Langer, xi). Yet they also constructed new connections between past and present in which the recognition of loss represented an attempt to find moral and intellectual authenticity.

Especially striking in Langer's remarks was the proximity of his analyses of disrupted narrative to attempts by Blanchot to contend with the Holocaust. For example, Langer's examination of Charlotte Delbo's feeling that the self who was in Auschwitz "isn't me, isn't the person who is here, opposite you" (Langer, 5) recalled the repeated statements by the narrator in Blanchot's *L'Arrêt de mort* (*Death Sentence*) about the removal he felt from wartime experiences that motivated an account of events he felt compelled to make. The internal division Langer analyzed in Delbo's account added a referential force to literary accounts that engaged the same period differently. Langer further acknowledged the binding of fiction and testimony when he began a chapter on anguished memory and the divided self by asking to whom the public memory of the Holocaust should be entrusted: "To the historian? The critic? The poet, novelist, or dramatist? To the surviving victim? Candidates abound, all in search of a common goal: the detour that will, paradoxically, prevent us from being led astray" (39). Curiously, Langer invoked Blanchot and a perilous threshold that kept the aforementioned candidates in the thrall of the impossible real by means of an unstory that "escapes quotation and which memory does not recall—forgetfulness as thought. That which, in other words, cannot be forgotten because it has always already fallen outside memory" (Langer, 39).[38]

Langer saw Blanchot's *Writing of the Disaster* as an attempt to contend with the consequences of an uncertain encounter with death expressed in the oxymoron of an "impossible real." Uncertainty derived here from a sense that, in Blanchot's words, "the disaster always takes place after having taken place" (cited in Langer, 40). Uncertainty also implied that those who survived the initial disaster remained in the thrall of an afterlife in which they "outlived" both those who persecuted them and those who did not manage to stay alive (Langer, 98). Furthermore, those who seemingly survived the disaster seemingly entered into the obverse of a paradox Langer invoked when he recalled the discovery by a former death camp inmate that one could still be alive without having survived (Langer, 159). If, for Langer, Blanchot wrote anguished memory as the unredeeming account of breakup between two incommensurable selves divided by and in knowledge of the disaster, Langer's remarks suggested that he had not drawn out the full implications of the extent to which the "impossible real" pervaded Blanchot's writings beyond the unredemptive project Langer classified in terms of anguished memory.

A concluding chapter allowed Langer to reflect on the understanding he derived from his suspicions. Yet even the countertheses of anguished, humiliated, tainted, and unheroic memory Langer developed did little to counter his grounding hypothesis of unredemptive retrieval. Once the full sense of this retrieval was accepted, what understanding of the past did Langer's analyses provide? One answer to this question involved Langer's admission that although the complexity of the Holocaust experience did little to confirm conventional theories of moral reality, it did much to question the reality of moral principles. Uncertainty and irresolution remained. Was the Holocaust an aberration to be dismissed? Or was it instead—as recent debate (Lyotard, Habermas) suggests—a realization of Enlightenment reason expressed in social formations such as Ulmer's post-age?

Langer ended his study by exploring the oral Holocaust testimonies in terms that openly asserted moral dimensions within what might otherwise have been taken for a narrower historical understanding:

> One of the unavoidable conclusions of unreconciled understanding is that we can inhabit more than one moral space at the same time—witnesses in these testimonies certainly do—and feel oriented and disoriented simultaneously. . . . History inflicts wounds on individual moral identity that are untraceable to personal choice or qualitative frameworks—though the scars they leave are real enough, reminding us that theoretical hopes for an integral life must face the constant challenge to that unity by self-shattering events like the Holocaust experience. (201)

These closing remarks link the variations of aftereffect I have discussed at the start of this chapter in terms of doubling and scandal to the uneasiness in debates over Vichy and the Holocaust. The widening of debate gave singular force to the unresolved memory of the interwar and wartime periods among historians, literary scholars, and others for whom Vichy and the Holocaust had seemingly grown more present while receding in time. Yet if, as Henry Rousso has argued, an informed critical understanding of Vichy has developed only within the past twenty years, France's national obsession with the memory of the period has also led to reassessments of earlier attempts to break with Gaullist accounts of a unified national resistance.

Among these reassessments, I want to conclude this chapter with remarks on Albert Camus's 1956 novel *The Fall* (*La Chute*). My choice of this novel is based on my sense that more than a decade before the Gaullist myth of Vichy was shattered in the 1970s, Camus's fictional portrait of Jean-Baptiste Clamence sketched the moral and historical dimensions of a duplicity whose implications are perhaps only now coming to full disclosure. To look again and anew at *The Fall* in this way is to reassess how it marked the force of aftereffect at an early moment in the postwar phenomenon of debate over Vichy's evolving memory.

The first-person narrator of *The Fall* was an updated Underground Man whose mastery at storytelling befitted his self-styled profession as judge-penitent. Jean-Baptiste Clamence prided himself on rhetorical skills that allowed him to manipulate both language and the law with impunity. Yet much like Dostoyevsky's Underground Man, a certain uneasiness cracked the veneer of irony and eloquence with which Clamence imposed himself on his interlocutor as a Frenchman more than happy to happen (fall?) upon a compatriot at the Mexico City bar in Amsterdam. Even more than Dostoyevsky's narrator, Clamence manipulated confession into self-definition by his audacious use of apophasis, the figure of ironic denial in which one claimed *not* to say or do exactly what one was saying or doing. Students of current critical theory may recognize in apophasis an antecedent of the strategy of simultaneous disclosure and dissimulation known as *mettre sous rature* (literally, "putting under erasure"). As executed by Clamence, apophasis generated an ongoing instability that allowed him to extend his disdainful confession indefinitely.

Rhetoric alone did not account in full for the force of confession in *The Fall*. Especially striking in Clamence's monologue was the incidence of appeals to history—to a real past—by which he tried to build the case for a self-portrait that turned increasingly toward self-defense. The aim of these appeals was set forth early in the novel when Clamence declared with mock irony that he had forgotten nothing of France's beautiful capital, or of its quays, a magnificent stage setting ("a real *trompe l'oeil*") inhabited by four million silhouettes. But if—as Clamence asserted several lines later—"all Europe is in the same boat," the image of four (or five) million silhouettes was also the first in a series of references to World War II.[39] Clamence initially cast his appeals to history as witty asides meant to establish complicity with his silent compatriot. When Clamence accompanied his interlocutor from the bar back toward the latter's hotel at the end of their first encounter, he stated that he lived in what used to be called the Jewish quarter until "our Hitlerian brethren" made room: "What a cleanup! Seventy-five thousand

Jews deported or assassinated; that's real vacuum-cleaning. I admire that diligence, that methodical patience! When one has no character one *has* to apply a method" (11).

Because appeals to the recent past were dispersed throughout the novel, their force was discernible by accumulation over and above any single statement. Clamence invoked "our Hitlerian brethren" as an ironic hyperbole to be taken both seriously and in jest—much hinged on the exact meaning that one attributed to the possessive adjective "our"! The complicity cast Clamence and his interlocutor as Frenchmen bonded against the Dutch in terms of national identity. Curiously, it also established an ironic second bond with ("our Hitlerian brethren") the Germans. In order to play down the latter, Clamence followed immediately with another witticism of shared culture recognizable when he referred to Descartes's *Discourse on Method*. But as in Clamence's earlier invocation of style as a cover for eczema, the reference cut two ways. Method still covered a lack of character.

Historical reference in *The Fall* bore directly on the distinction between imaginary and real events. A common view holds that Camus blurred that distinction in part to stop his readers from identifying him with his fictional narrator. Along these lines, I attribute the motive for Clamence's appeal to history to the form, execution, and objective of his tendentious confession. The question to be raised is exactly what—if anything at all—Camus's Clamence wanted to confess. Most readers of the novel answer this question by invoking the incident of the young woman whom Clamence passed on the Pont Royal one evening on his way home, moments before he heard "the sound—which, despite the distance, seemed extremely loud in the midnight silence—of a body striking the water" (70). Clamence's failure to save the woman may be nothing other than the staging of the ambivalence he directed toward his chosen role of generous lawyer. Quite possibly, the whole incident never happened. After he seemingly heard the splash, Clamence did not turn back to verify whether the sound he heard was real or unreal. Nor did he read the newspapers the following days to check for reports of the drowning. In both instances, Clamence's refusal to confirm the status of the incident as real or imaginary was explicit, almost as though his refusal to resolve the situation extended a wider refusal to engage the truth of a previous—and presumably originary—incident.

Did the young woman jump (fall?) from the Pont Royal? Or did Clamence only imagine it? In a compelling reading of the novel, Shoshana Felman described the incident on the bridge as an event literally missed; that is, witnessed exactly insofar as it was not experienced. Setting *The Fall* alongside the writings of Paul Celan and Primo Levi, Felman drew out the terrible irony that the account of the missed drowning in Camus's novel foretold both Celan's suicide in the Seine in 1970 and the title, *The Drowned and the Saved*, of the last collection of essays Levi wrote before he died from a fall at his home in 1987. Noting that behind the cry of the drowning woman it was possible to hear the lonesome, silenced cry of concentration camp survivors, Felman concluded: "Who is the saved, therefore, and who has drowned?"[40] Felman's reading combined the force of appeals to history in Camus's novel with personal accounts of the period by Celan, Levi, Hans Mayer (alias Jean Améry), and Jerzy Kosinski. The fact that, as Felman noted, these real-life survivors were also belated suicides enhanced the poignancy of comparisons to *The Fall*.

Yet having invoked Levi, it is surprising that Felman barely touched on his refusal to grant privilege to the saved over the drowned, as in the passage where he felt compelled to write that "we, the survivors, are not the true witnesses. . . . We survivors are not only an exiguous but also an anomalous minority: we are those who by their prevarications or abilities or good luck did not touch bottom. Those who did so, those who saw the Gorgon, have not returned to tell about it or have returned mute, but they are the 'Muslims,' the submerged, the complete witnesses, the ones whose deposition would have a general significance" (Levi, 83–84). Setting the passage by Levi against the ironic use of the first-person plural in Clamence's invocation of "our Hitlerian brethren" enhances the interplay of collective identity and difference imposed by the past onto those who live it and those who survive it.

A second reason against seeing disclosure of the incident on the Pont Royal as the motivation for Clamence's confession is the fact that its account occurred at the approximate midpoint of the novel. Thus it was less likely a final revelation than an initial confession inscribed within a more extensive gesture. The true objective of Clamence's elaborate confession was disclosure, not of the incident on the Pont Royal, but of the incident in the detention camp in North Africa that he let slip at the beginning of the novel's last chapter when he referred with understatement to the malaria he thought he had first caught at the time he was pope. Once again, it was difficult to determine with certainty whether this slip of the tongue was inadvertent or instead an intentional understatement—trope of litotes—meant to prick the interlocutor's curiosity. As though to corroborate the rhetorical ploy, Clamence followed the slip with a seemingly playful witticism: "No, I'm only half joking. I know what you're thinking; it's very hard to disentangle the true from the false in what I'm saying. I admit you are right. I myself . . . "(119). To joke only in part is also to be at least somewhat serious. Clamence's witticism was part play and part serious: a ploy of prejudgment—trope of prolepsis—that allowed him to retain control over what he called his useful confession. A related strategy in *The Fall* focused on unstable identity. The narrator stated at one point that Clamence was not his real name and that he had gone by several aliases. Elsewhere he asserted identity in collective terms that projected a presumptuous solidarity ("we children of the mid-century," 123) whose determination was openly historical.

I have argued that a number of rhetorical devices in *The Fall* posit an interlocutor who may, in fact, have been nothing more than a physical or imaginary reflection of the narrator. From another perspective, the transposition of Clamence from individual agent to historical type began in an epigraph with which Camus framed the central narrative. The epigraph took the form of a statement by Mikhaïl Lermontov in response to critics who had seen the central character of *A Hero of Our Time* as a fictional double of the author: "*A Hero of Our Time*, gentlemen, is in fact a portrait, but not of an individual; it is the aggregate of the vices of our whole generation in their fullest expression." The reference to Lermontov strengthened the ties between *The Fall* and *Notes from Underground* as exemplary instances of tendentious ambiguity. The self-contesting movement of both narratives could also be read as a parodic echo of Lermontov's *Hero*. All three cases—Lermontov, Dostoyevsky, and Camus—promoted ironic approaches that, in turn, complicated direct ("straight") identity between narrator and author. But while Clamence sought to hide his true identity as a fully particularized individual within a disdainful confession, the accumulation of specific historical signs refuted the claim that he was simply a modern Everyman.

The midcentury modernity found in *The Fall* was a consequence of Camus's decision on how best to use fictional narration to contend with history and circumstance. Exactly what, then, constituted the modern type whose historical determinacy Camus portrayed through Clamence's postwar confession? Where Primo Levi questioned the moral implications in distinctions between the drowned and the saved, Camus made Clamence into a voice that undermined stable determinations of innocence and guilt. In such terms, Clamence embodied the truth that World War II had made everyone guilty by implication. This was the case not only for those who had done nothing, but also for those who, like Clamence, "missed" the war while they knowingly committed dubious acts they would prefer to forget.

Reading *The Fall*, as Felman did, through *The Drowned and the Saved* brought the incident on the Pont Royal into line with the belated ambivalence I have referred to as aftereffect. The ambivalence of the survivor-witness uncertain about the reality of what may or may not have happened could easily become the useful ploy of those who knew all too well what they did and did not do. Even if the woman's drowning were only imagined, Clamence's actions prevented him from confirming whether the incident was real or imagined. At the same time, they enhanced the reality of his failure to act and intervene. In fact, Clamence was so preoccupied with his failure that he never questioned why the woman might have jumped from the bridge. As a result, his confession was redeeming only in the narrow sense that it allowed him to maintain a momentary advantage over an interlocutor whose claim to innocence he sought to undermine. Nothing in the confession eluded an irony that Camus seemed to understand some forty years ago: namely, that the fall in the title of his novel referred not only to the physical trajectory of those who drowned, but also to the moral trajectory of those who, seemingly saved, lived on to carry within them the images of drownings they may or may not have missed. Displacement became a central feature of Clamence's confession: his account of the incident on the Pont Royal inevitably carried traces of the story of the prison camp in North Africa that was disclosed only at a later point in the narrative. As Langer and others have argued, the kind of knowledge provided by Holocaust testimonials was less historical than metahistorical, representing "the activity of telling history, of organizing it, of being affected by both events and their pathos."[41]

Clamence's account of the incident on the Pont Royal at the midpoint of *The Fall* undermined the illusion of self-mastery he meant to convey in his account of the recent past he had survived. Yet the very uncertainty of the incident's outcome also enhanced Clamence's control because it motivated his interlocutor to keep listening in hopes of learning how the story ended. As Clamence extended his account, incompletion revealed the extent of his ambivalence and estrangement. The story never concluded because its end in terms of goal and ambition was nothing more or other than its telling. In this sense, Clamence embodied the harsh paradox of the survivor who, in Primo Levi's expression, was not the true witness. As a survivor, he carried not only the memory of his past actions, but also a certainty that the apparent privilege of "living on" imposed a burden of experience and knowledge with which he was forced to contend. Clamence fashioned the predicament he called his double profession when he devised an account of the past in which the interplay of truth and falsity ultimately undermined the claim to mastery he wanted both to attain and subvert. His double profession collapsed because the ostensible role of narration to contain the past was belied by the force of its return and immediacy (*actualité*).

Clamence's inability to hide the reality that his account was partial, selective, and self-serving linked him to the "children of the mid-century" with whom he identified himself. History in *The Fall* was neither identical with nor reducible to aftereffect. Yet the evidence that a certain past haunted Clamence turned the very duplicity of his account into an ambivalent and conflicted disclosure of a historical condition linked to France and World War II. Clamence's ambition to refashion a painful and unredeeming past into a partial truth failed because his attempt to forget by omission was belied by the experience and accountability that he—like other "children of the mid-century"—was forced to carry unresolved. Aftereffect extended this irresolution in time as the forceful return of a suppressed past disrupted an increasingly troubled sense of the present. The account of World War II in *The Fall* was a fiction both in terms of literary convention and because Camus's narrator revealed it as a fabulation. Yet if we consider this fiction as the account of a lived past, its affinities with and differences from the testimonies of Holocaust witnesses studied by Langer, Felman, and Laub can be clarified. Testimony occurs as an account in which fiction and history overlap: that is, a presumably reliable account related to events in a lived past. In addition to inexact references to World War II, what made Clamence's account unreliable from the perspective of historical practices was the absence of a specific framework of interpretation.[42] Clamence certainly emplotted his historical references when he set them in a confessional mode. But the truth of his account was intelligible less in its accuracy or completeness than in a structure of indefinite extension that withheld or repressed what Clamence's interlocutor-reader expected him to provide.

The absence in *The Fall* of a clear and consistent framework of interpretation enhanced the discrepancy between experience and account. Once Clamence revealed the duplicity of his double profession, his account of the past could only be seen as that of a failed witness who, in Felman's astute formulation, was unsure in his position as witness either if he perceived what he believed himself to be perceiving or even if he was speaking in his own voice (Felman, 139). Camus's fictional staging of an unresolved past returned to the present cast Clamence as a witness whose failure to intervene in the incident on the Pont Royal disclosed the force of irresolution I have called aftereffect. It is a sequence of irresolution over the recent past and the consequences of its return as scandal related to the writings of Martin Heidegger and Maurice Blanchot that I propose to explore in the chapters that follow.

CHAPTER TWO

Revising Martin Heidegger

The works that are being peddled about nowadays as the philosophy of
National Socialism but have nothing whatsoever to do with the inner
truth and greatness of this movement . . . have all been written by
men fishing in the troubled waters of "values" and "totalities."
Martin Heidegger, *An Introduction to Metaphysics*

Assembled in this book are seven writings that seem to be directly or
indirectly concerned with art. But appearances can be deceiving.
Martin Heidegger, *Poetry, Language, Thought*

Troubled Waters

Jean-Paul Sartre wrote in 1960 in his *Critique of Dialectical Reason* that the
case of Martin Heidegger was too complex for him to explain. What Sartre
did not—could not? would not?—address more than thirty years ago has
since returned as scandal and aftereffect. Until the late 1980s, the reception
of Heidegger's writings in France had bordered on the reverential for the
better part of six decades. Heidegger was seen as embodiment of the modern
philosopher-poet whose concepts and vocabulary made their way into the
works of writers and intellectuals from Sartre, Jacques Lacan, and René Char
to Michel Foucault and Jacques Derrida. For George Steiner, Heidegger belongs "to the history of language and of literature as much (some would say

more) than he does to that of ontology, of phenomenological epistemology or of aesthetics."[1] This literary dimension helps to explain how Heidegger became the object of a minor cult as a philosopher whose books were read as works of art and whose every pronouncement was scrutinized at length. It also suggests how the diversity of Heidegger's appeal may have stirred some readers to question the suitability of his work to the traditional concerns of philosophy. Alternative receptions have ranged from the skeptical to the frivolous. Logicians and philosophers of language such as Rudolf Carnap, A. J. Ayer, and W. V. Quine long ago objected to Heidegger's pseudostatements as "irrelevant to the legitimate practice of philosophy." Others dismissed Heidegger more or less outright as "the best comic example of the philo-sophical quack." An editorialist quipped in a recent issue of the *New York Times Book Review* that analytic philosophers were divided into those who believed Heidegger's writings were largely gibberish and those who believed they were entirely gibberish.[2]

Why, then, have so many readers—especially informed readers who presumably knew what they were getting into—taken the trouble to read these obscure and "difficult" writings? Steiner recognized this ambivalence when he wrote that "the question of whether Martin Heidegger is saying anything substantive and arguable *at all*, of whether his voluminous pronouncements upon man and *mundum* are anything but tautological incantations, lies deeper" (38). Dismissive irony toward Heidegger was the rule among professional philosophers, but it would be a mistake not to question the more serious concerns to which this irony pointed. The question, as Steiner put it, lay deeper. Ambivalence toward Heidegger's writings derived in large part from the fact that the (deeper) questions they raised often engaged the limits between philosophy and nonphilosophy or, as some might put it, philosophy and its others. Dismissal and irony responded to the perceived threat that Heidegger's writings posed toward practices of philosophy they presumed to correct. Yet the swipes at obscurity and "difficult" style only reinforced the provocation Heidegger's writings exercised, especially among readers who took them as examples of what philosophy should *not* be. If, as Heidegger contended, his work was profoundly open to question (*fragwürdig*), this was to be taken to mean both demanding and worthy of questioning.[3]

Where some readers dismissed Heidegger outright, others saw the notorious "difficulty" of his writings in a darker light as a mark of duplicity that masked a philosophical vision Heidegger never disclosed in full. Part of the problem involved the concept of *aletheia* (usually translated as "disclosure" and sometimes as "unconcealment"), which Heidegger came to see as a precondition for the emergence of claims to truth associated with language: "Propositional truth is derivative of and subaltern to the clearing as an original act of unconcealment. Before propositions can be formulated and states of affairs can be represented, beings must first be 'cleared.'"[4] The privileging of disclosure over propositional truth set Heidegger at odds with practices of philosophy founded on precise language and sustained argument. It also entered into what Theodor Adorno has called a jargon of authenticity in which words seemed always to say something more and higher than what they meant.[5] Heidegger's poetic exploitation of language removed his practice from those of fellow philosophers. Idiosyncrasy was also a mark of nonconformity by which Heidegger asserted his involvement with the phenomenon of emergent being loosely adapted from Greek antiquity against the authority of more recent traditions. Some took idiosyncrasy as a gesture of imperiousness that revealed the latently authoritarian tendencies of Heidegger's thought in general (Wolin, 20). At the very least, it marked the self-assurance with which Heidegger used language to control access to a philosophical vision fashioned at a polemic remove from those of his contemporaries more disposed toward Kant and Hegel.

"Difficulty" was also archival. It involved blocked access to materials and the existence of texts in multiple versions. With more than sixty volumes already in print, a complete edition (*Gesamtausgabe*) of Heidegger's writings is unlikely to occur for years! In such circumstances, reception has remained piecemeal and tentative. Christopher Fynsk identified some terms and assumptions of this reception when he wrote that the corpus of Heidegger's writings was a construct that had won "apparent unity and coherence of meaning through a conflictual process of differentiation and exclusion—a process that always leaves its marks in the form of gaps, inconsistencies, aporias, etc."[6] In another sense, this open-endedness undermines the allegations of difficulty made against Heidegger's writings if and when it reduces language and style to surface effects. This is especially the case when such charges are nothing more than elaborate excuses for refusing to take seriously writings that fail to conform to conventions of clarity and argument. Perhaps reading does not begin until, as Fynsk argued, the surface intelligibility of the writings is broken so as to follow "not the content, a series of propositions or theses (or even a series of what may seem to be poetic figures), but the very movement of thought in its becoming-other" (15).

How seriously, then, should Heidegger's writings be taken? What kind of reading might engage them without either trivializing them or simulating their tone and style? My approach to these questions seeks to clarify a number of assumptions underlying claims and counterclaims concerning the status of Heidegger's writings. The question of seriousness is one that I mean to take . . . seriously, even and especially when the ambiguities in Heidegger's writings make any answer to this question tentative. Apart from what Heidegger may or may not have intended, the issues raised by seriousness go beyond the authority associated with signature ("Heidegger's philosophy") and type ("Heideggerian philosophy"). Nor is the question of seriousness simply a matter of relating philosophy to other academic disciplines such as literature and history. A final caveat: my remarks are intended to introduce issues raised by various ways Heidegger's writings have been read and reread—by Heidegger himself, among others. Only by looking first at how these writings have been appropriated over time can any serious sense of current debate be understood. Only then might it be possible to situate—and presumably contend with—an ongoing polemic that has made Heidegger's writings a test case for the critical genealogy of a received modernity presently under intense scrutiny. A fuller sense of the corpus of writings in question is thus a prerequisite to any analysis of its evolving reception.

Heidegger's writings of the 1920s first raised issues of historicity by linking the question of what philosophy is (more exactly, what it was at the time) to claims regarding its proper task and the ambitions Heidegger held for what it might become. The initial formulation of these claims occurred in 1927 with the appearance of *Being and Time* (*Sein und Zeit*). Heidegger's desire that the book be read as an investigation of the character of the being of Being (*Dasein*) marked his view of it as the first in a series of critical engagements with a tradition of a metaphysics at its twilight end. Like Derrida after him, Heidegger saw himself both within and at a remove from this tradition. In more personal terms, Heidegger wrote in the shadow of his mentor, Edmund Husserl, and even more in that of Friedrich Nietzsche, whom he later referred to as the last metaphysician. Many readers have also seen *Being and Time* as an attempt to extract elements of Kantian and Hegelian thought in order to make a new beginning for philosophy. Yet even at this early stage of his evolution, Heidegger's links with tradition were already complex. It was as though he wanted to extract from the history of Western philosophy a conception that legitimized his readings of a particular Greek antiquity against those of a metaphysical tradition in decline. Like Kant, Heidegger sought to discover the conditions that made knowledge and action possible. But where Kant considered these conditions as abstract and unchanging,

Heidegger saw them as shaping human activities through an interplay of language and concepts that was decidedly historical.[7] Interplay here was not dialectic. Heidegger refused to inscribe it within a progression that, in Hegel's *Phenomenology*, culminated in the coincidence of reality and self-consciousness known as Absolute (sometimes referred to as Scientific) Knowledge (*Wissenschaft*). In other words, Heidegger shared Hegel's belief in a sense of historicity but not at all in the end toward which specific historical moments were directed. Heidegger followed Hegel concerning the extent to which specific modes of revelation defined the being of entities in time. Yet Heidegger refused to admit any single worldview as definitive, seeing it instead as the symptom of a deeper movement that was always hidden from view (Zimmerman, xiv). In sum, historicity in *Being and Time* was ongoing and never contained by any single moment. Its removal from the directedness or teleology of dialectic was among the most forceful differences setting Heidegger apart from Hegel and closer to the untimeliness of Nietzsche.

What might be the task of philosophy after the last metaphysician? For those who first read this question in *Being and Time*, it was linked to the initial notoriety (scandal?) that Heidegger willfully sought to promote. Emmanuel Lévinas studied philosophy under Husserl and Heidegger at the University of Freiburg in 1928–29 and was among the first in France to write about them. Lévinas was born in Lithuania in 1905 and came to France to study philosophy at the University of Strasbourg in 1925. Even though Lévinas eventually broke with Heidegger because of the latter's ties with National Socialism, his admiration for *Being and Time* ("one of the most beautiful books in the history of philosophy") has remained constant.[8] In an interview in 1982, Lévinas recalled how *Being and Time* defined a set of new problems on which Heidegger hoped to set the agenda of a philosophy grounded in ontology as a study of the state (*Verfasstheit*) as opposed to the whatness (*Washeit*) of beings. For Lévinas, this meant first of all looking again and more closely at language:

> The word *being* (*être*) is normally talked about as if it were a noun, although it is the epitome of a verb. In French, one says *l'être* (Being) or *un être* (a being). Heidegger reawakened the "verbality" of the word *being*; that is, what constitutes the event [*Ereignis*], the "Happening" [*"Geschehen"*], of Being in the word *being*. As if things and everything that is "have a certain way of Being," "practice a profession of Being." Heidegger accustomed us to the richness of these verbal tones. Although it might seem trite today, this reeducation of our listening is unforgettable! Consequently, philosophy would have been (although philosophy itself did not take this into account) an attempt to answer the question of the meaning of Being as verb. Whereas Husserl still

proposed—or seemed to propose—a transcendental program for philosophy, Heidegger clearly defined philosophy, in comparison with other methods of cognition, as "fundamental ontology." (Lévinas, "Admiration and Disappointment," 150)

Lévinas clearly identified the primacy of language and etymology in Heidegger's evolving conception of philosophy starting with *Being and Time*. The
heightened material sensitivity to the word "being" that Heidegger sought to
reawaken among colleagues and readers tied his ontology to the conjuncture
of philosophy and poetry he founded on his reading of classical Greek antiquity. Because language was a means to the "profession of being" Lévinas
identified with the reeducation of listening, it became a privileged site of
disclosure (event or happening) on which Heidegger hoped to reclaim philosophy as fundamental ontology. The beauty of *Being and Time* for Lévinas
was its depiction of human existence as a site of the disclosure of Being (*Dasein*) for which language served as a model. Depiction here meant not only
what, but how; that is, not only the image or representation of *Dasein* set
forth in *Being and Time*, but the conception and practice of language that
made this singular depiction so controversial ("difficult") among philosophers at the time.

If not language and the being of Being, who or what speaks when language speaks? In a strict sense, *Being and Time* inscribed human agency
within the disclosure of Being's essential truth. Whether Heidegger intended
this disclosure as a historical occurrence or whether he saw it instead in
more metaphysical terms is uncertain. Those who approach Heidegger's
writings of the 1920s and 1930s through his postwar texts often dehistori-
cize disclosures concerning the interwar period. They cite Heidegger's infamous dismissal of the 1933–34 rectorate—"the greatest stupidity [*die grösste
Dummheit*] of my life"—in order to avoid considering his philosophy in
conjunction with the rise of National Socialism in Germany. Allegations
over the past decade suggest that this avoidance is greater than many of Heidegger's earlier readers had thought. Recent debate has opposed received
opinion in order to reconsider the extent to which Heidegger's early writings
were marked with signs of historical and political thinking that he and his
followers displaced if not also suppressed. What might such a hypothesis
imply about Heidegger's personal agency and/or intentions? How might it
promote fuller understanding of the ontology set forth in *Being and Time*?
Finally, what might it suggest concerning the evolving reception of Heidegger's writings in France?

Being and Time is generally seen as the product of a traditional concern

with existence and being prior to Heidegger's 1929 conflation of philosophy
and ideological motifs. The priority of philosophical over political concerns
should not, however, be misconstrued as a direct consequence of chronology; it bears instead on a conception of agency and on specific actions Heidegger set forth more fully in the following decade. Yet three to four years
before he became rector under the Nazi regime in April 1933, Heidegger was
already considering how he could contribute as a professor of philosophy at
the University of Freiburg to the disclosure of *Dasein*. In the words of Jürgen
Habermas, "the switches are set for a national revolutionary interpretation
of what in *Being and Time* was a self-heeding and self-assertion sketched in
existential terms. Thus Heidegger, who had opted for the Nazi party before
1933, could explain Hitler's successful power-grab in terms of concepts *retained* from his own analytic of *Dasein*."[9]

Being and Time announced the high ambitions Heidegger already held
for philosophy in the late 1920s. Its acclaim among philosophers—some
might think instead of notoriety—also derived from Heidegger's skill at imposing a controversial perspective with which philosophers were subsequently forced to contend. Thus, by the midtwenties Heidegger was already
adept at manipulating controversy in order to legitimize his powerful professional presence within a German university system he identified in the
1933 rectorate speech as a prime site for spiritual and social change. If, as
Heidegger and many of his exegetes have since claimed, *Being and Time* was
an attempt to overcome metaphysics in the name of a negative ontology (a
de-ontology?), its disclosure of the social and/or political implications of
this overcoming was oblique. In retrospect and from the perspective of the
1930s, *Being and Time* founded an ontology whose relation to the political
and social issues of the period it disclosed only in part.

To what extent could the ontology set forth in *Being and Time* be described as political? Pierre Bourdieu answered the question by dropping the
distinction between philosophical and political approaches in favor of corresponding social and mental spaces:

> What is extraordinary in Heidegger's philosophical enterprise is the fact that
> he intended to mount a revolutionary philosophical coup in *creating*, at the
> heart of the philosophical field, a new position in relation to which all other
> positions would have to be defined. . . . In order to achieve such an upset of
> power relations at the heart of the philosophical field, and give a form of re-
> spectability to stances that were heretical and thus likely to appear vulgar,
> Heidegger had to combine the "revolutionary" dispositions of a rebel with
> the specific authority granted by the accumulation of a considerable amount
> of capital within the field itself.[10]

Bourdieu equated politics with language and the power of discourse, especially in view of the position he attributed to Heidegger regarding authority. Yet although the argument was compelling, discursive power and political power are not necessarily identical. Still, if the ontology in *Being and Time* was already political, attempts to relocate it within a discourse of "pure" philosophy enhanced the very ambiguities, resistances, and "difficulties" Heidegger exploited throughout his career. Initial obstacles to testing Bourdieu's hypothesis of political ontology are inscribed in the so-called difficulty of Heidegger's texts. It is not merely that different readers perform different readings or that literary and philosophical readings are always incompatible. Beyond specific differences among readers and readings, the density and opaqueness of Heidegger's writings seemingly render any single reading inadequate and provisional. Inadequacy extended here from exposition to demonstration and performance. It collapsed the distinction between the disclosure of Being designated by Heidegger's use of the Greek term *aletheia* and the mastery of disclosure performed by textual effects that departed from conventions of argument and logic upheld by other philosophers of the period.

Disclosure also relates issues of intention and agency to the uses to which Heidegger's writings have been put. As with Nietzsche, it is unclear to what extent appropriation after the fact extended beyond what Heidegger may have intended. Regarding Heidegger's postwar reception in France, the key role of Jean Beaufret remains suspect. Nevertheless, it is no coincidence that the literary ("poetic") qualities admired by many of Heidegger's French readers are often at the forefront of debate. As with Nietzsche before him, Heidegger is often dismissed as a "dangerous" philosopher whose ideas advanced the political ends of National Socialism. Current debate supplements earlier allegations with a sense that the difficulty of Heidegger's writings covers what Bourdieu studied as Heidegger's politics of ontology. Inscribing textual difficulty within a mechanism of disclosure promotes a change of perspective that—for better or worse—Bourdieu, Farías, and others have asserted against the grain of received opinion.

Ongoing debate since 1987 was touched off by *Heidegger et le nazisme* (*Heidegger and Nazism*), the translation into French of a text written in Spanish by a one-time student of Heidegger, Victor Farías. A German translation of the book appeared in 1988 and an English version a year later.[11] Lyotard has referred to the Heidegger affair as a "French" affair, but has linked it as well to a wider geophilosophy.[12] This displacement across borders and disciplines imposes strategies of reading that transpose aftereffect into the critical debate of which Heidegger's reception in France is an instance. Until recently, the sheer prestige enjoyed by Heidegger sufficed to dismiss most questions concerning his ties to National Socialism. Jean-Michel Palmier has noted that every study of and introduction to Heidegger inevitably mentioned his involvement with National Socialism, to a point where some readers tried to reread *Sein und Zeit* in terms of "this political engagement of 1933."[13] Palmier analyzed approaches to the problem via personal biography, the rectorate, and the political implications of Heidegger's philosophy. He even went so far as to mention Heidegger's postwar silence and his apparent lack of regret: "Everything suggests that instead of acknowledging he had been tragically mistaken on what Hitler's National Socialism had been, Heidegger considered that the error came from the fact that the movement had somehow not corresponded to the metaphysical truth that he had seen in it" (Palmier, 444). The interpretation is plausible, especially if the extent of Heidegger's political involvement were limited to the rectorate period and if Heidegger's postwar silence concerning the Third Reich were taken as a denial ("the greatest stupidity of my life"). What Palmier appears not to see is that this perceived lack of correspondence did not preclude Heidegger's commitment to a vision of National Socialism at odds with what the movement became as a historical phenomenon. Wolin has noted along similar lines that Heidegger continued throughout his life to distinguish between the "debased historical actuality" of Nazism and what he saw as its "true historical potential."[14] Because, for Heidegger, that potential never became reality, the extent to which his conception of National Socialism can be located within—or perhaps even between—the philosophical/theoretical and the political remains open and undetermined.

Current debate seems to substantiate allegations that Heidegger's allegiance to National Socialism extended well beyond the rectorate period. It also suggests that Heidegger's postwar silence concerning the Third Reich was consistent with a concerted program of partial and duplicitous disclosure perpetrated by him as well as by others on his behalf. To my knowledge, the first text by Heidegger to appear in France was a translation of "What Is Metaphysics?" that was published in 1931 in *Bifur* (no. 8) alongside "La Légende de la vérité" (The legend of truth), a philosopher's tale by the young Jean-Paul Sartre.[15] Following World War II, the divergence between Sartre's 1946 *Existentialism Is a Humanism* and Heidegger's 1947 "Letter on Humanism" moderated an influence Sartre had acknowledged in his 1939–40 war diaries and in the section of *Being and Nothingness* devoted to "The Three H's": Hegel, Husserl, and Heidegger.[16] A decade later, in 1955, Heidegger's

participation in a colloquium organized in his honor in Cerisy-la-Salle so-
lidified a reputation in France that remained more or less intact for thirty
years.

Much (though certainly not all) of the controversy surrounding the
Farias book masked what was perhaps all too evident: namely, that Heidegger's involvement with National Socialism was not news.[17] But if this was
true, then why all the fuss? Why was debate surrounding *Heidegger and
Nazism* so vehement and so sustained? Heidegger's prestige in France was
never uncontested, especially among those philosophers who tracked his interwar and wartime activities firsthand: "The French press has spoken of
Heidegger as a Nazi; it is a fact that he was a party member. If one had to
judge a philosophy by the political courage or lucidity of the philosopher,
that of Hegel would not be worth much. It happens that the philosopher is
unfaithful to his best thought when it becomes a matter of political decisions. . . . Yet it is the same man who philosophizes and who chooses in politics." Although this passage reads as if written in the wake of *Heidegger and
Nazism*, it appeared some forty years earlier, following the Liberation.[18]
How, then, could it come to pass that allegations made some four decades
earlier could suddenly take on the—belated—trappings of scandal?

Debate in France surrounding Heidegger *after* Farias has at times resem-
bled a mock trial played out in popular memory as a return of the repressed.
Earlier in the decade, press coverage of the New Philosophers (*nouveaux
philosophes*), Jean-Marie Le Pen's *Front National* party, and the New French
Right (*nouvelle droite*) had promoted an obsession with parallels—both real
and imagined—between the cultural politics of the 1930s and those of the
more recent "post"-age. Such parallels did not, however, account in full for
the recent furor in France over Heidegger, especially when his involvement
with National Socialism had already been known and debated on more than
one occasion. Much of *Heidegger and Nazism* drew on existing sources, such
as Guido Schneeberger's anthology *Nachlese zu Heidegger* (Supplement to
Heidegger) and the articles by Hugo Ott recently published in book form
under the title *Martin Heidegger: Unterwegs zu seiner Biographie* (*Heidegger:
A Political Life*).[19] Debate over *Heidegger and Nazism* has occurred as a *succès
de scandale* orchestrated by high media visibility.[20] The predisposition to
scandal enhanced an aftereffect Farías exploited to full advantage, as though
the allegations against Heidegger extended to his readers via a logic of cont-
amination. In the resulting atmosphere, debate focused less on engaging
ideas than on judging, and presumably condemning, the alleged actions of
an individual or group.

The inordinate desire to achieve closure on debate surrounding Heidegger drew repeatedly on the trope of anticipation known as prolepsis. In regard to Heidegger in particular, anticipation engaged a disclosure that was integral to the notion of truth as *aletheia*. Aside from its occurrence within the midthirties period of Heidegger's writings known as the turning point (*Kehre*), the interplay between closure and disclosure in "The Origin of the Work of Art" was inscribed in terms of the same social instabilities that dominated the revisionary atmosphere of recent debate. In some instances, the will to closure was clear and visible, as though the irruption of a suppressed or repressed past imposed what Herman Rapaport has referred to as the hermeneutics of detection.[21] The greater the resistance to the past, the more forceful its inevitable return. The point here is neither to condemn Heidegger nor to dispute or dismiss the allegations against him. Rather than filling in the blanks, we need to understand where the blanks come from and why we are only now beginning to see them.

The allegations set forth by Farías against Heidegger illustrate how aftereffect transposes a name and a corpus. In this sense, the extent to which Farías has reopened debate is surprising, especially when so much of the material he provides is biographic. Seemingly, Heidegger's prestige among the French has placed the burden of proof on his detractors. At the same time, however, Steiner has recognized that "owing to Farías's excavations, unscholarly and virulently selective as these often are, specific moments in Heidegger's abject treatment of endangered academic colleagues, in Heidegger's admiration for the Führer, and in Heidegger's cunning tactics of survival, can no longer be passed over" (Steiner, "Heidegger, Again," 45). In fact, Farías relied in large part on biography, using the seventeenth-century Viennese court preacher Ulrich Megerle (also known as Abraham a Sancta Clara) as the model figure around whom he constructed his account of Heidegger's spiritual and ideological evolution between 1910 and 1964 (see Farías, especially 39–55 and 292–301). In so doing, he privileged the closure afforded by biography over evolution and difference. Presumably, Farías framed his argument with Megerle because he wanted to show the constancy of anti-Semitism within Heidegger's writings. Yet he did little to help his reader understand whether this attitude derived from a traditional mistrust of urban worldliness among peasants or from an overt political discourse within Heidegger's philosophical vision before, during, and after the Third Reich.[22]

Farías tried to insert his reading of Heidegger within a number of historical contexts, but his dependence on chronology imposed a structure and a continuity—of the life, of the work—that were belied by the internal breaks undermining his implicit claim to systematic understanding. We may, for example, attribute a coherence to writings whose evolution we fail to recognize because we reduce them to partial expressions of a predetermined whole. Thus we tend by habit to impose identity and repetition over difference. In so doing, we displace, deny, and suppress difference to a point where scandal and controversy are the marks of a return that is ongoing and open-ended. As long as doubt and uncertainty remain, allegations such as those made in *Heidegger and Nazism* will continue to receive a minimal degree of serious consideration. The questions of whether they are stated convincingly and whether they further understanding of Heidegger, Nazism, or modernity remain separate and unresolved.

A Historical Matter

Because the fact of Heidegger's affiliation with the National Socialist party was not in itself news, the intense debate surrounding *Heidegger and Nazism* was less an aftereffect of revelation than of rereading. No more "poetic" readings, unless "poetic" were taken ironically as a cover for *aletheia* as duplicitous disclosure. Beyond whatever *Heidegger and Nazism* did or did not prove, it was no longer possible after Farías to read Heidegger as before. That is, it was no longer possible to detach Heidegger's practice of philosophy from political allegiances he seemingly preferred to disclose in part and long after the fact. Nor was it possible to dismiss in advance the place of these allegiances within a philosophical vision whose removal from political realities was proven in retrospect to have been illusory. A preliminary example of aftereffect by rereading is in order, and the one I have in mind predates current debate by almost twenty years. Hannah Arendt (1906–1975) was a political philosopher and critic whose books include *The Origins of Totalitarianism* (1951), *Eichmann in Jerusalem* (1963), and *Men in Dark Times* (1968). She also edited Karl Jaspers's *The Great Philosophers* (1962–66) and Walter Benjamin's *Illuminations* (1965). Arendt studied philosophy with Heidegger at Marburg and with Edmund Husserl at Freiburg before writing a dissertation with Jaspers at Heidelberg in 1929 on the concepts of love in the writings of Saint Augustine. The ties between Arendt and Heidegger were extensive and complex. Soon after they met in Marburg in 1925 they became lovers; this relationship continued until Arendt broke it off around the time Heidegger joined the Nazi party in 1933. After emigrating to France in the early 1930s, Arendt came to the United States, where she taught at the New School for Social Research and the University of Chicago.[23]

Heidegger once described Arendt as unmatched in her knowledge of the Greek language. She was also a German Jewish woman attentive to issues of assimilation, Zionism, and anti-Semitism. Presumably Arendt was in a privileged position to understand Heidegger's views and activities during as well as following his rectorate at Freiburg. At the very least, one imagines that she was an informed and interested reader of Heidegger's writings. Yet nowhere did Arendt state or even suggest that she was aware of the extent of Heidegger's involvement with the Nazi party after the rectorate episode. Her sharpest words on the subject appeared in a footnote to an article published in *Partisan Review* in 1946, "What Is Existenz Philosophy?":

> In his capacity as Rector of Freiburg University, [Heidegger] forbade Husserl, his former teacher and friend, whose lecture chair he had inherited, to enter the faculty, because Husserl was a Jew. Finally, it has been rumored that he has placed himself at the disposal of the French occupational authorities for the reeducation of the German people. . . . In view of the real comedy of this development, and of the no less low level of political thought in German universities, one is naturally inclined not to bother with the whole story. On the other hand, there is the point that this whole mode of behavior has exact parallels in German Romanticism, so that one can scarcely believe the coincidence is accidental. Heidegger is the last (we hope) romantic—as it were, a tremendously gifted Friedrich Schlegel or Adam Mueller, whose complete irresponsibility was attributed partly to the delusion of genius, partly to desperation. (Cited in Young-Bruehl, 217–18)

Twenty-three years later, Arendt added to her 1946 account in a text commemorating Heidegger's eightieth birthday.[24] She began by evoking an early figure of Heidegger as instructor (Privatdozent) and assistant working under Husserl at Freiburg in 1919. From the perspective of 1969, Arendt saw Heidegger's initial fame as based on the reputation of his lectures among students, a reputation that the publication of *Being and Time* in 1927 confirmed. Thus, she contended, it was Heidegger's thinking rather than his philosophy that "shared so decisively in determining the spiritual physiognomy of this century" (Arendt, "Heidegger at Eighty," 210).

For Arendt, the appearance of *Being and Time* replaced the cult of the teacher with that of the philosopher who *thought* metaphysics through to its end via a series of pathways or woodpaths (*Holzwege*) that were later invoked in the title of Heidegger's collected essays written between 1935 and 1946. Significantly, Arendt characterized Heidegger's project in the wake of *Being and Time* in terms that implied its distinctiveness: "This is a historical matter, perhaps even of the first order; but it need not trouble those of us who do not belong to the guilds, including the historical" (211). Is this sense of philosophical tradition the true limit of Heidegger's involvement with history? Arendt's text provides what I see as at least two answers to this question. A first answer portrays a pursuit of the so-called "abode" or residence of thinking as a "coming-into-nearness to the distant" (Arendt, 214). The passage is taken from Heidegger's *Discourse on Thinking*, a text from 1959 that Arendt set alongside another from *Introduction to Metaphysics* (1935–36) in which the question of thinking was set "out of order" and thus apart from everyday life. The temporal removal between the two accounts was curious, almost as though Arendt inadvertently extended Heidegger's ambiguity via inversion. This interpretation was strengthened when Arendt wrote that "this nearness-remoteness relation and its inversion in thinking pervades Heidegger's whole work, like a key to which everything is attuned. Presence and absence, concealing and revealing, nearness and distance— their interlinkage and the connections that prevail among them have next to nothing to do with the truism that there would be no presence unless absence was experienced, no nearness without distance, no revealing without concealing" (214–15). Arendt did not set the paired terms in the preceding passage within a dialectical progression of thesis, antithesis, and synthesis; instead, she asserted the extended interplay that Heidegger had developed in the midthirties as the concept of disclosure.

"Heidegger at Eighty" provided a second account of Heidegger's involvement with history when Arendt referred directly to the rectorate episode. She did this with surprising understatement: "As far as the world is concerned, [Heidegger] was served much worse than Plato, because the tyrant and his victims were not located on the other side of the ocean, but in his own country. As far as he himself is concerned, I believe the matter is different. He was young enough to learn from the shock of the collision, which drove him back to his inherited abode after ten short hectic months thirty-five years ago, and to settle what he had experienced in his thinking" (216). With all due respect to Arendt, her assessment was inaccurate. The Freiburg rectorate episode occurred when Heidegger was in his midforties; Arendt was overly charitable to treat it as a youthful error. Furthermore, it is known today that Heidegger remained a member of the Nazi party through 1945. As a result, the so-called withdrawal to the abode of thinking may have been less of a retreat from the world of history and politics than Arendt and others thought. Even if Heidegger did nothing more than pay membership dues to the party, suspicion over the extent of his involvement now extends toward the meaning to be imputed to his postwar silence concerning the Nazi policy of extermination.

Curiously, Arendt's direct attempt to contend with Heidegger's "error" performed its own displacement. The brief passage in the main text of her article was supplemented by a pagelong footnote that began as follows:

> There are many aspects to this escapade, which today—now that the embitterment has died down and, above all, the numerous false reports have been somewhat corrected—is usually called an "error." Among them are aspects of the Weimar Republic, which did not at all show itself to its contemporaries in the rosy light it now has for us, against the horrible background of the years that followed it. The contents of this error differed significantly from the "errors" that were then common. Who else but Heidegger came up with the idea that National Socialism was the "encounter between planetarily determined technology and modern human beings"—except perhaps those who read, instead of Hitler's *Mein Kampf,* some of the Italian futurists' writings, which fascism, in contrast to National Socialism, referred to here and there. (284)

Arendt's desire to set things straight concerning Heidegger was consistent with her views on the "dark times" of interwar Germany, the Third Reich, and the Holocaust. Yet it is difficult to read her article today without noting the fallibility of her insight. I have invoked Arendt because her desire in the 1971 text "to honor the thinkers" (216) illustrates the extent to which the claims made in *Heidegger and Nazism* have undermined previous accounts that had been taken as informed, if not also authoritative. This *risk* of subverted understanding raises the stakes of debate surrounding the Farías book and aftereffect. *Heidegger and Nazism* promoted a hermeneutic of suspicion that consistently extended beyond what Farías actually succeeded in proving. As the gap between claim and demonstration only added to the controversy, emphasis was displaced from Heidegger's writings to the various receptions they have received. Arendt's two accounts can be read—in retrospect and against her explicit intentions—as blind to the very political and social realities of interwar Germany to which Heidegger was responding, first in *Being and Time* and later in the texts of the Freiburg rectorate. It is the issue of how such blindness can be appropriated—that is, the uses and causes it can be made to serve—that has raised debate over *Heidegger and Nazism* to the point of scandal.

Scandal II

Heidegger and Nazism was at least as scandalous in what it implied about the French reception of Heidegger as in what it revealed about Heidegger himself. In this sense, the question "Why, Heidegger and the Nazis?" might be rephrased as "Why, Heidegger and the Nazis . . . *now?*" It was likewise important to consider the social, political, and institutional conditions that made the (serious) reception of a book like *Heidegger and Nazism* possible. For what is regarded as meaningful depends not only on historical context, but also on a recognition that this context is itself problematic. Rüdiger Bubner addressed this issue in discussing the evolution of modern German philosophy: "The historicity of contemporary philosophy finds its expression in the shape of its problems. In the range of the problems that are recognized as actual, contemporary philosophy defines itself as against tradition and at the same time puts itself into a relationship to it."[25] In Bubner's terms, the problems of philosophy were not just those that legitimized by tradition, but also and especially those that were unforeseen and for which there might be no simple or immediate solution. The suspicion that Farías projected onto the "other" Heidegger—that is, the Heidegger who seems *not* to have retreated from politics after the rectorate period—extended toward a wider condition of engaging exactly those unforeseen problems that irrupted as scandal and aftereffect.

Debate over Heidegger in the wake of *Heidegger and Nazism* has inevitably engaged issues of revision and, in particular, the extent to which the claims made by and for Farías have altered our understanding of the interwar past. Once again, revision affected not just what we may, or may not, have come to understand about Heidegger, but also how we have come to view those whose intellectual debts to Heidegger were seemingly compromised. This means that we should not exclude the resistances that mediated revision by displacing or even dismissing "difficult" questions for which there were no easy answers. Resistance here was often indirect and inadvertent. Alternatively, it was open and an effect of suppression. On this side of the Atlantic, Richard Rorty has asserted the preeminence of moral concerns bearing on revision in the wake of the Farías book when he asked why anyone should care whether Heidegger was a self-deceptive egomaniac:

> A good reason for caring about such matters is that the details about the attitudes of German intellectuals toward the Holocaust are important for our own moral education. It pays to realize that the vast majority of German academics, some of the best and brightest, turned a blind eye to the fate of their Jewish colleagues, and to ask whether we ourselves might not be capable of the same sort of behavior. . . . A bad reason for caring is the notion that learning about a philosopher's moral character helps one evaluate his philosophy. It does not, any more than our knowledge of Einstein's character helps us evaluate his physics. You can be a great, original, and profound artist or thinker, and a complete bastard.[26]

Rorty clearly identified the moral stake in debate over *Heidegger and Nazism*. Yet his apparent desire to reject Heidegger the rector and Nazi party member in order to redeem ("save") the philosopher and author of *Being and Time* was questionable (*fragwürdig*) in the two senses noted earlier. What remained unquestioned for Rorty—and this in spite of his straight-talking allusions to good and bad reasons—was the perceived exemplarity of Heidegger's writings over and above their author. Absolute categories of good and bad as Rorty used them were forceful, yet it was hard not to see the extent to which Rorty invoked them to trivialize the more complex ("diffi-cult") question of how Heidegger came to identify his fundamental ontol-ogy with what he later described as the inner truth and essence of National Socialism. Even if Heidegger had willfully sought to dissociate his philoso-phy from his political views or from the politics of the Third Reich and post-war Germany, their articulation could not be dismissed as neatly as Rorty suggested. It remained hard ("difficult"?!) to dismiss the extent of Heideg-ger's involvement with Nazi cultural politics during and after the rectorate. In response to Rorty, Christopher Norris rightly protested what he saw as an attempt to trivialize an extensive and serious involvement into a sentimental error, a species of category mistake.[27] Good and bad reasons notwithstand-ing, Rorty's defense of Heidegger simply did not hold.

How (seriously) were Heidegger's writings to be taken in the wake of de-bate following the Farías book? Should they be dismissed outright because of political allegiances of their author that many found to be reprehensible? Or were they instead untimely meditations and part of a philosophical vi-sion with little or no ties to the politics and social realities of interwar Ger-many? These questions were raised by the appearance in France of numer-ous articles, dossiers, and more than a dozen studies that followed the publication of *Heidegger and Nazism*. The specificity of Heidegger's political allegiance—its extent and duration—almost mattered less than the fact that debate made it more and more difficult to deny or refute what Karsten Har-ries has referred to as the essential connection between Heidegger's embrace of National Socialism and his philosophical thinking (Harries, "Introduc-tion," xviii). Aftereffect was staged as the shock or scandal at recognizing the elements of piety and the pastoral in Heidegger's writings as poses that dis-simulated a more dangerous vision of political and social change for which Nazi Germany could easily have served as a test case. Resistance on the part of Heidegger's sympathetic readers transformed this dissimulation into cen-sorship so that only the infrequent irruption of scandal afforded insight that tendentious reverence otherwise suppressed.

Some used *Heidegger and Nazism* as evidence to condemn or defend Heidegger and his writings; others used it to develop wider projects. Luc Ferry and Alain Renaut argued in *Heidegger and Modernity* that the Farías affair was one result of a Heidegger revival whose ties with a disenchanted French left they viewed with bemusement. By what strange inversion, they asked, had someone who was more than a fellow traveler of the Nazis become a principal philosopher of the Left? The question was provocative. It was also disingenuous and self-serving, especially when Ferry and Renaut inscribed their discussion of debate over Heidegger within a critique of modernity whose philosophical model found exemplary expression in his writings:

> The deepest significance of the debate, for which the Farías book and even the Heidegger case are merely the occasion, becomes clear: it hinges on—we can see this clearly in Derrida—the criticism of modernity, and what defines it philosophically, culturally, and no doubt also politically, namely the outbreak of subjectivity and the values of humanism. The Heidegger controversy merely stands in the foreground of a controversy that has a quite different impact, involving nothing less than the significance attributed to the logic of modernity; if we argue so much about it today, isn't it because Heidegger's deconstruction of modernity provided a considerable part of the French intelligentsia with the bases and style of its criticism of the modern world?[28]

For Ferry and Renaut, Heidegger's critique split between positions they described as postmodern and antimodern. Heidegger was postmodern to the extent that his call to Nazi revolution promoted an end to and transcendence of modernity. He was antimodern in that his call for a return to the Greek tradition responded to and rejected European decadence. Both positions were taken as critiques of modernity and, in particular, of democracy as its political expression. Where the postmodern Heidegger liquidated subjectivity by passing from democracy toward authoritarian movements, the antimodern Heidegger responded to a vision of decline with laments of rootlessness and lost traditions that led him to his attempts at renewing a certain Greek antiquity.

The critiques of modernity Ferry and Renaut attributed to Heidegger revealed little more than what was set forth as philosophy often took on ideological—if not openly political—status. Though they stated that the time for polemicizing was over, Ferry and Renaut seemed more concerned with the new-look Heideggerians they wanted to discredit than with the philosophical issues they claimed to address. This fall into polemic was a symptom of place and time, pointing to a wider coming to terms with a political past visible in Heidegger's writings but certainly not limited to them. Where Rorty took Heidegger's philosophy seriously over and against the man who wrote it, Ferry and Renaut were more interested in upbraiding self-styled Heideggerians whom they seemed to take almost *too* seriously!

The institutional context of Philippe Lacoue-Labarthe's *Heidegger, Art, and Politics* was significant. The book began as a supplement, a statement Lacoue-Labarthe was asked to write by the committee of examiners to which he had submitted his candidacy for a *Doctorat d'Etat* on the basis of cumulative work *(sur travaux)*. This context also transformed what might otherwise have been misconstrued as a statement of faith *(profession de foi)* into a reflection on the claim to philosophize imposed by authority of the French university system. Ironically, Lacoue-Labarthe questioned this claim by staging his engagement with Heidegger's writings as a potential measure of philosophy's limits. Attentive readers recognized the gesture as deconstructive in that it posited the problem of a provisional end or closure that Derrida and others have modeled on Heidegger's notions of *Destruktion, Zerstörung,* and *Abbau*. The gesture was neither respectful homage nor stylistic indulgence; it was most certainly not arbitrary. For the question of determining philosophy's limits openly engaged the very kinds of ambitions that Heidegger held for philosophy from the late-twenties period of *Being and Time* through the interview that took place in 1966 but was not published in *Der Spiegel* until after his death in 1976.

Lacoue-Labarthe approached the question of philosophy's limits within and especially outside the university: "And it is outside the University, or on its fringes, that at the same time an imitation twice removed has assumed the title of philosophy (Sartre) and that thinkers of an otherwise rigorous exigency and of a completely different sobriety have continually tested, at its limit, the capacity-to-philosophize [*le pouvoir-philosopher*] (Benjamin and Wittgenstein, Bataille and Blanchot, for example)."[29] Two remarks are in order. First, the spatial metaphor associated with the terms "limit" and "fringes" in the preceding passage characterized legitimation as centrifugal (decentered) rather than centripetal (centered). Second, legitimation was tied to practices of autobiography and confession that elided the distinction between "man" and "work" that Farías (and Rorty, in his wake) seemed intent on maintaining.

Early in his account, Lacoue-Labarthe identified the origin of his own (modest) claim to philosophize when he wrote that a reading of Heidegger gave him a first jolt (11); he used the French word *choc* and added *Stoss,* the

German term for push or shove that he may well have borrowed from "The Origin of the Work of Art." At about the same time, he learned that Heidegger had been a member of the Nazi party. From the start, then, Lacoue-Labarthe read the Heideggerian text in view of a political commitment that he could not abide. This meant also that he refused both to separate the political from the philosophical and to reduce the former to the status of an aberration:

> My hypothesis is as follows: it lies, on the one hand, in the tenor and style of the commitment of 1933 which are precisely (because it is a commitment that is involved) philosophical, and as a consequence produce statements that are philosophical in type and can be located as such in the tradition. The commitment of 1933 is founded on the idea of a hegemony of the spiritual and the philosophical over the political itself (this is the theme of *Führung* of the *Führung*, or of the *Führer*), which leads us back at least to the Platonic *basiléia*, if not to Empedocles. His statements (on Germany, on work, on the University, etc.) are purely and simply programmatic and are, moreover, organized in a number of "Appeals." On the other hand, if it is true that certain of these calls (the most immediately political or the least removed from the National Socialist program) will subsequently be unequivocally abandoned and repudiated, in its deep intention and the essential nature of its aspirations, the injunction of 1933 will be maintained to the end. (13)

Lacoue-Labarthe began by asserting that a serious commitment to National Socialism pervaded the 1933–34 rectorate period, a period that some —including Heidegger—have trivialized as a lapse. Yet, Lacoue-Labarthe continued, the status of the period in question remained ambiguous. For while the seriousness of Heidegger's commitment had been documented over and above his own statements to the contrary, it had also been invoked in order to dismiss Heidegger's writings outright and thus precisely in order *not* to read them. In both instances, a gesture of avoidance foreclosed textual analysis according to criteria that were motivated at least as much by moral as by historical and/or political concerns. Lacoue-Labarthe's conclusion was unequivocal: in 1933, Heidegger neither slipped nor faltered. He willingly committed himself to the rectorate and to what he might accomplish by making the university a prime site of National Socialism's transformation of German society: "In 1933 Heidegger is not mistaken [ne se trompe pas]. But he knows in 1934 that he was mistaken [s'est trompé]; not about the truth of Nazism but about its reality" (20).

To resume at this point, Lacoue-Labarthe saw Heidegger's commitment to National Socialism as unequivocal and serious when he made it, even if one limited its direct political expression—that is, its impact on the institution of the German university system—to the ten months of the rectorate. For Lacoue-Labarthe, the position set forth on Heidegger's writings of the rectorate period was consistent with a philosophical vision that retained a disposition for the "essential truth and greatness" of National Socialism long after he resigned from the rectorship. But what was this disposition and how might an understanding of its evolution help to account for the intensity of recent debate? More pointedly, was Heidegger's withdrawal following the rectorate only an accommodation that removed him from public view without moderating his support of National Socialism?

Lacoue-Labarthe's remarks concerning the coincidence of politics and philosophy in Heidegger's writings were clearly more incisive than the topical concerns that Ferry and Renaut expressed in *Heidegger and Modernity.* Yet Lacoue-Labarthe did not, I believe, follow through the full implications of his argument. Although he grasped the seriousness and extent of Heidegger's commitment, his reference (in the passage previously quoted) to "a number of 'Appeals'" was surprisingly elliptical. The same held true for the "deep and essential expectations" of the 1933 injunction. Why did Lacoue-Labarthe stop short at the rectorate period? If Heidegger's commitment to the rectorate was unequivocal and serious when he made it, what might explain his resignation less than a year later? Lacoue-Labarthe's answers to these questions were surprisingly indirect and understated. They focused on a sense of the discrepancy between the "truth" and the "reality" of Nazism as he referred to them in the passage just quoted. Presumably, the discrepancy resulted from Heidegger's recognition of National Socialism as a political *reality* whose philosophical *truth* he had mistaken as compatible with *Being and Time* and his subsequent writings. Such an account was generous and forgiving almost to the point of apology. It implied that Heidegger's resignation marked a refusal on his part to allow ontology to serve political ends unworthy of it. Self-critique led to self-correction and to the withdrawal from politics associated with the *Kehre.* Yet this was certainly not at all the only way to interpret the 1933–34 transition, especially if the *reality* of National Socialism were seen as less committed to the political and social changes that Heidegger had hoped (however idealistically) to enact via the rectorate.

Heidegger's 1933 rectorate speech supported this second interpretation by asserting the role that the university's self-determination might play in promoting a National Socialist conception of nationhood. In fact, self-determination was so strongly asserted that one could argue, via the trope of crossover known as chiasmus, that Heidegger came to see the philosophical *reality* of National Socialism as inadequate to the implied *political* truth of *Being and Time*. In such terms, Heidegger might well have become more Nazi than the Nazis and thus a liability by extremism that the party program could not tolerate. Long after the fact, Heidegger reported that Otto Wacker, Nazi secretary of education during the rectorate period, accused him of subscribing to a "'private National Socialism' that circumvented the perspectives of the Party program" (Harries, "Introduction," xxxii). As with the statement from Sartre's *Critique of Dialectical Reason* cited at the very beginning of this chapter, the case of Heidegger may already have been too complex even in 1933–34 for the Nazis to explain! Neither Lacoue-Labarthe's motives nor his fairness strike me as questionable. Yet it is as though the institutional context of Lacoue-Labarthe's statement placed a burden of accountability on him that ought instead to have been projected onto Heidegger and his texts. The initial call to accountability was directed toward the candidate-critic whose claim to philosophize set him into a mediating role between the institution and a complex ("difficult"?) figure. Heidegger was both a fiction constructed cumulatively through Lacoue-Labarthe's readings and a figure of the institution, discipline, and tradition that located those readings—even uneasily—within the history of German philosophy. This complexity did not hide the relation to power staged as a rite of passage within the French university system. Lacoue-Labarthe's recourse to autobiography erased the distinctions between work and man (text and author) that Rorty sought to maintain. It was also a disarming move in a tradition that engaged philosophy in the experience of everyday life. At the same time, however, autobiography internalized a vulnerability imposed by the setting of the defense (*soutenance*) as a call to justify a claim to knowledge that the university could either accept or reject. The result—despite Lacoue-Labarthe's candor—moderated the direct and extended encounter with Heidegger to which he clearly aspired.

Getting Serious

Debate in the wake of the allegations made by Farías continues to transpose Heidegger into an exemplary figure. Depending on the commentator, Heidegger can be made to stand for deconstruction and continental philosophy, as well as "theory" and, by implication, against hermeneutics and analytical philosophy. Such transposition distorts to the point of caricature, and also suggests why many positions for or against Heidegger are so weak and beside the point. Transposition becomes a symptom of the extent to which debate as polemic conflates the ostensible issues at hand (namely, the extent and duration of Heidegger's involvement with National Socialism) and a more general struggle over cultural legitimation ranging from canon, genre, and medium to national and disciplinary practices. For some, this struggle is a constant, the deep structure or true stake in all discourse grounded in what Foucault termed the inevitable relation between power and knowledge. For others, more localized concerns direct debate toward struggles related to institution, discourse, and discipline. The continuing controversy over a book as weakly argued as *Heidegger and Nazism* suggests that current debate is seriously flawed. It is not merely that the wrong kinds of arguments are being used to address the right kinds of issues; the peculiarities of debate related to Farías on Heidegger are related to the uneven reception of deconstruction in the Anglo-American academy. In such terms, the name or figure of Heidegger can be made to stand for something like deconstruction before the fact, if not also for a conflated "continental" practice that purportedly threatens traditional distinctions between philosophy and literature.

The distortions and transpositions surrounding Heidegger thrive because many who do not know the history of deconstruction might wish for it to be scandalous. While I see no simple or quick way to be done with the current scandal of aftereffect surrounding Heidegger, a number of considerations strike me as worthy. To begin, future debate should strive less to determine a definitive meaning than to trace an ongoing movement intelligible through a series of changes. This is not to say that the true meaning of Heidegger's writings will appear only gradually and after a certain period of time will have passed. Nor does it suggest that rereading is always already mediated by the passage of time and thus at a necessary remove from an originary meaning it can never expect to attain. To the contrary, debate over Heidegger is very much a current affair engaging the claim to authority that Farías makes against the uneven grain of received opinion. The point would be to recognize instead the scope of this unevenness in order to determine the extent of common ground it might also contain. Lacoue-Labarthe wrote that it would be better to stop seeing fascism in pathological terms and instead recognize in it not only "one of the age's possible political forms—and one no more inadequate or aberrant than any other—but [also] the political form that was most able to provide enlightenment regarding the essence of modern politics" (Lacoue-Labarthe, *Heidegger, Art, and Politics,* 107).[30]

Lacoue-Labarthe correctly specified the political form of fascism as the unnamed object around which various receptions had circulated as instances of what Heidegger might well have dismissed as idle chatter *(Gerede).* Aside from straight denial, the failure to contend with the full political implications of fascism occurs most often when politics and art blend together into a kind of staged epic. This staging, often close to a phenomenon of national aestheticism, draws on affect to arouse responses that transform direct political ends into more nebulous terms of nation, homeland, and patriotism. In addition, it allows the individual agent or subject of history to dissolve within a group so as to avoid personal accountability for actions undertaken collectively. For Lacoue-Labarthe, Heidegger consented to this staging during the rectorate period despite misgivings concerning the discrepancies between his vision of National Socialism and those of party ideologues.

An additional concern points to the past and to narration of it as a series of operations on—and with—language. Because the act of writing history inevitably manipulates elements of narrative, what end does such manipulation serve? What motivates it? What claims to legitimation—either explicit or implied—does it make? Hayden White has raised these questions in conjunction with remarks on the authority attached to certain accounts that imposed on real events the forms and coherence more commonly associated with stories about imaginary events. For White, the authority of historical narrative arose from a desire to make experience meaningful and coherent, a desire whose origin White located in wishes, daydreams, and reveries. Historiography allowed this desire for the imaginary and the possible to be considered against the imperatives of the real and the actual: "If we view narration and narrativity as the instruments with which the conflicting claims of the imaginary and the real are mediated, arbitrated, or resolved in a discourse, we begin to comprehend both the appeal of narrative and the grounds for refusing it."[31] White reached no definitive conclusion concerning the function of narration, but the questions he raised about the appeal of narration and narrativity in the representation of events construed to be true rather than imaginary bear directly on current debate.

The turn to a contested past I have sketched in discussing recent debate over Vichy and Heidegger should not be mistaken for a historicism with scientistic ambitions of objectivity. This is especially the case because the turn is imposed rather than chosen, a precondition rather than a situation resulting from individual or collective agency. Furthermore, attempts to attain rapid closure derive from claims to mastery and appropriation that are often unexamined. Much of the problem comes from a mentality of detection that winds up being more or less ineffectual.

In the case of Heidegger, debate over *Heidegger and Nazism* has disclosed the extent to which growing resistance had undermined the prestige Hei-

degger and his writings had enjoyed among artists and intellectuals following World War II. This was especially, but certainly not solely, the case in
France. That Farías argued his case weakly and that he provided little
archival material that others such as Hugo Ott had not already provided
mattered little. What mattered was what the hyperbole and media visibility
made all too clear: namely, the defenses with which Heidegger and his apologists had countered allegations as far back as the 1946–47 debate in *Les
Temps Modernes* were refuted by documentation that attained the status of
undeniable fact. Revised perception after Farías transformed Heidegger's involvement with National Socialism from a minor episode into a permanent
taint (Wolin, "The French Heidegger Debate," 137). The timing of this revised perception also extended the progressive engagement of aftereffects
Henry Rousso has referred to as the Vichy syndrome. Following the 1985 release of *Shoah* and the belated trial of Klaus Barbie for wartime crimes after
his forced return to France in 1983, the revelations in *Heidegger and Nazism*
reconfirmed France's obsession with a wartime past with which it had not
yet fully contended. As detractors gloated, it was as though a disclosure of
disclosure had turned against the philosopher for whom it had once served
as a model of experience.

   The deaths of Barthes, Sartre, Lacan, and Foucault between 1980 and
1984 marked the decline of a generation of postwar intellectuals that some,
such as Ferry and Renaut, had come to see as antihumanist. Lacoue-
Labarthe argued in passing that a number of "great figures" from Drieu and
Brasillach to Benjamin, Bataille, and Malraux were all duped by history and
that, all things considered, Heidegger's merit will have been that he suc-
cumbed for only ten months to "the Janus-headed illusion of 'new times'"
(Lacoue-Labarthe, *Heidegger, Art, and Politics,* 22). Belatedness here bordered on the banal, and Lacoue-Labarthe admitted as much. It is also important that belatedness served as an alibi that elided the specificity of commitment. After the fact, not all errors are identical, nor are they always to be
equated with wrongdoing. Differences of ideology, time, and place are likewise anything but negligible. Whether or not we want to admit it, we are
likely to learn little from debate surrounding Heidegger until we question
the assumptions that keep National Socialism a taboo we would rather dismiss than examine. Geoffrey Hartman redirected debate along such lines
when he described a postwar Heidegger who wrote as the bystander-thinker
or middle voice he always was "after a calamitous brush with politics," before
adding that the enormity of the destruction unmentioned in Heidegger's
1947 "Letter on Humanism" has created a change "we are still trying to as-

sess."[32] Thinking Nazism is more than rethinking or evaluating it, for, in La-coue-Labarthe's words, "the phenomenon was not born out of nothing, but came from us, 'good Europeans that we are'" (*Heidegger, Art, and Politics,* 127).

Where to go from here? One option among others is visible in a conver-gence of Nazism and modernism surrounding the figure of Heidegger in the titles of the books by Farías and by Ferry and Renaut. Dropping Heidegger in the sense of deleting the concerns of biography is necessary if only be-cause insufficient documentation reduces serious inquiry to speculation. Lacoue-Labarthe avoided this pitfall only in part because he used the auto-biographical to ground his assessment of Heidegger in terms of the very kind of personal involvement that Ferry and Renaut took to be compromis-ing. The confessional nature of Lacoue-Labarthe's account emphasized the reality of the relation to—or even *with*—Heidegger in lived and/or existen-tial terms that Ferry and Renaut simply failed to engage.

We might prefer to believe otherwise, but admitting fascism and/or Na-tional Socialism as integral to certain conceptions of recent modernity is one of our big cultural nightmares. It is not just that we might be implicated indirectly at a remove of time and place. We are always contaminated in ad-vance through Heidegger and de Man as well as through all those who in one sense or another made common cause with the project of a revolution from the extreme right. This is, I imagine, an unpopular message among readers who style themselves as liberals. Yet the ongoing debates over Hei-degger and de Man will be of little more than passing interest until we ad-dress the resistance imposed by liberal biases that fail to contend with the full implications of what it means to associate fascism with modernity. This means taking a longer and harder look at our cultural past than many of us are willing to do. In the end, the scandalous disclosure of a certain past sur-rounding Heidegger and de Man is not simply "theirs"; through them, it is very much ours as well. This is the primary sense of what it means to take Heidegger—and the scandal of aftereffect—seriously.

CHAPTER THREE

White Out

Dispersal and Doubling

Before the work, the writer does not yet exist; after the work, he is no longer there: which means that his existence is open to question—and we call him an "author"! It would be more correct to call him an "actor," the ephemeral character who is born and dies each evening in order to make himself extravagantly seen, killed by the performance that makes him visible— that is, without anything of his own or hiding anything in some secret place.
Maurice Blanchot, *Après coup*

History does not withhold meaning, no more than meaning, which is always ambiguous—plural—can be reduced to its historical realization, even the most tragic and the most enormous.
Maurice Blanchot, *Après coup*

Some books lead to revolutions, others to scandal. Response to the October 1987 appearance of Victor Farías's *Heidegger and Nazism* divided between hostility directed toward Farías himself and the revised figure of Heidegger portrayed in his book. Editorials and follow-up coverage in the scholarly and even popular press extended into the winter, sometimes on a daily basis. Many who had read the book (as well as others who had not) took strong position for or against it. An interview with Jacques Derrida in the November 6–12, 1987, issue of the mass-circulation weekly *Le Nouvel Observateur,* was of special interest. Derrida had been writing on Heidegger since the 1960s and two books by him, *De l'esprit* and *Psyché,* were released within weeks of the Farías book. The coincidence was so striking that it was hard not to read *De l'esprit* and the sections on Heidegger in *Psyché* in tandem with *Heidegger and Nazism.*[1]

The interview showed Derrida attentive to the moral issues and the emotion surrounding the resurgent debate. In this sense, Derrida asked whether condemning Nazism outright did not foreclose the extended analysis that was desirable in place of what, in some cases, was nothing more than intellectual posturing in the guise of moral judgment. Concerning the nature and extent of Heidegger's ties to National Socialism, such posturing extended patterns of proleptic avoidance that bordered on the pathological. For many, it was as though any serious attempt to engage the issues raised by and surrounding the Farías book—even to the point of invoking National Socialism at all—was perceived as tainted and objectionable. Denial was the just measure of questions and issues that, as Derrida put it, many of Heidegger's readers seemingly preferred to neglect, if not also forget.

> How can it be denied? Why cry out that so many "revolutionary," audacious, and unsettling works of the twentieth century—in philosophy and in literature—have ventured, even committed themselves in regions haunted by what is diabolical for a philosophy confident of its liberal and democratic left-wing humanism? Instead of erasing or trying to forget it, should one try instead to account for this experience, in other words, for our times? without believing that all this is henceforth clear for us? The task, the duty, and—in truth—the only new or interesting thing, is it not to try to recognize the analogies and possible breaks between what is called Nazism—this enormous, plural, and differentiated continent whose roots remain obscure—and, on the other side, a Heideggerian thought that is just as multiple and that will remain for a long time provocative, enigmatic, still to be read? Not because it might hold in reserve, ever encrypted, a correct [*bonne*] and reassuring politics, a "left-wing Heideggerianism," but because it opposes to the Nazism that was a Nazism of its own that is more "revolutionary" and purer?[2]

For Derrida, the issue of Heidegger's involvement with National Socialism opened onto the multiple relations ("analogies and possible breaks") between National Socialism and practices of cultural modernity, relations that remained either unexamined or appropriated in the name of a "correct and reassuring politics." Beyond these options, Derrida sketched a third inquiry—decidedly provocative and *in*correct—that rejected the thesis of a ("reassuring") left-wing Heideggerianism in favor of an unequivocal commitment to a more radical ("more 'revolutionary' and purer") conception of National Socialism than many readers of Heidegger would care to confront. Close to three months after the interview with Derrida, a *Nouvel Observateur* dossier on what had by then become L'Affaire Heidegger appeared under the title "Heidegger et la pensée nazie" (Heidegger and Nazi thought). The dossier contained contributions from a variety of Heidegger scholars including Derrida, Philippe Lacoue-Labarthe, and François Fédier. A second set of contributions came from former students and acquaintances such as Hans-Georg Gadamer, Jürgen Habermas, and Emmanuel Lévinas. Blanchot contributed to the dossier by submitting a text in the form of a letter. Neither a philosopher by profession nor a former student, friend, or colleague of Heidegger, Blanchot had written on Heidegger, notably in *L'Entretien infini* (*The Infinite Conversation*), and had contributed a short passage (later published in *L'attente l'oubli*) to a collection commemorating Heidegger's seventieth birthday in 1959. Who, then, was Heidegger for Blanchot and what might it mean for him to write a letter in 1988 on Heidegger and National Socialism?

Blanchot first acknowledged that the format of essay and tone of personal remembrance conveyed a false sense of authority to speak on what he referred to in passing as the H. and H. (Heidegger and Hitler) affair. Yet his choice of epistolary form also clashed with the rhetorical force of a title, "Penser l'apocalypse" ("Thinking the Apocalypse"), whose reference to the Final Solution was hard to misconstrue. The title also tempered the implicit claim to modesty that the letter asserted against both the erudite article and eyewitness testimonies. In so doing, it resisted direct attempts to determine stable meaning in what only appeared to be a simple and uncomplicated text. Blanchot began by acknowledging that Farías had indeed provided unpublished information—"with a polemical intent, it is true" ("Thinking the Apocalypse," 475)—before registering his surprise at the relative silence surrounding Lacoue-Labarthe's *Heidegger, Art, and Politics*. In defense of the latter, Blanchot analyzed an account in Karl Löwith's memoirs that questioned the thesis that Heidegger's commitment to National Socialism had been limited to the 1933–34 period of the Freiburg rectorate.[3] Blanchot referred in particular to Löwith's account of a discussion in Rome in 1936 during which Heidegger agreed with Löwith's view that he (Heidegger) had sided with National Socialism because he saw it in agreement with the essence of his philosophy: "Heidegger told me unreservedly that I was right and developed his idea by saying that his concept of historicity (*Geschicht-*

lichkeit) was the foundation of his political involvement" (cited in "Thinking the Apocalypse," 477).

Blanchot invoked Löwith because the account of his 1936 meeting with Heidegger supported Lacoue-Labarthe's hypothesis that political involvement had transformed Heidegger's thought into *philosophy* (Blanchot's emphasis), adding that Löwith's account was written in 1940 without any explicit view toward future publication. Blanchot's efforts to justify his invocation of Löwith emphasized the moral credentials he felt impelled to establish for Löwith, as in the following passage: "It would be worthwhile to quote this overwhelming account, the words of a man whose intellectual and moral probity are unquestionable" (476). These efforts also pointed to the strong moral tone in which debate surrounding National Socialism in the wake of the Farías book was cast within and outside the academy. Concerning the postwar period, Blanchot wrote that he followed Lacoue-Labarthe in condemning Heidegger's refusal—Blanchot called it a "determined silence"—to address the Final Solution policy of extermination carried out especially, but not exclusively, against the Jews:

> Allow me after what I have to say next to leave you, as a means to emphasize that Heidegger's irreparable fault lies in his silence concerning the Final Solution. The silence, or his refusal, when confronted by Paul Celan, to ask forgiveness for the unforgivable, was a denial that plunged Celan into despair and made him ill, for Celan knew that the Shoah was the revelation of the essence of the West. And he recognized that it was necessary to preserve this memory in common, even if it entailed the loss of any sense of peace, in order to safeguard the possibility for relationship with the other. (479)

For Blanchot, Heidegger's postwar silence marked a willful refusal to engage—that is, to name, evoke, or even see—the Final Solution except in terms whose inadequacy Blanchot described as scandalous. Yet even this willful silence broke on occasion, as in the infamous 1949 speech in which Heidegger purportedly characterized agriculture as a mechanized food industry whose essence was "the same thing as the manufacture of corpses in the gas chambers and the death camps, the same thing as the blockades and the reduction of countries to famine, the same thing as the manufacture of hydrogen bombs" (cited in "Thinking the Apocalypse," 478). The sentence was made especially horrifying by a repeated phrase—"the same thing as" ("la même chose que" in French and "das Selbe wie" in German)—that reduced the extermination of the Jews to an operation of technology without even mentioning the Jews by name. Blanchot remarked: "It is indeed true that at Auschwitz and elsewhere Jews were treated as industrial waste and that they were considered to be the effluvia [*la décharge*] of Germany and Europe (in that, the responsibility of each one of us is at issue)" (478).

Blanchot's letter to *Le Nouvel Observateur* showed who Heidegger was for him in terms of the issues surrounding *Heidegger and Nazism.* Of particular interest was Blanchot's invocation of Löwith and Lacoue-Labarthe as correctives to Farías. Still unresolved, however, was the peculiarity of the epistolary format and Blanchot's decision to write in terms that were so clearly motivated by considerations of voice and authority. This choice of format was, in turn, complicated when Blanchot concluded that the Holocaust placed responsibility on "each one of us." The original French formulation ("la responsabilité de chacun de nous est engagée") suggested strongly that the responsibility and commitment involved ("at issue") were distinctly collective. Yet Blanchot never clarified the progression from individual to collective accountability. Instead, he ended his letter with a postscript that reverted to terms of the singular, as though his invocation of collective responsibility merely multiplied a personal confession. Any resulting sense of the collective was tentative and unstable. Here is the postscript in full:

> P.S.—A few more words concerning my own case. Thanks to Emmanuel Lévinas, without whom, in 1927 or 1928, I would not have been able to begin to understand *Sein und Zeit,* or to have undergone the veritable intellectual shock the book produced in me. An event of the first magnitude had just taken place; it was impossible to diminish it, even today, even in my memory. This is certainly why I took part in the homage for Heidegger's seventieth birthday. My contribution was a page from *L'attente l'oubli.* A little later, Guido Schneeberger (to whom Farías owes a great deal) sent me or had sent to me by his publisher the speeches Heidegger had made in favor of Hitler while he was rector. These speeches were frightening in their form as well as in their content, for it is the same writing and the very language by which, as in a great moment of the history of thought, we had been present at the loftiest questioning, one that could come to us from *Being and Time.* Heidegger uses the same language to call for voting for Hitler, to justify Nazi Germany's break from the League of Nations, and to praise Schlageter. Yes, the same holy language, perhaps a bit more crude, more emphatic, but the language that would henceforth be heard even in the commentaries on Hölderlin and would change them, but for still other reasons. (479–80)

My previous remarks have already suggested that I see Blanchot's postscript as something other than a simple supplement. Understatement—"a few more words concerning my own case"—did not hide Blanchot's desire to legitimize his statements just as he had legitimized those of Karl Löwith that he invoked earlier. Taken at face value, Blanchot's letter to *Le Nouvel Observateur* was a personal account that presupposed identity between the first-person singular in the text and the name of the real author under whose signature it appeared. In this sense, the letter recounted Blanchot's early access to *Sein und Zeit* via Lévinas and the reaction ("the veritable intellectual shock") that the Heideggerian text produced in him. Yet sixty years after the fact, Blanchot set the value he had placed on his reaction—"an event of the first magnitude had just taken place"—alongside his postwar discovery of the speeches Heidegger had made in support of Hitler during the rectorate. Curiously, Blanchot cast his reaction to disclosure of Heidegger's rectorate speeches in the very terms of equation—"the same writing and the very language . . . the same language . . . yes, the same . . . language . . . " he had cited via Lacoue-Labarthe from Heidegger's 1949 remarks on agricultural technology! Was the resemblance inadvertent or intended? Somewhere between the two, ambiguity resulted from the progressive disclosure precipitated by Blanchot's 1927 reading of *Sein und Zeit*—"an event of the first magnitude"—and later by his postwar discovery of the rectorate speeches. The insights derived from Heidegger and Schneeberger fulfilled the function of jolt that Blanchot referred to openly in the case of the former. In the terms used by Blanchot, agency seemed to be equated with reaction.

Retrospection and the change of critical perspective through time suggest that Blanchot's 1988 letter to *Le Nouvel Observateur* was not simply confessional, but at least as much apologetic in the sense that it attempted to explain rather than merely describe his evolving engagement with Heidegger's writings. In this sense, the perspective on the Heideggerian "event" in the letter bore an uncanny resemblance to the following passage in a text by Derrida from 1980: "It is also true that the living *thinkers who gave me the most to think about or who provoked me to reflection,* and who continue to do so, are not among those who break through a solitude, not among those to whom one can simply feel oneself close, not among those who form groups or schools, to mention only Heidegger, Lévinas, Blanchot among others whom I shall not name. It is thinkers such as these to whom, strangely enough, one may consider oneself most close; and yet they are, more than others, other. And they too are alone."[4] That Derrida made this statement some seven years before the Farías book appeared helped to clarify the extent to which controversy surrounding *Heidegger and Nazism* resulted in large part from the reactions of some readers to aspects of Heidegger's career of which others such as Derrida, Blanchot, and Lacoue-Labarthe were already aware. Belatedness here was determinable both in time and as a gap or blind spot of knowledge whose disclosure was scandalous.

The choice of an epistolary format both disclosed and displaced Blanchot's long-term involvement with Heidegger's writings. His 1988 letter responded to an outside call (*demande*) that carried an imperative within its ostensible tone of cordiality. Curiously, Derrida was soon to use similar terms to describe his reaction to a call concerning Paul de Man's wartime writings: "When I received, in December [1987], the telephone call from *Critical Inquiry* which proposed, singular generosity, that I be the first to speak, when a friendly voice said to me: 'It has to be you, we thought that it was up to you to do this before anyone else,' I believed I had to accept a warm invitation that resonated like a summons."[5] Like Derrida—who added that he felt "unable not to accept" the request to write—Blanchot wrote reactively. Like Derrida again, Blanchot's response ultimately exceeded the demand. In both instances, the engaging of unnamed readers through a specific correspondent marked a powerful substitution. The text to the journalist Catherine David also addressed the wider readership of *Le Nouvel Observateur* so that David became the coincidental correspondent of a letter directed *through* or *around* as well as *to* her.

The postscript enhanced the complex rhetorical force of Blanchot's letter. It may, in fact, have been the very point for which the letter served as a pretext. Blanchot's gesture of modesty ("I prefer to put this in a letter to you instead of writing an article that would lead anyone to believe that I have any authority to speak") displaced a claim to authority that he redirected toward his postscript. A letter instead of an article: the disclosure conveyed by the postscript ("a few more words concerning my own case") was neither suited to nor contained by a footnote. Nor could a footnote have conveyed the same intimacy as a postscript. It is, of course, possible to read Blanchot's contribution to the *Nouvel Observateur* dossier as a series of remarks by a non-specialist who wrote ostensibly to assert Lacoue-Labarthe's reading of Heidegger against that of Farías. My emphasis on the personalized nature of Blanchot's contribution—"a letter instead of an article"—suggests otherwise. The discrepancy between demand and response was simply too great to be dismissed as coincidental. Blanchot's text signified in and by excess. In saying this, I do not want just to read the letter ironically and by inversion in order to show how it invariably contradicted itself. Instead, the letter illustrated the multiple meanings traversing what appeared initially to be a stable and unequivocal text. As in the words with which Jacques Lacan ended his seminar on "The Purloined Letter," there was little doubt that Blanchot's letter ultimately arrived at its destination.

Blanchot's letter on Heidegger also engaged a set of problems related to what Michel Foucault has referred to as the author function. My previous

remarks on the letter in *Le Nouvel Observateur* were meant to test an interpretive strategy I want now to direct toward a number of texts from different
periods of Blanchot's career. My intention here is neither to deconstruct nor
reconstruct an author, but instead to construct an author function by exploring selected writings by Blanchot from the early 1930s to the present.
My decision to use the January 1988 letter in *Le Nouvel Observateur* as a first
example was meant to illustrate how one might read and write (reread and
rewrite) Blanchot as "he" has read and rewritten others. The status of the
pronoun "he"—that is, what motivated the quotation marks that set it apart
from unmarked pronouns in conventional usage—is another issue around
which I have organized my choice of texts. In tension with the authority imposed by conventions of chronology and genre, the texts I analyze here and
in the following two chapters emphasize traces and aftereffects related to
conceptions of history and writing that recent debates surrounding Heidegger and de Man have staged in terms of controversy and scandal.

Transposing a textual corpus into an author function also allows me to
address questions surrounding what I want to call Blanchot's politics. Yet the
politics to which I refer are less a matter of party and ideology than of the
textual effect of disclosure. In an essay written in 1986, Blanchot argued that
Foucault's *Discipline and Punish* marked a transition from the study of isolated discursive practices to that of the social practices on which they were
grounded: "It is the emergence of the political in the work and life of Foucault."[6] In the pages that follow, I take my cue from Blanchot by tracing the
relations between literary discourse and social practice whose emergence is
disclosed in Blanchot's postwar writings. A first remark involves the associations linking the concept of emergence with visual models and with stable
subjectivity criticized by Foucault and Blanchot, each in his own way. In
1986, Blanchot wrote:

> It is accepted as a certainty that Foucault, adhering in this to a certain con-
> ception of literary production, got rid of, purely and simply, the notion of
> the subject: no more oeuvre, no more author, no more creative unity. But
> things are not that simple. The subject does not disappear; rather its exces-
> sively determined unity is put in question. What arouses interest and inquiry
> is its disappearance (that is, the new manner of being which disappearance
> is), or rather its dispersal, which does not annihilate it but offers us, out of it,
> no more than a plurality of positions and a discontinuity of functions. (Blan-
> chot, "Michel Foucault as I Imagine Him," 76–77)

The passage provides an initial sense of how one might read Blanchot.
But if we take seriously its admonition that "things are not that simple,"

emergence needs to be tempered with dispersion. If we are looking for indications on how to read and interpret, these indications must address the binding of text and author. Reading and interpretation are not always linear. Stable chronology still constitutes a privileged order of meaning, but chronology alone cannot found understanding unless it is set against other orders that often tend to be nonlinear. If the subject disperses rather than disappears, inquiry needs to focus on the textual effects produced by dispersion in the form of traces. The temporal expression of the nonlinear would thus work against strict chronology. In proposing this, I want also to emphasize that the understanding promoted by nonlinearity is constructed through textual practices and effects rather than through reference to a consistent authorial entity. The case of Blanchot is of particular relevance because his writings have often been seen as resisting interpretation derived from an authorial identity taken to be stable and unproblematic.[7]

The phenomenon of dispersal in Blanchot's 1988 letter on Heidegger was far from isolated in his writings of the past two decades. *Après coup* (*Vicious Circles*) was a 1983 reprint of two short fictional narratives, "L'Idylle" and "Le Dernier Mot," written in the midthirties and published together as a book in 1951 under the title *Le Ressassement éternel*.[8] A fifteen-page addendum for the 1983 reprint recast the earlier texts, first by inverting the title as *"Après coup" précédé par "Le Ressassement éternel."* The gesture gave to the afterword an effect of authenticity, as though "Blanchot" were commenting long after the fact on texts published under his signature some fifty years earlier. Yet like the postscript to Blanchot's letter on Heidegger, the addendum was far from simple. For while it added to the two narratives, it derived much of its rhetorical force from the same trope of digression—parabasis—that Blanchot was to use again four years later in "Thinking the Apocalypse." Parabasis in *Après coup* conveyed a will to truth in a critical voice that ostensibly altered how the two fictional narratives were to be read (reread). Moreover, it did this against the grain of critical approaches that cast Blanchot's narratives as allegories of interpretation and thereby elided an earlier vision of interwar France in the 1930s texts that remained under erasure. Finally, the mode of aside bore the signs of self-critique that promoted a consistent authorial identity above and beyond change in time. The effect was one of logical identity such that Blanchot was—seemingly still and always—the Blanchot he had always been.

Après coup also recast problems of interpretation associated with the two interwar narratives in terms of historical reference that invoked a post-Holocaust condition:

That is why, in my opinion—and in a way different from the one that led Adorno to decide with absolute correctness—I will say there can be no fiction-story ever about Auschwitz (I am alluding to *Sophie's Choice*). The need to bear witness is the obligation of a testimony that can only be given— and given only in the singularity of each individual—by the impossible witnesses—the witnesses of the impossible. . . . From this it would seem that all narration, even all poetry, has lost the foundation on which another language could be raised—through the extinction of the happiness of speaking that lurks in even the most mediocre silence. (*Vicious Circles*, 68)

The opening assertion—"no fiction-story [*récit-fiction*] ever about Auschwitz"—can be read as either an imperative or a challenge. In the former case, it might refer to the Final Solution and those for whom survival was no longer life because life had undergone the "decisive blow that leaves nothing intact" (*Vicious Circles*, 68). In the latter, it might be closer to a recognition that no narrative could describe or otherwise account for the enormity of what had taken place surrounding the name and place of Auschwitz. Yet if instead, as the challenge to fiction in *Après coup* suggested, the need to bear witness could never be filled adequately, its consequences for narration remained unclear. As Blanchot added, "it would seem" that another kind of narration was imposed. The question would then be one of determining what that other narration might be. The claim that narration could no longer raise another language seemingly undermined a capacity to account adequately for a condition whose historicity was perhaps less explicit than might have been assumed. Thus, while the word "Auschwitz" openly invoked the site of the Nazi concentration camp in southwestern Poland, it also conveyed a conception of postwar culture whose status remained uncertain.

Writing Death

We can conceive of nothing except in terms of our own life, and beyond that,
it seems to us everything is wiped out. Beyond death, in fact, begins
the inconceivable which we are usually not brave enough to face. . . .
We know that death destroys nothing, leaves the totality of existence intact,
but we still cannot imagine the continuity of being as a whole except beyond
our own death, or whatever it is that dies in us. We cannot accept the fact
that this has limits. At all costs we need to transcend them and
maintain them simultaneously.
Georges Bataille, *Erotism*

Après coup challenged interpretation along lines that destabilized rereading through belatedness. Blanchot transposed the challenge into a ploy when he wrote in no uncertain terms: "In a completely different context I have written: *Noli me legere.* A prohibition against reading that tells the author he has been disposed of. 'You will not read me.' 'I do not remain as a text to be read except through the process that slowly devours you while writing.' 'You will never know what you have written, even if you have written only to find this out' " (*Vicious Circles*, 59). A few pages later, Blanchot reiterated the challenge: "*Noli me legere.* Does this impossibility have an aesthetic, ethical, or ontological value?" (61). This reiteration had a moderating effect, as though the prohibition—"a polite appeal, a strange warning"—were always already violated.

The direct challenges to reading in *Après coup* also echoed an earlier challenge in Blanchot's afterword to his 1948 narrative *L'Arrêt de mort* (*Death Sentence*). The brief passage in question was set apart from a central narrative of some 120 pages. It was uttered by a narrator onto whom one may or may not impose the identity of a writer often called *Blanchot l'obscur* in reference to another of his early narratives, one that was published first in 1940 and again ten years later in a drastically shortened version, both times under the same title, *Thomas l'obscur* (*Thomas the Obscure*). Here is Lydia Davis's translation of the afterword to *L'Arrêt de mort*:

> These pages can end here, and nothing that follows what I have just written can make me add anything to it or take anything away from it. This remains, this will remain until the very end. Whoever would obliterate it from me, in exchange for that end which I am searching for in vain, would himself become the beginning of my own story, and he would be my victim. In darkness, he would see me: my word would be his silence, and he would think he was holding sway over the world, but this sovereignty would still be mine, his nothingness mine, and he too would know that there is no end for a man who wants to end alone.
>
> This should therefore be impressed upon anyone who might read these pages thinking they are infused with the thought of unhappiness. And what is more, let him try to imagine the hand that is writing them: if he saw it, then perhaps reading would become a serious task for him.[9]

The doubling that pervaded *L'Arrêt de mort* started with the twin meanings of the French term *arrêt*, derived from the infinitive *arrêter* (to stop) or as the noun *arrêté* (decree or sentence) used in the context of a tribunal or administrative decision. Blanchot's title translated as *Death Stop* and/or *Death Sentence*. An additional doubling occurred in the persistent equation of narrator and authorial entity, with the latter understood as voice, signature, or function. Deletion of the afterword starting with the 1971 reprint of the book complicated this equation.[10] Interpreting *L'Arrêt de mort* in the wake of the deleted afterword has pointed to the evolution of Blanchot's writings, with special attention to the texts of the interwar and Occupation periods. In 1976, two issues of the French journal *Gramma* provided an extensive listing of Blanchot's interwar articles in periodicals such as *Le Rempart, La Revue du XXe siècle, La Revue Universelle, Combat, Le Journal des Débats,* and *L'Insurgé.* Four years later, Jeffrey Mehlman maintained in "Blanchot at *Combat*" that Blanchot had seriously considered an offer from Pierre Drieu La Rochelle to help edit the *Nouvelle Revue Française* under Drieu's direction.[11] Even though he considered only a very few of the interwar texts, Mehlman was instrumental in raising questions concerning Blanchot's early writings that (despite clear differences) later resurfaced surrounding Heidegger and de Man. Along with Michael Holland, Mehlman was among the first to make the case for closer historical analysis as a necessary supplement to readings that approached the postwar writings through concepts and/or hermetic textuality.

Because it asserted historical concerns as integral to the challenge of disclosure it performed, *L'Arrêt de mort* marked a point of convergence between interwar and postwar practices. Notable in this regard was the narrator's invocation of the September 1938 Munich agreement at which Neville Chamberlain and Edouard Daladier, on behalf of England and France, respectively, sacrificed the Sudetenland to Hitler and Mussolini in what proved later to be a vain attempt to avoid armed conflict. Chamberlain returned to London reassured that the signatures of Hitler and Mussolini guaranteed "peace in our time." Less than a year later, Chamberlain joined the French in declaring war on Germany and Italy after Hitler invaded Poland. The opening pages of the narrative identified an interval of nine years during which the narrator sought to account for events he described as difficult to disclose. The events in question were presented as having started in October 1938: that is, almost a full year before the phony war and some twenty months before France fell to German forces in June 1940. Blanchot's first-person narrator was a writer/journalist whose coverage seemingly reduced historical circumstances to a backdrop for more personal concerns.[12] Yet this displacement of history and "public events" in the name of the personal and the everyday was partial and temporary. From the start, the narrator stated that he wrote freely because the story he wanted to tell concerned no one but himself. Furthermore, it was a story, he claimed, that could be told in ten words: "That is what makes it so awful. There are ten words to say. For nine years I have held out against them" (*Death Sentence,* 2). At a later point, however, Blanchot's narrator disrupted his narrative when he explicitly related his postwar account to the political history of the wartime and Occupation period: "I would like to say something else now. I am talking about things which seem negligible [*infimes*], and I am ignoring public events. These events were very important and they occupied my attention all the time" (46). Juxtaposing these two passages underscores a significant instability between narrator and narrative. Although the opening pages of *L'Arrêt de mort* set forth a project of writing that was personalized to the point of compulsion, the latter passage disclosed the narrator's passivity as a historical agent. In this sense, it becomes increasingly hard not to explore this fictional evocation of France in the late 1930s in conjunction with Blanchot's interwar journalism on French and economic foreign policy.

From the perspective of *L'Arrêt de mort*, *Après coup* extended an earlier attempt on Blanchot's part to disclose a certain interwar past. Specifically, such disclosure occurred in the historical references within the personalized account of events leading to the ten words the narrator had sought to formulate—"A ces dix mots, j'ai tenu tête"—for nine years. But how exactly was this disclosure to occur? The opening paragraph of *L'Arrêt de mort* invoked a determinate date before embedding it within the narrator's more personalized story:

> These things happened to me in 1938. I feel the greatest uneasiness in speaking of them. I have already tried to put them into writing many times. If I have written books, it has been in the hope that they would put an end to it all. If I have written novels, they have come into being just as the words began to shrink back from the truth. I am not afraid to tell a secret. But until now, words have been frailer and more cunning than I would have liked. I know this guile is a warning; it would be nobler to leave the truth in peace. It would be in the best interests of the truth to keep it hidden. But now I hope to be done with it soon. To be done with it is also noble and important. (1)

The "things" referred to in the first sentence of this passage were events concerning the narrator's encounters with a number of women and especially with a certain J. whose sickness and death seemed to coincide with the historical fate of France after the election of the Popular Front government under Léon Blum in May 1936. Even if we questioned what constituted an event, historical reference and/or allegorical functions would nonetheless supplement what was primarily a confessional project.

A lingering sense of guilt undermined the reliability of a narrator whose use of disclosure recalled the loophole phenomenon Mikhail Bakhtin had analyzed in Dostoyevsky's fiction.[13] From the very start, Blanchot's narrator admitted that he had written a first account of the 1938 events some two years later "in a state of lethargy" in July and August 1940. But after writing this account, he destroyed it. Elsewhere, the narrator expressed his desire to control the extent of disclosure he wanted to produce: "I shall go on with this story, but now I will take some precautions. I am not taking these precautions in order to cast a veil over the truth. The truth will be told, everything of importance will be told. But not everything has yet happened" (31). Such interruptions extended parabasis while promoting the artifice of a tendentious account the narrator was unable (or unwilling) to bring to closure. Each aside undermined the continuity of the narrative by drawing attention to the control exercised by the narrator to construct a presumably true and accurate account of events that had not yet—"not everything has yet happened"—come to closure. Similar breaks marked *L'Arrêt de mort*'s distance from conventions associated with the first-person narration known in French as the *récit*. Each successive break destabilized the statements that preceded it and realigned the narrative in view of other statements ("the truth will be told") that deferred the closure presumably afforded by a definitive account. This same deferral undermined the possibility of determining an authentic voice that openly worked to overcome distortion.

The second half of *L'Arrêt de mort* described a series of encounters between the narrator and a number of female characters. Consistent with the pattern of disclosure and traversal already noted, infrequent references to the time and place of wartime "events" set the account of these encounters within a historic specificity whose function goes well beyond setting. Toward the end of his account, the narrator invoked unmistakable geographic markers in a passage recounting a search for shelter: "I crossed the rue de la Paix, which was extraordinarily quiet, and without light. How quiet it was, and how tranquil I was, too. I could hear my footsteps. The rue d'O was quiet, but gloomy: the elevator was not working and in the stairwell, from the fourth floor on up, a sort of strange musty smell came down to me, a cold smell of earth and stone which I was perfectly familiar with because in the room it was my very life" (66). The invocation of the rue de la Paix was direct and seemingly descriptive. The rest of the passage, however, destabilized description in terms of an affective fallacy that projected the narrator's personal disorientation onto the urban setting of wartime Paris. The opening reference to the rue d'O connoted a coding on a par with the narrator's quasi-systematic reference to female characters according to the first letters of their names: J., N. (for Nathalie), C. (for Colette). The final sentences of the passage returned to the atmosphere of morbidity that inscribed the real-

ity effect within a mood of personal crisis. Similar progressions occurred repeatedly throughout the *récit*.

L'Arrêt de mort* ended without resolving the dilemma announced in its
opening pages. In place of resolution, the afterword challenged the reader to
interpret exactly what the narrator remained unable—if not also unwilling—to disclose in full. When the afterword was deleted starting with the
1971 edition, the interplay between revelation and withholding extended toward interpretation of the entire narrative. Once deleted, the challenge
"under erasure" (*sous rature*) raised new questions and problems. Yet as in
Blanchot's remarks on Foucault and stable subjectivity in 1986, dispersal
was not identical with disappearance. While stable interpretation no longer
seemed possible, alternative practices were adjusted to dispersal and frag-
mentation. Among other consequences, this meant that interpretation constructed fragments into various configurations and clusters of meaning for
which any and all claims would remain tentative. The insights afforded
would vary from one configuration to another, both in terms of the pre-
misses that organized individual readings and of the documentation that
might revise understanding. In the case of the latter, Blanchot's writings
since *Le pas au-delà* (*The Step Not Beyond*) can be read as ongoing responses
to the postwar challenge set forth in—and later deleted from—*L'Arrêt de
mort*.

The evocation of interwar and wartime France in *L'Arrêt de mort* exploited the marking of historical reference in fiction that Roland Barthes
termed the reality effect (*l'effet de réel*).[14] This historical marking, in turn,
contrasted with the ghostlike quality of Blanchot's characters and a passivity
that has been linked to the posthistorical. What was the end of history, and
how might a reading of *L'Arrêt de mort* from the perspective of the posthistorical help to account for aftereffect in Blanchot's writings of the past
twenty years? My answers to these questions begin at the end or, more precisely, at *one* end of history. Hegel first wrote the end of history in 1807 in the
concluding chapter of his *Phenomenology of Mind*. He wrote it as Absolute
Knowledge (*Absolut Wissen*): that is, as a final embodiment of spirit (*Geist*)
that ended the progression toward an ideal society attained by means of the
dialectic interplay of thesis, antithesis, and synthesis. Spirit for Hegel was
not identical with history, but variable in time and closer to collective phe-
nomena such as nation and people. In the *Phenomenology*, the concept of
Absolute Knowledge or Science (*Wissenschaft*) referred to a phase or stage at
which reality and thought coincided to the point of identity. For Hegel, this
coincidence reconciled experience and self-consciousness. It also brought

the Hegelian system to a halt: "Absolute knowledge . . . unites the objective form of truth and the knowing self in an immediate unity."[15] It was sometimes claimed that the concept of Absolute Knowledge was reinforced—if not inspired—by the historical reality of the approach of Napoleon's troops toward Jena. Yet it turned out that history did not end in 1807 and that Hegel outlived the so-called end of history by over thirty years. But if Hegel's timing was off, this hardly detracted from the accuracy of his affirmation that the developments of material reality conformed to rather than determined the emergence of ideal principles.[16]

More than a century later, Alexandre Kojève returned to the end of history in lectures on Hegel's *Phenomenology* given between 1933 and 1938 in the Section des Sciences Religieuses at the Ecole Pratique des Hautes Etudes in Paris. According to Vincent Descombes, Kojève was such a talented storyteller that he succeeded in turning the austere *Phenomenology* into a serialized philosophical novel whose dramatic scenes and reversals kept up suspense for readers avid to learn what happened at the end of the story (*à la fin de l'histoire*).[17] Because the French term *histoire* translates into English as both "story" and "history," the point made by Descombes could also be recast more fully as the end of the *story* of history (*la fin de l'histoire de l'histoire*). Hegel may have *lived* a first end of history, but it was really Kojève who formulated the fuller consequences of posthistory, as in the following passage:

> In point of fact, the end of human time, of History—that is, the definitive annihilation of Man properly speaking, or of the free and historical Individual—means quite simply the cessation of Action in the full sense of the term. Practically, this means the disappearance of wars and bloody revolutions. And also the disappearance of *Philosophy;* for since Man himself no longer changes essentially, there is no longer any reason to change the (true) principles which are at the basis of his understanding of the world and of himself. But all the rest can be preserved indefinitely; art, love, play, etc.; in short, everything that makes man *happy.*[18]

Happiness derived for Kojève from an end to the alienation that Hegel had seen as dominating all states of self-consciousness prior to Absolute Knowledge. As the collective human agency of Spirit achieved the coincidence of self and other, it also tamed the natural world. The resulting state of inaction extended indefinitely because there was neither need nor desire of further change. The posthistorical world was one in which nothing remained to be done: a world of permanent leisure such as that evoked by the title of Raymond Queneau's 1952 novel, *Le Dimanche de la vie* (The Sunday of life).

(Queneau edited the notes taken during Kojève's 1930s lectures that were published in 1947 as *Introduction to the Reading of Hegel.*)

Kojève's vision of a posthistorical world raised its own problems. Even as Kojève followed Hegel in seeing Absolute Knowledge as the overcoming of alienation, the temporal extension of vacation (*vacances* in the plural) remained subject to the void (*vacance* in the singular) of inaction within it. If the end of history precluded further action, then what—if anything—remained to be done? Perhaps, as Perry Anderson has argued in reference to Lutz Niethammer's *Posthistoire,* the end of history was a condition, less a theoretical system than a structure of feeling (Anderson, *A Zone of Engagement,* 279). Could *L'Arrêt de mort* formulate this passivity? Descombes noted the resonances of a posthistorical sensibility in Blanchot: "Kojève already said that the end of history was equivalent to the death of man. In all his works Blanchot described this life after death which is the lot of man in the aftermath of history, and to which modern literature, in his view, is the supreme testimony. After the end of history, said Georges Bataille, human negativity does not disappear—it only becomes 'unemployed' " (112–13).

Kojève's skills at storytelling helped him to transmit Marx's reading of Hegel to an interwar generation of intellectuals and writers including Bataille, Sartre, Lacan, Queneau, and Maurice Merleau-Ponty. These skills should not, however, obscure what Hegel himself had written in the *Phenomenology* concerning narration and history. After describing Absolute Knowledge in terms of coincidence and reconciliation, Hegel added the following remarks on history as *Geist* externalized and emptied in time:

> This way of becoming presents a slow procession of spiritual shapes [*Geistern*], a gallery of pictures, each of which is endowed with the entire wealth of Spirit, and moves so slowly just for the reason that the self has to permeate and assimilate all this wealth of its substance. Since its accomplishment consists in Spirit knowing what it is, in fully comprehending its substance, this knowledge means its concentrating itself on itself [*Insichgehen*], a state in which Spirit leaves its external existence behind and gives its embodiment over to Recollection [*Errinerung*]. In thus concentrating itself on itself, Spirit is engulfed in the night of its own self-consciousness; its vanished existence is, however, conserved therein; and this superceded existence—this previous state, but born anew from the womb of knowledge, is the new stage of existence, a new world, and a new embodiment or mode of Spirit.[19]

Reference to shapes (*Geistern*) and, in particular, to a picture gallery (*Gallerie von Bildern*) endowed with the entire wealth of Spirit, gave visual expression to the self-concentration (*Insichgehen*) that served as a prerequisite for Absolute Knowledge. Remembrance (*Errinerung*) likewise lent force and coherence to events transposed into elements of a traditional narrative (*récit*), whether that narrative was taken as historical, fictional, or a combination of the two. The terms used by Hegel on the final page of the *Phenomenology*'s final chapter thus conveyed the capacity of representation to impose closure and meaning after the fact (onto "previous states") in order to birth anew existence, world, and Spirit.

A final reference to the end of history was almost contemporaneous with *L'Arrêt de mort* and opened onto more recent considerations. It appeared in "An Age of Doom," an essay written in 1950 in which Hendrik de Man—the onetime socialist, leader of the Parti Ouvrier Belge, and uncle of the literary critic and theorist Paul de Man—commented on the concept of *poste-histoire* whose invention he attributed to the nineteenth-century French mathematician Antoine Augustin Cournot. De Man wrote:

> The term posthistorical seems adequate to describe what happens when an institution or a cultural achievement ceases to be historically active and productive of new qualities, and becomes purely receptive or eclectically imitative. Thus understood, Cournot's notion of the posthistorical would, in a more general way than intended by him, fit the cultural phase that, following a "fulfillment of sense," has become "devoid of sense." The alternative, then, is, in biological terms, either death or mutation.[20]

De Man's sense of the pertinent alternative ("either death or mutation") extended the atmosphere of passivity implied by the posthistorical formulated by Hegel and Kojève, and also helped to explain the way Blanchot portrayed this afterlife in *L'Arrêt de mort*. The narrator's opening reference ("These things happened to me in 1938. . . . There are ten words to say. For nine years I have held out against them") identified the ostensible origin and moment of narration in historical terms that framed ("contained") the prewar and wartime periods. Outside the limits of this identification, the narrator constructed a postwar account whose tendentiousness culminated in the afterword and the challenge to interpretation reminiscent of the final pages of Dostoyevsky's "Notes from Underground." Where the afterword challenged interpretation, its deletion as of 1971 precluded even this possibility. Yet if, as in Blanchot's remarks on Foucault, we were contending with dispersal rather than disappearance, critical reading might look instead to account for traces of dispersal in Blanchot's writings of the past two decades, starting in 1973 with *Le pas au-delà*.

The elements of structure and rhetoric that made *L'Arrêt de mort* an open-ended narrative suggested that an early version of this dispersal occurred in the immediate aftermath of World War II. They also pointed to some major consequences of posthistory related to interpretation. For as the historical references in *L'Arrêt de mort* accumulated, the invocation of real times and real places clashed increasingly with the narrator's unstable account. What, then, can be made of the reality effect promoted by historical reference in Blanchot's *récit*? How is historical reference to be understood? Does it constitute anything more or other than local color or background? The first sentence of *L'Arrêt de mort* ("These things happened to me in 1938") had suggested a more integral function, especially in light of the nine years separating them from the moment of narration. From the very start, then, a determinate and ongoing duration—from 1938 to 1947—surrounded the interwar and wartime periods in relation to which Blanchot's narrator was a surviving witness. In the terms used by Hendrik de Man, the choice imposed by the narrator's survival could be seen as that of death or mutation.

As *L'Arrêt de mort*'s narrator constructed his account in terms of revelation and withholding that resisted closure, each break in narration deferred closure toward the progressive inaction conveyed by the term *arrêt* in the title. *L'Arrêt de mort* performed—showed rather than asserted—an equation of mutation and death embodied in a narrator whose capacity to "live on" also asserted the impending death he was loathe to admit. The ten words *L'Arrêt de mort*'s narrator sought to say were perhaps the very words that would express openly the inner death his narration suspended somewhere between suppression and disclosure.

Commonality

Blanchot's *La Communauté inavouable* (1983) displayed a number of aspects of the aftereffect visible in *L'Arrêt de mort* and *Après coup*. Neither simply a reprint nor a new edition, the book was divided into two essays, the first an essay on a negative community and the second on a community of lovers. Each responded to ("accompanied") a specific text: Jean-Luc Nancy's "La Communauté désoeuvrée" and Marguerite Duras's *La Maladie de la mort* (*The Malady of Death*), respectively. Rather than being elements or moments of a dialectic, however, the sections of *La Communauté inavouable* supplemented each other. What their interaction disclosed—even if it was unavowable (*inavouable*) within confessional writing—was the historicity of the interwar period that Blanchot staged only indirectly. The first essay "La Communauté négative" ("The Negative Community") staged this historicity in conjunction with Georges Bataille's explorations into the dynamics of social groups. By means of experiments conducted between the wars in the name of groups such as Contre-Attaque, Acéphale, and the Collège de Sociologie, Bataille sought to grasp the nature of communal existence in relation to what Blanchot termed the memory of the Soviet experience and the premonition of what had already become fascism. Alongside these two experiences Blanchot set the privileged example of the surrealists, formed in multiple configurations around ideas and dominant individuals: "Ideal community of the literary community. . . . The Surrealists, André Breton before all the others, had foreseen it and theorized it prematurely."[21] For Blanchot, then, the negative community exemplified by the surrealists was one of witness-readers who understood their experience only in the aftermath of its occurrence. Forever belated—*nachträglich*—in relation to what brought them together, the surrealists foreshadowed the nonconformist phenomenon of interwar writers disenfranchised from the Catholic church and mainstream political parties. The instability of these groups asserted the transitory nature of community when it was conceived on the model of political and/or social activism. Moreover, this first phase in Blanchot's search for community in history pointed to a reduced model based on friendship. The reduction evolved from the epic development of *Geist* in Hegel's *Phenomenology* and Marx's transposition of *Geist* into the class struggle to the heroic figure of Kojève's nihilating consciousness. Blanchot continued the progression in 1962 in an essay on the death of his friend Georges Bataille that inspired the collection of essays later published as *L'Amitié*.

From avant-garde to counterculture. A follow-up to the negative community associated with interwar and postwar movements from surrealism to *Critique* transposed ideology into joyous communication. The transposition occurred with singular force during the Red Spring (*printemps rouge*) of 1968. Ironically, it was as though the collective rituals that had fascinated members of the negative community during the College of Sociology period of the late 1930s were suddenly being staged on the boulevards of the Latin Quarter in Paris. The initial expression of ritual was liberating: "May '68 showed that, without a project or conjuring, an *explosive communication* could be affirmed (affirmed beyond the usual forms of affirmation) in a sudden and fortuitous encounter: an opening which allowed everyone— without distinction according to class, age, sex, or culture—to make his or her way with the first passerby as with someone already loved, precisely because this person was the familiar unknown" (*Communauté inavouable*, 52; emphasis in the original). Explosive communication resulted from a dissymmetry of desire that Blanchot took as essential to the ethic of all relations with others. This was why he set the text by Duras alongside that by Nancy. *La Maladie de la mort* recounted the very paradoxes that made desire both vital and fatal, thereby placing desire into what Bataille might have called a sovereign function above or removed from law and/or convention. Blanchot took this notion of desire to its extreme by invoking Jacques Lacan in order to assert that desire as communication transcended willful sacrifice as well as abandon: "To desire is to give what one does not have to someone who does not want any of it" (*Communauté inavouable*, 71).

The transition from individual to collective action also had affinities with Abraham's leap of faith as Søren Kierkegaard recounted it in *Fear and Trembling* (1843). What interested Blanchot in Kierkegaard's account was a faith so intense that it was unintelligible—uncommunicable—to others. Those who lacked Abraham's love of God could not understand, except in terms of paradox or silence, his willingness to sacrifice his son Isaac. From the perspective of those around him, Abraham's faith was threatening because it presupposed a direct communication with God from which other humans were excluded. For Blanchot, the community of lovers who embodied desire as communication threatened a social order built on or out of the reciprocal exchange of language. As in *Fear and Trembling*, the silence surrounding Blanchot's community of lovers was meaningful and overdetermined as an ethical precondition yet to be expressed through language.

If the events of May and June 1968 were the precedent for a future communication yet to pass, an obvious question was when—if ever—a full transition would occur. Blanchot's conclusion was suitably equivocal; it extended by direct allusion the paradox contained in Ludwig Wittgenstein's precept that what cannot be spoken of must be kept silent. For Blanchot, Wittgenstein could not impose silence upon himself because "in order to keep silent, one must talk" (*Communauté inavouable*, 92). By substituting Blanchot for Wittgenstein, the previous sentence can be seen as staging the very interplay between silence and talk whose evolution I want to trace in Blanchot's writings from the 1930s to the present. Not surprisingly, the author function derived from Blanchot's early writings resonated strongly with the Heideggerian topoi of disclosure and, in particular, with the interplay between silence and talk in Blanchot's attempts since the late 1960s to contend with the cultures and politics of interwar France.

CHAPTER FOUR

From Reaction to Militancy

Interplay

Aftereffect has been characterized in previous chapters as the scandalous return of what is left out—displaced or suppressed—when philosophy and literature are considered as self-contained disciplines and/or practices. Concerning Heidegger in France, a major reason for the persistence of debate surrounding *Heidegger and Nazism* is the lack of evidence to prove or disprove the allegations that Farias brought to wider disclosure.[1] While apologists went through predictable contortions of denial, cynics gloated that Heidegger and those who claimed to speak in his name had perpetrated a major deception whose exposure they could no longer defer. Evidence to resolve differences, if it existed at all, might remain inaccessible ("lost") for years. Uncertainty and irresolution thus implicated not only the figure of Heidegger as modernist philosopher-poet, but all those in France and elsewhere whose readings of Heidegger since the 1930s were seemingly complicitous with a hoax whose intellectual and moral ramifications were dizzying. Whether this complicity was willful or inadvertent mattered little to those who took malevolent pleasure in the effects of scandalous disclosure on future considerations of Heidegger's reputation as a major philosopher-poet of interwar and postwar modernity in France.

Allan Stoekl has argued that modernist texts (his examples include writings by Bataille, Blanchot, and Leiris) were the locus of an irresolvable struggle between different ideological forces rather than the repository of a single force.[2] I would take Stoekl one step further by considering each text within a corpus or an invented series as the restaging of a cumulative struggle. Thus it would be one thing to read representations of interwar France in Blanchot's journalism of the 1930s and quite another to analyze how these representations were recast some fifty years later in *Après coup* and *La Communauté inavouable*. A fuller analysis of this recasting might explore various structures and tropes within specific texts. It might also seek to account for the constraints on reception imposed by genre, discipline, and reading formation. Finally, such an analysis might beg the question of the extent to which conflicting appropriations of a text devolved from the historical embeddedness of writing and reading. The break with dominant conceptions of literature that critics and theorists heralded starting in the late 1960s was far from absolute. From Foucault and Derrida to Deleuze and Baudrillard, those who questioned whether stable interpretation was possible were accused of a nihilism that often revealed as much about the accusers as it did about those they accused. Fredric Jameson wrote in *The Political Unconscious* that the close reading of a text amounted "less to a wholesale nullification of all interpretive activity than to a demand for the construction of some new and more adequate, immanent or antitranscendent hermeneutic model."[3] Elsewhere in the same text, Jameson specified the nature of that new model by identifying a key assumption that many self-styled "new" historicists had only begun to explore: namely, that "history is *not* a text, not a narrative, master or otherwise, but that, as an absent cause, it is inaccessible to us except in textual form, and that our approach to it and to the Real itself necessarily passes through its prior textualization, its narrativization in the political unconscious" (35; emphasis in the original). Jameson's remarks suggest that the inadequacy of certain models of interpretation was not correctable merely by adjustment or refinement. Their inadequacy was less of detail than of type. What Jameson called the political unconscious provided one way of rethinking the questions concerning literature and philosophy. Furthermore, it suggested the type of model ("immanent or antitranscendent") on which alternative practices of interpretation might be founded.

My intention in this and the next chapter is to follow Jameson's lead by rethinking—that is, by thinking again and differently—my earlier remarks on aftereffect in terms that emphasize their grounding in the material practices of culture in a specific context. By material practices, I mean the variety of books, newspapers, paintings, films, and songs of a specific time and place as well as the conceptions, technologies, and processes of symbolic representation that bear on their circulation. Questions of not just how but also when and where literature articulates with politics contain their own articulation. They imply, in turn, a conception of literature as a set of practices whose links with social and discursive formations are multiple and changing. Heidegger's evolving reception in France over the past sixty years illustrates the extent to which moral and/or political assumptions concerning an individual figure have promoted identifications that were often judgmental and misleading. The scandal that erupted in the wake of the Farias book was, of course, as much about literature and philosophy in France in the 1980s as about whatever Martin Heidegger may or may not have done some fifty years earlier. Recent controversy surrounding Heidegger has resulted not only from a condition of belatedness as a lack of perspective that the passage of time alone might correct. In the case of France since 1930, belatedness has evolved at least as much from patterns of displacement and blockage related to the conjuncture of modernist culture and right-wing politics. Ongoing debates about Vichy are a point of entry for what I see over a longer duration as an interwar phenomenon whose full significance remains yet to be determined.

How might a clearer sense of Maurice Blanchot's writings contribute to the articulation of the literary and the political in interwar France? A first distinction between politics and the political points to questions and issues raised, admittedly in different ways, by Derrida and Lacoue-Labarthe concerning Heidegger, de Man, and the scandal of aftereffect. If the very notion of Blanchot's politics sounds close to oxymoronic, we might counter by asking to what extent literary space (*l'espace littéraire*) coincides with political space (*l'espace politique*). If I write as though this distinction were invalid, ill-advised, or otherwise dubious, it is not simply because I find it in each and every instance to be false. Instead, I want to force a conjuncture of the literary and the political by considering what might be learned—about writing, about history, about the notoriously obscure "Blanchot"—by looking at a sizable portion of his writings that is seldom, if ever, studied.

It has long been known that Maurice Blanchot's postwar career as novelist and literary critic was preceded by an extensive period of journalistic activity. In 1969, Jean-Louis Loubet del Bayle provided the following biographical sketch in his monumental study of the young *non-conformistes* of the 1930s:

MAURICE BLANCHOT: Born in 1907 in Quain (Saône-et-Loire). Between 1930 and 1940, foreign affairs editor for the *Journal des Débats*. Close to certain quarters of *Action Française,* he works on *Réaction* and on *La Revue Française* between 1930 and 1934, then, regularly, on *Combat* from 1936 to 1939. On the eve of the war, he is one of the principal editors of *Aux Ecoutes*. During the Occupation, he is, in the Northern zone, Literary Director of *Jeune France,* a cultural association funded by Vichy's Secretariat General for Youth. In 1941, he publishes a novel, *Thomas l'obscur,* start of a second career as novelist and essayist. Disengaging himself from politics, he draws near to the existentialists. At the Liberation, he participates in the first issues of *Les Temps Modernes,* but distances himself from militant existentialism by refusing all political commitment. Since the war, interpreter notably of Sade and of Lautréamont, he has devoted himself totally to his work as writer and as critic, publishing articles and columns regularly in the new *Nouvelle Revue Française*.[4]

Between 1931 and 1937, Blanchot wrote some 160 articles in a variety of dailies, weeklies, and monthlies that included *Combat, L'Insurgé, La Revue Française,* and *La Revue du XXe siècle.* Approximately half of the articles were short reviews of fiction and essays by writers from Roger Martin du Gard, Julien Benda, and Pierre Drieu La Rochelle to Denis de Rougemont, Albert Thibaudet, and Virginia Woolf. A second group of articles addressed nonliterary issues ranging from Hitler's rise to power to French economic policy and the Popular Front government. Blanchot's journalistic career extended into the German occupation of France. Between April 16, 1941, and August 17, 1944, he wrote some 172 articles for the "Chronique de la vie intellectuelle" column in *Le Journal des Débats.* Of these, three reappeared as the pamphlet *Comment la littérature est-elle possible?* published by José Corti in 1942, and were reprinted with fifty-seven others the following year by Editions Gallimard as *Faux pas.*

Well before the recent debates surrounding Heidegger and de Man, critical portraits by Tzvetan Todorov and Jean-Paul Aron had cast Blanchot as a prime figure in revisionary accounts of postwar French modernity. These portraits raised the stakes of relating the literary and the political. A chapter in Jeffrey Mehlman's *Legacies* likewise transformed Blanchot's 1930s journalism into an apology for anti-Semitism and collaboration. At worst, the existence of the early writings seemed to taint Blanchot by a logic of prefiguration similar to that directed more recently toward Heidegger and de Man. Whatever the short-term results, controversy surrounding Heidegger and

de Man is likely to promote more extensive inquiry into the politics of interwar modernity in Europe and, in particular, the cultural ambitions that
permeated the interwar French right. Yet the case against Blanchot (at least
as Mehlman made it after qualifying his project as exploratory) overshot its
ostensible goal of sketching "a hypothetical path—or series of paths—
through Blanchot's writing to the very different incarnation that has figured
so centrally for a generation of literary critics."[5] The sheer volume of these
early writings is a mark of the serious consideration and extended analysis
they warrant. There is no reason why what Mehlman referred to as "the in-
augural silence in Blanchot's sense of literature" should not undergo fuller
disclosure.

Crossing the Rhine

In the celebrated expression of Caesar concerning the Rhine that separates
Gaul and Germany, who will decide how the truth, psychological or political,
will be divided up?
Lucien Febvre, *La Terre et l'évolution humanine* (1924)

E. J. Hobsbawm argued in *Nations and Nationalism since 1780* that the phenomenon of nation was a relative newcomer in human history, that its initial formulation was in the main Eurocentric, and that its evolved expressions were products of localized historical conjunctures. An emergent sense
of nation—or "nation-ness"—could thus be seen as integral to processes of
nation-building that hovered between cartographic fantasy and what Benedict Anderson has termed imagined communities. Hobsbawm put it suc-
cinctly when he wrote that "nations do not make states and nationalisms,
but the other way around."[6] What interests me in Hobsbawm's remarks is
less the assumed precedence of nationalism over nation than an extended
interplay of the two, an interplay whose understanding is crucial to the "national question" as debated in recent years by historians, philosophers, and
social scientists. (I am thinking here, in addition to Hobsbawm and Anderson, of Fernand Braudel, Eugen Weber, Ernest Gellner, Zeev Sternhell, Herman Lebovics, and Anthony Smith; among theorists of culture, the names
that come to mind are Gayatri Spivak, Homi Bhabha, and Robert Young.)

Hobsbawm considered nationness very much of a made thing, an effect
or product of invention and social engineering. Moreover, because nationalism occurred as a grounding principle and thus prior to the nation, there
was always a gap in time between the construct of nation it projected and

the historical phenomenon of nation to which this projection gave rise. As a result, if the nation projected by nationalism was intelligible prospectively, the historical nation was recognized only after the fact. What, then, might it mean to look at the national question as Blanchot raised it in articles published under his name between 1932 and 1937? More than a half-century later, how might a closer look at the construct of nationness in these early writings contribute to clarifying what remains for many of Blanchot's readers a marginal practice? In order to situate this construct, I want to approach it, so to speak, from across the Rhine.

Ernst Robert Curtius (1886–1956) is best remembered for his encyclopedic study *European Literature and the Latin Middle Ages* (*Europäische Literatur und lateinische Mittelalter*), written in 1948. Along with Leo Spitzer and Erich Auerbach, Curtius was part of a generation of Romance philologists whose studies on topoi and stylistics marked a key phase in the evolved practices associated in France after World War II with *la nouvelle critique*. Among the three, Curtius most openly engaged a wider sphere of general readers. After World War I, studies on Valéry Larbaud, Charles Du Bos, and Marcel Proust testified to the seriousness with which Curtius took on the critical task of initiating the German public to "new" French writing. (Additional studies on James Joyce and on T. S. Eliot broadened the scope of national practices toward comparative philology.) Literature as Curtius conceived it a decade after World War I was not an isolated practice, but a means of access to wider social and political issues. The opening pages of *Einführung in die französische Kultur* (*The Civilization of France*) engaged these wider issues as follows:

> It goes without saying that political realities have not been absent from my thought. If my book were given to contribute in its modest way to clearing the ground where the Franco-German dialogue is sought, then my effort would not have been superfluous.
>
> Millions of French and Germans are unanimous in calling with all their will for the harmony of our two countries. If we fail to establish it, we know all too well what lies in wait for us: the collapse of our civilization. We must all contribute to bring forth a five-year plan to reconstruct our common heritage: Europe. It is in this thought that our civilizations should understand and approach each other.[7]

The tone of the passage was generous and its intent conciliatory. Curtius took ostensible pains to bring two recent enemies to a degree of shared understanding. Along similar lines, the call to dialogue at the start showed the extent to which Curtius considered political realities integral to his wider mission as a humanist, especially when he added that the presence of these realities was to be assumed as a given. The force of this opening call to a dialogue between nations across the Rhine was underscored by the unqualified possessive adjective (*notre*) invoked as "our civilization," "our common heritage" ("notre civilisation," "notre commun patrimoine") in each of the final two sentences. The usage was not, I believe, an instance of decorum or formality, as in the first-person plural known in French as *le nous magistral.* Nor should it be overlooked that the Alsace in which Curtius was born changed hands between France and Germany four times from 1870 to 1945, that he studied at the University of Strasbourg, and that when he wrote in 1930 of "notre commun patrimoine: l'Europe," he was already the author of *Französischer Geist im neuen Europa* (French Spirit in the New Europe), published in 1925.

I want briefly to examine the elements and structure of the vision of France set forth by Curtius in his *Einführung.* In particular, I want to examine how Curtius, as a German humanist predisposed to the task, theorized the key concepts of "culture" and "civilization" in relation to France. I do this for several reasons. First, because I mean to situate attitudes toward culture in interwar France in conjunction with what has come to be known after the work of Touchard and Loubet del Bayle as the spirit of the 1930s (*l'esprit des années trente*). Second, I want to test a hypothesis related to concerns for national identity among intellectuals on the French right and nonconformist dissidents during the 1930s. Over a somewhat longer duration, my choice of the *Einführung* is motivated by the complexity of Franco-German relations following World War I as a test case for France's evolving identity over the last two decades of the Third Republic. Finally—and not at all coincidentally—Curtius is of special relevance because his 1930 study was the object of a three-page review signed by Maurice Blanchot under a heading of "Controverses" in the March 27, 1932, issue of *La Revue Française.* Crossing the Rhine, then, is an attempt to explore a geographic and cultural border as formed in the words of a Frenchman writing in 1932 about a German writing about France. More pointedly, it is meant to provide a means of thinking through in detail the attitudes and assumptions at work in an early text by Blanchot in which national difference was a prime concern.

Linked by Curtius to nation, difference occurred as well in a slippage of title from German (*Einführung in die französische Kultur*) to French (*Essai sur la France*) and English (*The Civilization of France*). Translation here was perhaps nothing more or other than a surface effect. Yet Curtius implied otherwise when he identified the misunderstanding that occurred whenever essentializing terms such as "the French" and "the Germans" were left un-substantiated. Keeping this potential for slippage in mind, he considered how best to understand a foreign civilization not just in its isolated elements, but in its inner form of development. To this end, Curtius asserted that the error of disregarding fundamental differences between German and French conceptions of civilization led to countless other errors. And nowhere was this difference more pronounced than in the antithesis between *Kultur* and *civilisation,* where the latter represented the specific temper of an elevated social situation to which the former added the creative elements of science and art.

To this neohumanist conception invoked via Wilhelm Von Humboldt, Curtius contrasted Nietzsche's prophetic view in which tragic and Dionysiac values set culture apart from ideals of civilization associated with the common herdsman:

> On the German as well as the French side both these words and conceptions were set in opposition to each other. In both countries this was admitted, but the estimate formed in each nation was exactly the opposite. We rate *Kultur* higher than *civilisation.* France places *civilisation* in a higher category than *Kultur.*
>
> To the Frenchman the word *civilisation* was both the palladium of his national idea, and the guarantee of all human solidarity. Every Frenchman understands this word. It inflames the masses, and under certain circumstances it has a sacredness which exalts it to the religious sphere. (14)

For Curtius, then, *Kultur* belonged to the sphere of the educated elite set apart from the German people as a whole. *Civilisation* in the French conception summarized all that separated human existence from barbarism. It extended the Greco-Roman tradition that remained within it as a formal category of its nature. As a result, the historical development of *civilisation* tended toward universal categories that fused with and dominated the national idea. In seeking to fulfill its national ideal, France annexed the universalizing mission it inherited from ancient Rome. Likewise, for Curtius, the emotional force of this fusion of national and universal ideas produced a mystical nationalism enhanced by a religious prerogative in the form of a cult identified with the Catholic faith and the figure of Joan of Arc: "France alone, of all Christian nations, has achieved an emotional fusion of this kind. And this Nationalist Catholicism has recently again increased in power. The cult of the Sacred Heart, and the reverence shown for the Maid of Orleans, who was canonized in 1920, gives it its color at the present time. It is one of the strong elements in the Action Française" (22).

This emotional fusion did not simply transpose the idea of nation into religious sentiment. In the *grand siècle* following the Renaissance, it exalted the idea of nation into a universal significance embodied by Louis XIV and grounded in the undisputed authority of the monarchy, the church, and the state. From the Crusades through the revolution, the idea of civilization ordered the whole of national history in the light of an illuminating aim expressed as a mission to civilize. And this to a point where, Curtius wrote, the World Exhibitions of 1889 and 1900 seemed to illustrate that "all the peoples of the earth were bringing their gifts to the altar of French civilization" (32). To translate *deutscher Kultur* into *culture allemande* was to reduce something universal into a restricted context. National designations, expressed either as German *Kultur* or French *civilisation,* opposed a French notion of civilization that was integrally generalized and universal.

Curtius ended his remarks on *Kultur* and/against *civilisation* by prophesying that while the notion of France as the supreme representative of civilization persisted among right-wing figures such as Henri Massis, the best minds among the young in France were no longer hampered by traditional ideals. The successor to this conception of France's cultural preeminence was not yet clearly defined because France remained a land of gerontocracy. Yet between the generation of those born around 1900 and their predecessors there existed a very tangible difference of attitude: "Economic and political problems, as well as problems of ideals, everywhere required new solutions. The old ideas must be thought out afresh, even the conservative ideas of tradition" (41–42). Because he saw a similar process of self-examination taking place in Germany, Curtius hoped that resolving the controversy between *Kultur* and *civilisation* would further mutual understanding among the two nations.

In separate chapters devoted to geography, history, religion, education, and the city of Paris, Curtius devoted special attention to literature and intellectual life. In fact, it would be more accurate to state that Curtius equated literature with intellectual life, as he argued that all the national ideals of France were colored and shaped by literary form. Thus, concerning Descartes he wrote that even if the virtues of the *Discours de la méthode* were equated unfairly with clarity of expression, this quality held its own in a general public alongside the technical or esoteric knowledge prized among specialists: "The Frenchman will allow himself to be instructed in all forms of knowledge if the literary form is good. In France, in the ranks of intellectual types, the writer ranks higher than the scholar" (127). What motivated this predisposition was, Curtius concluded, a peculiarly French tradition of the man or woman of letters as exponent of the national spirit and thus of a role to which neither the philosopher, the musician, nor the scholar could make an equivalent claim.

Blanchot's remarks on Curtius changed abruptly from exposition to critique fueled by a surprisingly aggressive nationalism. After praising the impartiality and insights of *Essai sur la France,* Blanchot wrote that the book had probably appeared too late and that such ventures (*démarches*) from abroad only aroused suspicion: "We were expecting judgments about us that were possibly unpleasant or unjust, but yet susceptible of being true . . . Conclusions excessively preoccupied with an immediate advantage soon revealed their clear intent. There was no way to imagine that they might ever bring to us any insight into our country or the way other countries judge it. They could only teach us to be mistrustful."[8] Blanchot's tone was judgmental and defensive, its force grounded in an assumed equation of "we" that bore the marks of chauvinism in a strict and narrow sense. If Curtius really believed that literature played a more important role in France than elsewhere, the idea was far from original.

As Blanchot saw it, the central thesis of a common European legacy on which Curtius grounded his essay rang hollow because the recent past had contradicted it in advance. Blanchot substantiated his misgivings by invoking turn-of-the-century remarks by Charles Maurras in *L'avenir de l'intelligence* that prophesied the misery and degradation that the future was preparing for intelligence. In fact, not only did Blanchot invoke Maurras, he also contrasted him with Paul Claudel, whose diplomatic career, he added, was unlikely to revive the prestige that literature had lost since its high point in the eighteenth century. Blanchot could not contain his irony: "As for the eighteenth century where M. Curtius sees the 'origin of this narrow fusion of literature and the State,' 'the willful intention of Richelieu and Louis XIV,' it was valid for the literature of illustrious names and honorable duties, but watched jealously that the only credit they received was in the realm of pure fiction" (363). What Curtius took for the equation in France of literature with civilization was, Blanchot wrote, really of very little importance. For the equation was upheld at the cost of a perceived absence of a passion for philosophy and metaphysics, which meant, for example, that a Hegel, a Schopenhauer, or a Nietzsche would never have emerged in France. As Blanchot summarized, "Let us consider, at least, where the observation by M. Curtius leads: our impotence in philosophy that makes us pay a high cost for our love of literature, even compromises our literary superiority" (364).

In what Blanchot took for a more serious misperception, Curtius deprived literature of poetry via a prejudice toward clarity that, for Blanchot, had led writers and critics alike astray. This prejudice grew from practices of rhetoric and style as well as from a reading of the *Discours de la méthode* that had less to do with Descartes as philosopher than with norms and practices to which his name was subsequently linked. Blanchot took these norms as restrictive because they prescribed not only how—in terms of poetics—language could be used, but also, more fundamentally, how it related to experience. The remark was grounded in assumptions concerning the experience of language that, in turn, pointed to corollary notions of literary space and the future book. This early gesture of resistance to normalized clarity suggested that Blanchot was already formulating in 1932 a version of the distinction between everyday and essential language that he would develop considerably in postwar essays on Mallarmé, Proust, and Kafka. In the review of Curtius, however, the initial formulation was topical to the point of polemic:

> A prejudice toward clarity has continually misled writers and critics. Today where this prejudice yields, it encourages by a sort of challenge in authors of good will the obscure enterprises and singular expressions that do not always respond to the will of their inspiration. But beforehand, to what idiocies, to what slipshod constructs has it made us complacent! Neither the ambition of an effective harmony, the concern for a true purity, nor the search for this beauty that—millenary—seems born with each new writer, does not always succeed in winning out over the desire to touch the greatest number without being tiresome. (364)

The vocabulary of this passage contained a torsion or a change of register from categories of the aesthetic to the social and even the political. The prejudice toward clarity dominated a certain conception of French literature, but this domination was far from absolute. Blanchot's rhetorical questions expressed an impatience that, in the last sentence of the passage, were openly critical of the extent to which values of harmony, purity, and beauty associated with poetic language had been degraded in favor of access and intelligibility. When Blanchot responded that literature was not clear, he associated clarity with the intellectual equivalent of a universal suffrage he was loath to tolerate. The just measure and cost of this clarity was nothing less than abdication and compromise: "What is his idea of the average European so readily sensitive to that which is unique and incompatible in our literature?" (364). For Curtius to equate clarity with accessibility and to consider this equation a prime virtue of French literature was to grant too much to the average European and too little to the specificity of French practices. It was, in sum, to equate literature with prose and thus to make of it *un art du milieu* in the pejorative sense of something mediocre.

To consider literature in terms of a universal clarity was moreover to relegate it to the realm of a psychology and to an *analyse des passions* that reduced human activities to an abstract and timeless "continuous discourse on Man." The claim also set the psychologizing essence Curtius attributed to French literature at odds with a metaphysical tendency on the German side. Blanchot responded in no uncertain terms and once again with irony: "It is a fine privilege, but is it everything? Our subtlety would be worth the worst kind of crudeness if it did nothing more than isolate shades of detail and delicate features of feelings without seeking there as well the trace of the eternal" (365). French literature—Blanchot wrote "our" (*notre*) literature— was not a mere inventory of psychological states but rather aimed at something more ambitious: "It becomes a matter of hoping to attain the human at a point where the pure and the essential are conceived in the concrete harmony of a real action or the passions of some concrete being" (365).

Blanchot's rejection of Curtius was threefold. First, he considered Curtius wrong in describing the analysis of feelings and/or passions as the primary if not also the essential quality of French writing. Second, Blanchot questioned the analogy by which Curtius cast the metaphysical and philosophical tendencies he attributed to German literature as equivalent to the French tendency to psychologize, especially when this analogy cast these tendencies on opposite sides of the Rhine as mutually exclusive. Finally, Blanchot asserted that what Curtius took for an abstract difference at the level of national practice was valid only in specific instances. In such terms, Blanchot's defense of French literary practices did not, then, simply adjust or refine aspects of what Curtius argued. Nor was the level of abstraction in itself susceptible to the misreading for which Blanchot held Curtius accountable. In sum, if Curtius was right that French literature was in essence a "continuous discourse on Man," he was right for the wrong reasons. This objective was not attained, as Curtius asserted, via psychology and an analysis of emotions, but by a balanced discourse of reason in which neither the ardor of poetry nor the resources of philosophy were lacking: "[Literature] does not renounce richness, abundance, the variety of inspiration: nor does it renounce being perfect. Without losing anything, without sacrificing anything, it animates the body of goods that form our civilization" (365). In direct opposition to what Curtius had held in *Essai sur la France*, Blanchot concluded that literature in France attained its distinctive character of universality and humanity as a unique and all-encompassing synthesis.

With a Vengeance

Blanchot's review of Curtius's book raised a major question of border related to national identity as at least part of the nonconformist French right conceived it in the early 1930s. The border in question was really two: one geographic, the other a more unstable construct of politics and culture. In terms of the former, I have already suggested the extent to which Franco-German relations during the Third Republic served as a measure of evolving national sentiment. This was so despite the fact that the practices to which national sentiment gave rise were continuously divided between two political traditions that, following Zeev Sternhell, I want to designate as republican and nationalist. On the side of the former was a tradition of universal rights and the inalienable worth of the individual, a tradition supported by liberal and democratic impulses rooted in the French Revolution. On the side of the latter was a political tradition in which the primacy of the individual with regard to society yielded to the particularist and organistic collectivity, which, as Sternhell put it, was often dominated by a "local variant of cultural, and sometimes biological and racial nationalism, very close to the *völkisch* tradition in Germany."[9]

Sternhell's sense of these rival traditions identified the difficulty of ascribing stable correspondences to expressions of nationalist ideologies along a spectrum from left to right. This was especially the case because universalist and particularist traditions on the right were often linked, even at times within the works of a single writer. Sternhell also saw the extent to which sentiment of nation—a variant of Hobsbawm's "nation-ness"—was polyvalent, in that it was capable of appropriation in various ways and by different groups all along the political spectrum. Examining the sentiment of nation in Blanchot's 1932 reading of Curtius helps to account for the complexity of national identity at a moment of political, economic, and spiritual crisis. Because this sentiment evolved in response to conditions imposed by circumstance, I want to trace its changing expression in a series of articles published under Blanchot's name a year after his review of Curtius.

Between April 27 and August 29, 1933, Blanchot wrote sixty-one articles for *Le Rempart*, a Parisian daily described by Loubet del Bayle as openly anticapitalist and antiparliamentary.[10] The paper was the organ of a militant splinter group of the "Jeune Droite" movement that sought alternatives to what it perceived as the inert and conservative elements of Action Française. Blanchot's work at *Le Rempart* brought him into contact with Jacques Talagrand (alias Thierry Maulnier), for whom he was to work on *Combat* three years later. By June 1933, the failure of France's delegation to protect national interests at an international economic conference in London heightened popular dissatisfaction with parliamentary rule dominated by a party that was radical in name only. Seven months later, that dissatisfaction erupted into the demonstrations of February 1934. Outside France, Hitler's seizure of power in January 1933 and his dissolution of all but his National Socialist party imposed a new urgency on the growing calls for a stronger France. Circumstances at home and abroad thus lent themselves increasingly to calls by a militant right for economic, political, and spiritual change for which national revolution became a necessary means.

Analysis of the articles in Le Rempart by title and content reveals a nearly equal distribution between foreign and domestic issues. Economic policy entered into fifteen of the articles, and another six explicitly addressed revolution either in terms of Third Republic France or post-Weimar Germany. The copresence of domestic and foreign perils illustrated the difficulty of treating Blanchot's critique of the government's domestic policies apart from international concerns. "La Révolution nécessaire" (Necessary revolution), published in the issue dated June 22, 1933, displayed marks of a manifesto in its call to mobilize opposition to government policies more and more at odds with the best interests of the French nation. For Blanchot, a recognition of crisis was the prerequisite for change: "It becomes increasingly evident that the country is today witnessing the death throes of a system. Tomorrow, by its revolt and by its anger, that each will have occurred [il l'achèvera]" (2). The party in office held power, he wrote, but was incapable of decisive action. It demanded full powers but could not implement them because it had neither a doctrine nor a program. As a result, any and all expectations were lowered in view of a democratic state that had repeatedly displayed its incompetence for a half-century.

"La Révolution nécessaire" responded to conditions that went beyond economics or politics and thus toward what even the more moderate Esprit group around Emmanuel Mounier referred to with irony as the established disorder (désordre établi):

> The greatest weakness of this regime is to no longer promise anything, to no longer have revolutionary parties on its left. Our greatest hope, today, is that, for a free nation, for the defense of mankind, for spiritual wealth, rises the magnificent promise of revolution. While socialism submits to democracy and to dictatorship as it repulses the very idea of insurrection, while communism slowly abandons the force of its founding myths, the ideas of nation are allied with all that is battle, rebellion, and mistrust of established positions,

with violence, with excess. They alone today propose to a discouraged youth reasons to hope and a new fate. The spiritual revolution, the national revolution, is no longer an image and a symbol. Each day, events bring it closer, each day they make it more necessary. And little by little, they teach us what it will be: hard, bloody, unjust, our last chance of salvation. (2)

The reference to spiritual revolution echoed other right-wing intellectuals whose estrangement from organized political parties and the Catholic church had led to dissidence in response to government policies of economic reform that Blanchot saw as ill-founded and desperate, the symptoms of a crisis of authority on the part of a weak democratic state that had lost the confidence of the people.

"La Révolution nécessaire" was one in a series of nine texts in *Le Rempart* that openly invoked national revolution as an alternative to a parliamentary system whose dependence on private interests compromised its ability to rule. Here, for example, was how Blanchot, in an article published on May 31 entitled "La Révolte contre le pouvoir," analyzed comments by Prime Minister Edouard Daladier concerning demonstrations by shopkeepers and other taxpayers against proposed tax reforms they saw as excessive and unwarranted:

> The French have just shown the great power they have at their disposal. . . . By refusing, as they have just noted their intentions, to pay up to a certain point what they consider to be unjust taxes, they will have a healthy defensive reaction.
> Because one does not pay a government that lives by plunder and that organizes pillage.
> One does not pay a government that works against itself and against the nation.
> One does not pay a government when it no longer represents anything but an arbitrary power persistent in destroying everything it has a mission to safeguard. (1)

For Blanchot, threats of government reprisal only extended the solidarity among demonstrators they were intended to put down. Evoked in popularist terms and without reference to specific parties or ideologies, it was as though the French state itself became revolutionary to the extent that the vacuum created by the government's abdication of authority called for a new order: "We believed there still existed a government capable of justice, exercising its authority and maintaining its prerogatives. But we find before us only a delegation of private interests, watched over jealously by their representatives: there is no longer any government [il n'y a plus d'Etat]" ("Quand l'Etat est révolutionnaire" [April 29]: 2).

Suppression was a last-ditch attempt on the part of a weak regime that sought to maintain an illusion of order in circumstances that called for direct intervention against parliamentary rule: "Therefore, when power is in the hands of the abettors of disorder, when it is an instrument of oppression, force becomes the only means of guaranteeing order and of serving true authority" (April 29). The significant detail here was the trope of inversion by which Blanchot referred to a state whose self-destruction imposed a new order: "Mortal perils threaten us from within and without. Never has it been more useful for the French to have a strong sense of the changes that are necessary for France to return to itself and to find again a society without socialism and a government without anarchy" (April 29). The range of problems faced by France in the spring of 1933 made it difficult to isolate Blanchot's critique of economic policies from political concerns at home and abroad. Moreover, France's various domestic crises pointed to deep-seated political and spiritual problems whose resolution Blanchot also pondered on occasion in light of post-Weimar Germany.

I base this last remark on two articles: "Des Violences antisémites à l'apothéose du travail" (Anti-Semitic violence at the May Day celebration) and "La Vraie Menace du Troisième Reich" (The true threat of the Third Reich), which appeared in *Le Rempart* on May 1 and June 29, respectively. The first of these articles denounced the demagoguery and racism that Hitler used in place of substantial political reform, as in his attempt to appropriate the ritual celebration of labor: "What Hitler cannot give in real reforms, he tries to find in psychological equivalents. He consecrates the dignity of the 'worker' and praises him in great speeches . . . It would be wrong to see these celebrations as nothing more than childish demonstrations. The apotheosis of work is a symbol whose meaning is not lost for the Germans. It expresses the revenge of collective forces, the limitless devotion to an ideal of greatness and of domination" (3). Persecution added to a rhetoric of racial specificity that Blanchot saw as crude and effective: "The celebration of work is also the celebration of the army, declared the Minister of Defense—and this word gives meaning to all of these demonstrations" (3).

"La Vraie Menace du Troisième Reich" was more complex and ambivalent. Blanchot coupled his misgivings over Hitler's charismatic success—my expression, not Blanchot's—with his view that France's inability to understand Germany was yet another symptom of liberal democracy's weak rule: "For more than a century, France has had difficulty in understanding the Reich's intentions. . . . Since the Armistice, all diplomacy has consisted in looking for a Germany that did not exist." For Blanchot, writing in the spring of 1933, Hitler's rise to power exemplified a strong rule and thus a potential threat to France's national security. Yet this threat did not seem to preclude a certain degree of admiration on Blanchot's part for the success with which Hitler had mobilized a generation of young Germans in search of alternatives to inept liberal government.

> Hitler offers German youth a new religion that is one of a perverted nationalism, of a race superior to all others: in sum, of Germanism. He has given a new form to the age-old dream in which Germany, proud and immense, dreams of imposing on the world the culture it has chosen for itself. And, ambitious heir to Luther and to Bismarck, it pursues an enterprise that is a danger to peace and a threat to Western civilization.
>
> It is not at all by affront and by ineffectual violence that the French will prepare to rectify these errors. Instead, it is by opposing to this revolution that claims to give us the model of a new society, a deeper revolution such as the one France wants. And it is also by a strong diplomacy—unfaltering and without idle threats—that the two countries will reestablish a balance that has been broken for a long time.[11]

Even when qualified as in this passage, Blanchot's willingness to invoke the example of Germany was a measure of the deep disaffection within a generation of those on the French right whose inability to find an acceptable model of national sentiment at home led them to look across the Rhine. When Blanchot invoked Hitler's appeal to a mythic German past, he was not at all endorsing National Socialism as a political regime. Instead he looked to Germany in order to appropriate in the name of France a future identity for which the deeper revolution he foresaw was a necessity. Once again and so as to avoid any misunderstanding, it bears repeating that Blanchot gave every indication of having seen through the artifice of Hitler's appeal to "a new religion . . . of a perverted nationalism" grounded in an assumption of racial superiority that threatened France and European civilization. It is also curious that despite such misgivings, Blanchot seemed to admire in Hitler's ploy an appeal to strength toward which he sought to direct efforts in France to reestablish diplomatic balance with Germany. Balance here was not synonymous with complicity or collaboration, but the mark of strength and prestige for which Blanchot saw revolution as a prerequisite.

The articles under Blanchot's signature in *Le Rempart* projected identity for a French nation and a people apart from—and against—various ruling bodies in Paris. Even as he identified the menace that a National Socialism represented for France and for Europe, Blanchot was thinking how to appropriate for France the intense national sentiment that Hitler had mobilized in Germany. Blanchot invoked Germany under Hitler as an example (largely, but not absolutely, negative) against which he measured what he perceived as France's shortcomings. In this sense, the articles in *Le Rempart* show the complexity of a position that, over the spring and summer of 1933 and thus seven to nine months before the February 1934 riots, typified the antiliberal, antidemocratic, and nonpartisan stance associated with the non-conformist phenomenon of the 1930s. Moreover, the articles illustrated the extent to which deep opposition to a series of weak French regimes on the part of a generation of disaffected right-wing intellectuals was grounded in a conviction that the problems devolving from economic and political mis-management were inscribed within a wider "spiritual" threat to Western civ-ilization.

It is curious that when Blanchot invoked the menace of Germany against a weak France, he used the very terms of culture and civilization to which Curtius had attributed a providential resonance. What I have argued con-cerning Curtius, Blanchot, and perceptions across the Rhine was intended to substantiate the scope and extent of debate over cultural difference in France and Germany at a particular moment in a decade during which the politics of renewal on both sides of the river moved toward national revolu-tion. A desire to substantiate the nature of Blanchot's nationalist sentiment in the early 1930s motivates my reading of the articles in *Le Rempart*. Yet my conclusion points less to the extent of a Germanophilia than to a clearer sense of what Germany and National Socialism represented in 1932–33 to a young Maurice Blanchot who invoked the necessity of revolution in hopes of breaking with the mediocrity of republican governments he—and many others on the interwar French right—found unbearable.

The articles in *Le Rempart* also include at least one text, "Les Chances du néo-socialisme" (The chances of neo-socialism), published on August 29, 1933, in which Blanchot pondered what Hitler's mobilization of German youth might mean for future attempts to mobilize the disaffected *non-con-formistes* of his own generation. Renewal was thus a prime factor in what he saw as a praiseworthy renunciation of convention and partisan concerns in favor of a new political thought. At the same time, however, Blanchot ex-pressed impatience with a reluctance to break completely with residual forms of Marxism and democracy he took for symptoms of decadence: "What is disappointing is all that is residual, artificial, and equivocal in this thought that seeks itself. National Socialism should appear as an important sign. It does not yet appear as a hope" (3).

Blanchot's contributions to *La Revue du XXe siècle* and *Le Rempart* were set within the Jeune Droite offshoot of Action Française, which regrouped in

1936 to publish *Combat* and, a year later, *L'Insurgé*. The positions taken in the texts on Curtius and on post-Weimar Germany suggested that Blanchot's perception of political and spiritual crisis had not yet in 1932–33 hardened into the militant dissidence that he and others who wrote for *Combat* and *L'Insurgé* directed toward the Popular Front some three to four years later. While Blanchot watched the rise of a National Socialist regime across the Rhine, he watched as well the rise in France of equivalent efforts at national renewal. In 1933, Blanchot's call to revolution—"une révolution plus profonde et telle que la France la veut" ("a deeper revolution such as the one France wants")—was still tempered by the possibility of peace through diplomacy. Over the next four years, the evolved positions Blanchot was to take in articles written for *Combat* and *L'Insurgé* traced a militant turn in response to the Popular Front and what he perceived as its shortcomings. The nature of that turn—to the left? to the right? or, as Zeev Sternhell puts it provocatively, "neither left nor right"—will be studied in chapter 5.

Caveat

My reading of Blanchot's articles in *Le Rempart* is not intended as objective or aloof. Nor should the desire to move prudently toward fuller disclosure be mistaken for timidity. The question of how to approach the "early" or "militant" Blanchot of the 1930s is not simply one of historical details. At the same time, precipitous judgment—especially when it takes the tropic form of prolepsis—strikes me as an unworthy and irresponsible response to the ambivalent politics linked to the cultures of France in the 1930s that are all too often denied their historical complexity. What, then, are the limits of objectivity in historical inquiry and how do they evolve with the passage of time? What can be claimed as irreducibly factual and self-evident? As Fritz Stern has noted, the health of nations as of individuals depends on some measure of release from the wounds of the past. As memories fade, they are also rearranged in accordance with perceived needs of the present: "Historians abet—and sometimes correct—the rearrangement of the past so that a society can find a tolerable or livable past for itself, for 'try as we may, we cannot, as we write history, escape from our purposiveness.'"[12] My account of Blanchot's articles in *Le Rempart* revises by force of circumstance and the retrospection that the passage of time asserts. But it does so in terms that I am willing to defend against what I see as attempts to aestheticize the political. If anything, my approach to the articles in *Le Rempart* has asserted the specificity of the political against the literary and the aesthetic. The tactic—

intended as provisional and provocative—still needs to be justified in view of the more frequent approaches to Blanchot via his fiction and essays.

I also admit to a certain uneasiness with the key concept of articulation. For while I mean to assert how Blanchot's interwar texts can and should be related to his fiction and essays, I am not suggesting that they simply be appended to or inserted uncritically within his total corpus. In this sense, an approach that asserts the political can be misleading if and when it is taken as an absolute apart from other discourses and practices such as philosophy and literature. The issue is that of setting practices we associate with certain genres and disciplines within a relevant context. Articulate, connect, join, attach, or link: whatever the term, the point is to account as much as possible for the full scope and variety of mediations that inevitably bear on specific practices. My second thoughts on articulation derive from my decision to approach Blanchot via Heidegger and from what this ordering implies concerning the phenomenon of aftereffect. To read Heidegger via Farias and then to direct this mediation toward Blanchot is doubtless convoluted, but such convolution also illustrates the inherent limitations of treating the political apart from practices of philosophy and literature. The limitations are especially clear in attempts to engage what received understanding of cultural modernity has systematically displaced. Articulation is, then, not by necessity an ill-chosen ("wrong") term. Instead, the problems it raises point to ongoing inquiries into the political (*le politique*) undertaken in the wake of deconstruction. For example, we may take this statement written by Lacoue-Labarthe and Nancy in 1981:

> Inquiry into the political or into the essence of the political is, on the contrary, what should bring us back to the political presupposition itself of philosophy (or, if one prefers, of metaphysics), toward a political determination of essence. But this determination does not make a political position: it is the very position of the political, of the Greek *polis* toward what has unfolded in the modern age as the qualification of the political by the subject (and of the subject by the political). What remains for us to think, in other words, is not a new institution (or instruction) of politics (*la politique*) by thought, but the political institution of so-called Western thought.[13]

The binding of *le politique* and *la politique* goes well beyond wordplay. The wordplay destabilizes concepts and distinctions much as the supplement of the early ("political") writings destabilizes dominant approaches to Blanchot's total corpus. Although the provisional effect of this gesture is disruptive, it should not be equated with an extended paralysis or inaction. If,

as Nancy Fraser has put it, one's *politics* inevitably encroaches on one's conception of the political, determining when and how this encroachment occurs will be possible if and only if inquiry into *le politique* ventures forth
from its transcendental safehouse.[14] In the case of Blanchot, such a venture
first occurred in the texts that appeared under his signature during 1933.

CHAPTER FIVE

Under Erasure

What about the *other* history, wherein nothing of the present ever happens, which no event or advent measures or articulates? Foreign to the succession of moments, which is linear even when it is hindered and as zigzagging as it is dialectical, the other history is the deployment of a plurality which is not that of the world or of numbers. It is a history in excess, a "secret," separate history, which presupposes the end of visible history, though it denies itself the very idea of beginning and of end.

Maurice Blanchot, *L'écriture du désastre*

I am not summoning up these hard facts merely so that they will not fade from memory, but also so that the memory of them makes us more aware of our responsibility.

Maurice Blanchot, "Our Responsibility"

The Essential Perversion

René Char marked his 1964 reading of Maurice Blanchot's 1958 article "La Perversion essentielle" (The essential perversion) by praising Blanchot's ability to keep politics in a temporal perspective. Politically, Char wrote, Blanchot could only go "from one disappointment to another—that is, from one courage to another—because he is not prone to the forgetful mobility [mobilité oublieuse] of most contemporary writers."[1] Char praised Blanchot in terms of difference that cast him as a model figure of constancy and endurance. But as a counterpoint to forgetfulness, memory is not by necessity either uniform or stable. Varying with circumstance, it can be individual or collective, acknowledged or denied. When memory displaces the strong affect associated with loss and absence, it also extends the work of mourning and grief. The displaced term in Char's remarks was the term of history. And the issue I mean to raise via Char is the curious place of a certain past in Blanchot's writings. More pointedly, I mean to argue that the exemplarity of Blanchot to which Char referred in 1964 was possible only by displacing toward forgetful mobility a determinate past for which Blanchot has never fully accounted. How, then, are history and memory bound up in Blanchot's writings?

"La Perversion essentielle" expressed Blanchot's views on the power offered to Charles de Gaulle in May 1958 to contend with circumstances surrounding attempts to end France's colonial presence in Algeria. Because Blanchot considered this presence as a mutation of political power, the pertinent question was not how de Gaulle might resolve the volatile situations at home and abroad, but how it came to pass that his presence responded to something beyond the political matters on which he might be expected to act: "The power invested in a providential man is no longer a political power, it is a power of salvation. Its presence as such is salutary in itself and not because of what it will do" (21). Terms of salvation and providence added messianic elements to an explicit discourse of secular politics. The effect evoked a holy war or crusade that resonated with a rhetoric of spiritual crisis recalling the political upheavals of the 1930s that Blanchot had lived as a young adult.

Char's remarks also revealed a force of mutation between "La Perversion essentielle" and Blanchot's writings of the 1930s on politics and literature. They pointed to the complex binding of postwar texts by a Blanchot who wrote critically of de Gaulle's providential return in 1958 and articles of twenty years earlier in which Blanchot had called for the overthrow of the Popular Front regime. The temporal gap separating these two sets of articles raised questions of order and priority, for to read the interwar essays back through the postwar corpus risked reducing them to a supplement in the weak sense of something derived or inessential. To follow chronology in a straightforward order was likewise to flatten the force of resonance and displacement of a corpus that extended over sixty years. Chronology also tended to privilege a signature—"un certain Maurice Blanchot"—grounded in a historical figure whose identity was neither stable and consistent nor purely broken and fragmented, but continually dispersed.

How might Blanchot's articles of the 1930s be approached without granting to them a privilege of predetermining origin? Were texts such as "La Perversion essentielle" written to compensate for an interwar extremism that Blanchot subsequently disavowed? If so, was this compensation willful and explicit or was it indirect and displaced? These questions haunt Blanchot as they have haunted many of his generation because substantial evidence suggests that our understanding of interwar and wartime France remains not merely incomplete in detail, but defective through denial and suppression. To what extent, then, might the early writings legitimize accusations directed toward another Blanchot ("un Blanchot autre")? What difference might these accusations make in reassessing his place in French literary modernity? The answers I propose in this chapter trace an evolving interplay between politics and literature grounded in articles Blanchot wrote for *Combat* and *L'Insurgé* from February 1936 to December 1937. The articles, many of which dealt with the Popular Front government headed by Léon Blum, are best understood in conjunction with practices of a French right that ranged from conservatives and neoroyalists to others who saw themselves as neither right nor left.

The interwar monthly *Combat*—not to be confused with the clandestine Occupation publication of the same name—emerged in January 1936 from the Action Française offshoot known as La Jeune Droite (The young right). Under codirectors Jean de Fabrègues and Thierry Maulnier, it published thirty-seven issues through July 1939. Most of *Combat*'s contributors belonged to a generation of Catholic intellectuals born between 1900 and 1910 who were disenfranchised from the French right in 1926 after Pope Pius XI placed *Action Française* on the Vatican's list of prohibited publications. Over the following decade, these young writers and organizers rejected a liberal capitalist mentality they saw as a prime cause of the world war they had witnessed as children. Increasingly at odds with inept republican regimes that threatened to deprive France of anything but an abject future, they established journals, associations, and movements whose visions of renewal ranged from the neoroyalism associated with Action Française to the ambiguous politics of personalism of the *Esprit* group established in 1932 under Emmanuel Mounier.

Jean de Fabrègues, born in 1906, studied philosophy at the Sorbonne and served as a secretary to Charles Maurras while maintaining ties with the Catholic intellectual circles around Jacques Maritain and Georges Bernanos.

Thierry Maulnier (born Jacques Talagrand in 1909) was a classmate of Robert Brasillach and Roger Vailland at the Ecole Normale Supérieure. The author of acclaimed studies on Nietzsche and Racine, Maulnier wrote extensively after the Liberation as a theater critic for the right-wing journal *La Table Ronde*. From 1964 until his death in 1988, Maulnier was a member of the Académie Française. According to Zeev Sternhell, Maulnier belonged to a generation of fascistically inclined intellectuals who undermined democracy in France between the wars "without assuming direct responsibility for membership in a fascist party or organization."[2] Maulnier's itinerary—the *Petit Larousse* described him as a writer and journalist, "defender of a classical ideal"—illustrated the extent to which engagement on the militant right during the 1930s remained under erasure in relation to a postwar literary career seemingly removed from active political involvement. After the fact, Maulnier's militancy of the 1930s remained ephemeral and unseen: either deleted from early accounts and thus actively forgotten, or never added to others for which literature and politics were presumably kept apart.

What passed for a progression from politics to literature among intellectuals who militated on the interwar French right was neither universal nor absolute. Some remained openly politicized and moved ostensibly toward the left, while others remained unchanged and unrepentant. Here, for example, is how Alice Kaplan began her account of meeting Maurice Bardèche, a contemporary of Maulnier and coauthor with Robert Brasillach of *Histoire du cinéma* in 1935: "Maurice Bardèche makes it clear to me that he is *not* a surviving fascist activist from the 1930s. From the first, he explains, his political writings per se are radically outside any signifying context: he declares himself against the Resistance in 1947, and against the Jews in 1948. Finally, in 1961, he writes, as the opening sentence of a book entitled *Qu'est-ce que le fascisme?*, 'I am a fascist writer.'"[3]

Combat was founded as a review of theory and criticism, a self-styled "laboratory of ideas" on the political right. Like many ephemeral publications of the period, it never stabilized its finances. By the end of 1936, the monthly had 1,051 subscribers and outlets in forty-two cities. Repeated price increases, from 15 francs in 1936 to 20 francs in 1937 and 30 francs in 1938, suggested that the goal of two thousand readers announced for 1937 was never attained.[4] Despite its limited circulation, *Combat* made its mark by combining elements of the "antidemocratic and anticonservative spirit" of *Je Suis Partout* with an intellectual content whose prestige seemingly compensated for the invective it shared with the protofascist weekly (Sternhell, 229). The virulence that *Combat* shared with *Je Suis Partout* also set it apart from the more stolid *Action Française*. Between these two, *Combat*'s positions were often taken to be closer to the fascist than to the neoroyalist right. At the same time, however, articles critical of Hitler's rise to power suggested that the monthly's endorsement of fascism clearly stopped short of supporting National Socialism as a political regime (Sternhell, 229). In sum, the primary orientation of the monthly was nationalist.

An editorial statement in *Combat*'s first issue in January 1936 left little doubt concerning its hostility toward the Popular Front coalition that, five months later, would form the first French government headed by a member of the Parti Socialiste:

> Every day we see the growing danger of a future servitude of intelligence. The signs of this servitude do not appear only in the great dictatorial nations where the community, the state, the masses require from the intellectual the total adherence of thought. Even in France, writers are not content simply to take a stand—which is consistent with their rights and their status—in political struggles. In numerous circumstances, we have seen many in whom we used to honor the elevation of mind, the acuity of analysis and scruples, accept to keep their reason silent in the face of what sentimentality requires, the alleged urgency of positive action, or the orders of a political party. . . .
>
> Thus have we recently seen intellectuals whom we would have believed more conscious of the dignity of their condition advocating that their readers boycott works by their adversaries, guilty of having signed a manifesto that had displeased them. Every day, we see them prefer the demagogic call to the discussion of ideas, and popular sentiment to objective truth. These base compromises are possible only because intelligence has penetrated the world of social and political realities, not to rule it and to organize it, but to forget itself there and to serve it. . . .
>
> Intelligence must not put itself in the service of the masses, but should inform and lead them; it should not follow the evolution of history, but rather make the evolution of history. If idealism displays the impotence of the mind before a world in relation to which it no longer knows any attitude other than that of disinterest, materialism displays an equal impotence because, incapable of restoring to intelligence its sovereign domination over reality, it abandoned it willy-nilly to uncontrolled feelings, class hatreds, and antagonisms of interests. . . .
>
> The struggle to be waged here is the struggle for a new synthesis, for a reconciliation of intelligence and the real in their necessary union and in their true relations. It means that this review will be devoted neither to games of pure intelligence, nor to the tasks of enlisted intelligence. It means that it will try to reestablish the mind and the world, intelligence and politics, man and society in their true subordination and unity. In the face of idealist bankruptcy and the materialist peril, it is time to restore a new realism.

The editorial openly took to task ideals and practices it saw as detrimental to the intelligence of a France subjected to corrupt republican regimes. It also asserted the monthly's independence from party loyalty as a means of transcending ideology and doctrine. To this end, *Combat* sought whenever possible to take a clear stand on specific issues that often went against the grain of imposed adherence (*embrigadement*). From 1936 to 1939, the monthly supported the cause of Francisco Franco in Spain and applauded the 1938 Munich agreements as a victory of reason ("victoire de bons sens") and a viable alternative to war. In addition, it warned that Germany's imperialist intentions threatened the rebuilding of France from within that it saw as a prime necessity.[5] In retrospect, *Combat*'s self-styled nationalism asserted many of the values of national revolution that were later appropriated in the cause of the Etat Français government established in 1940 at Paris and Vichy.

Like other offshoots of Action Française, *Combat* saw itself as a weapon (*machine de guerre*) defending the French nation against a decadent and corrupt republic. To this end, it promoted a renewal of values for which the political struggle against democracy and capitalism was a prerequisite. This renewal derived from the nineteenth-century figures Georges Sorel and Pierre Joseph Proudhon: "When it wants to give an idea of its revolutionary orientation whose principle is that of reconciling nationalism and socialism, the *Combat* team prefers to invoke the example of the Cercle Proudhon. [Pierre] Andreu, for one, gathers the mass of these prewar references and sees in them the marks of a '1913 fascism' (February 1936)" (Leroy and Roche, 66).[6] *Combat*'s vision of nationalist renewal set it at odds with Popular Front policies on almost all domestic issues. Differences also surfaced among older members of Action Française who found *Combat*'s tone too strident for their tastes: "Maurras, between the wars, had enlisted these young men on a crusade which, earnest in concept, was in fact a great romantic adventure, a children's crusade. He had tamed them a little, he had taught them some things, he had endowed them with a revolution of their own—that of counterrevolution. Now they were fulfilling what they thought they had derived from him, carrying his teachings to what seemed to them their logical conclusion when actually it was only one of several possible conclusions. No wonder they were as disillusioned in him as he was in them."[7] By the mid-1930s, the deep disillusionment with the Third Republic shared by Maurras and his nonconformist offspring no longer compensated for differences of militancy and generation.

Between February 1936 and December 1937, Blanchot contributed eight articles to *Combat*, all of them devoted primarily to politics. "La Fin du 6 février" (The end of February 6) in the second issue (February 1936) assessed the failed opportunities for political change following the February 6,

1934, demonstrations precipitated by the Stavisky affair: "It could be judged that the demonstrations of February that were magnificent by virtue of their fervor, devotion, and sublime actions were mediocre in their conclusion" (26). Because Blanchot accepted that the truth about Stavisky would never be known, he concluded that the controversy surrounding Stavisky's death was yet another reminder of France's progressive decline: "For some, this honorable anniversary seems an event whose remembrance suffices and which continues to dominate all politics. This is not true. This date, simultaneously painful and great, is no longer anything more than a symbol. It is time, in the order of revolt, to think about something other than pious commemorations" (26).

Such misgivings concerning February 1934 extended toward a series of ongoing diplomatic blunders that Blanchot feared were drawing France into a war it neither wanted nor could successfully wage. In "La Guerre pour rien" (War for nothing) in *Combat* 3 (March 1936), he wrote that the Franco-Soviet pact left France without protection against future attack, presumably from Nazi Germany. Along the same lines, "Après le coup de force germanique" (After the German takeover) in *Combat* 4 (April 1936) chided the government of Albert Sarraut for placing too much value on the false security afforded by worthless treaties and by a League of Nations ("this inhuman, annoying, and impotent institution") incapable of taking preventive action against Hitler. Some two months before Blum took office, Blanchot reserved harsh words for the Popular Front coalition that he portrayed with open disdain: "What it will not do is direct a new politics founded on moral and material strength. And the regime will continue to go from provocations to failures, until it calls for war out of weakness or until another national revolt puts an end to its abuses" ("Après le coup," 59).

Blanchot increased the vehemence of his opposition after the Blum coalition took office in the summer of 1936. Two articles published later that year sketched a composite portrait of deep disaffection. "La Grande Passion des modérés" (The grand passion of the moderates) in *Combat* 9 (November 1936) applauded neutrality as a refusal to follow the rhetoric of those on the left whose desire to intervene in Spain threatened to lead France into an international conflict at odds with what Blanchot saw as its best interests: "What the leftists have tried to do in an unleashing of democratic interests has been judged and repressed as it should have been. No one doubts that the Popular Front wanted war, that it missed its opportunity, and that it awaits its vengeance" (147). The same moderates who in the past condemned insurrection and violence had seemingly found a new taste for blood. For Blanchot, this acquired taste was nothing less than a new thrill ("c'est le frisson nouveau") that played into Moscow's strategy of promoting international war.

"Le Caravensérail" (The caravanserai) in *Combat* 10 (December 1936) left little doubt concerning Blanchot's attitude toward the French and foreign communists under the new coalition government: "Since the accession of the Popular Front, since the entry into the French Chamber of seventy agents of Moscow, the nationals have a subject of preoccupation, communism, an object of terror, communism, and a rallying point, anticommunism" (171). While Blanchot justified anticommunism as "a police action, a matter of hygiene" and expressed admiration for those committed to it, he also noted the shallowness of those ("imbeciles and opportunists") who came to it out of self-interest. Anticommunism, then, fell short of the position Blanchot and *Combat* sought to promote. In fact, Blanchot went so far as to state that communism itself was a minor concern—"le cadet de nos soucis"—in view of a necessary revolution to come. This move beyond an oppositional stance was noteworthy because it showed the extent to which Blanchot wanted to mobilize those for whom anticommunism was a means rather than an end. Anticommunism was secondary to the task of removing the latest in a series of governments that had continually betrayed French interests: "Those on whom we set our eyes from now on are those who direct and decide officially. That is where one day it will be necessary to strike" (171). This call to violence was also unsettling because it echoed a similar call for "the necessary revolution" made three years earlier in Blanchot's article in *Le Rempart* on June 22, 1933. It was as if the interval had only worsened matters by adding betrayal to ineptitude.

Blanchot elaborated his call to revolution in late 1937, in two articles published in consecutive issues of *Combat*. In "La France, nation à venir" (France, nation of the future), from *Combat* 19 (November 1937), he chided the government for France's nonintervention, first in the Rhineland and later in Spain. In both instances, he saw abstention from preventive action as the result of a growing irreality that drew France toward a major conflict it could only lose. What some took for a pacifist diplomacy of self-protection was also a dangerous refusal to maintain the material conditions and substructure on which the future of France as a nation depended. For Blanchot, pacifism amounted to nothing more than an alibi for a politics of absence:

> France exists today neither in the regime, nor in the state or in its customs. It is absolutely not coincidental with legal France, it hardly has any more reality

in what is called real France. It has only the slightest effectiveness and a very weak presence in most minds and social groups. Its principal reality is in the past where history keeps it intact and in the future where it represents itself by some prospects and various images of what it should be. Real France can be felt today only as a possible France. (131)

The reality Blanchot saw in Blum's foreign policy was that of a willingness to do the bidding of others, especially when that bidding advanced the cause of party politics. Passivity at the level of people or nation thus ensured the triumph of Marxism or fascism in Spain while promoting the apparent absence of any true French cause. The resulting compromises were nothing less than disastrous to an inert France whose only future was extinction.

Blanchot's final contribution to *Combat*, "On demande des dissidents" (Dissidents wanted), published in the twentieth issue of the monthly (December 1937), expressed a last-ditch effort to counteract passivity with dissidence by drawing out those truly committed to revolution among the opportunists and others who claimed to be "above the fray." Dissidence was a position Blanchot upheld against both the left and the right: "It will be seen under such conditions that the true form of dissidence is that which abandons a position without ceasing to observe the same hostility in view of the opposite position or which abandons it in order to accentuate this hostility" (157). In the form Blanchot gave to it in late 1937, dissidence was the precursor of revolution within a political right that alone claimed to uphold France's true interests. Like Maulnier, Blanchot held faith that popular opposition to party politics would drive the national revolution to come. A logic of paradox thus made hatred of France the truest form of a dissident nationalism.

From Revolution to Literature

L'Insurgé: politique et social was a weekly offshoot of the *Combat* group. Between January 13 and October 27, 1937, it produced forty-two issues in an attempt to build on *Combat*'s reputation in order to reach a wider audience. The weekly format and a desire to mix cultural and social commentary put *L'Insurgé* into direct competition with established right-wing publications such as *Candide, Gringoire,* and *Je Suis Partout.* The new venture was motivated by interests that were commercial as well as ideological. It recalled Gaston Gallimard's decision to launch *Marianne* as an offshoot of the *Nouvelle Revue Française* in 1932.[8] Similarities between *Marianne* and *L'Insurgé* were, however, largely limited to format. For while both periodicals commented on politics and culture, the pacifism promoted by *Marianne*'s first editor, Emmanuel Berl, was distinctly at odds with the virulence in the latter publication's reactionary call to resistance: "*L'Insurgé* prefers instead of ten thousand bourgeois who will read it in front of their fireplaces a thousand resolute men . . . who will make it live the only life suitable to a journal of combat: the life of the street."[9] Politically, *L'Insurgé* went beyond *Combat* in opposing what it perceived as a working-class dictatorship. Invoking the threat of a Communist-style takeover, *L'Insurgé* played heavily on the fears and ambitions of a lower middle class it sought to mobilize and represent (Leroy and Roche, 76).

Blanchot contributed no fewer than sixty-seven texts to the weekly during the nine and one-half months of its existence, often writing editorials and book reviews in the same issue. His editorials—thirty by my count— were signed and usually appeared on the front page. The book reviews (a total of thirty-seven) appeared under the headings "Chroniques de la vie intellectuelle" (Chronicles of intellectual life) and "Lectures de *L'Insurgé*" (Readings of *L'Insurgé*). Listings in *Gramma* 5 attributed an additional number of collective editorials, signed *L'Insurgé*, to Blanchot.

The convergence of politics and literature in Blanchot's contributions to *L'Insurgé* marked a departure from his articles in *Le Rempart* and *Combat*. Alongside editorials whose hostility toward the French government remained high, the choice of writers and of texts under review composed a sampling of culture along a wide political spectrum. The French writers reviewed by Blanchot in *L'Insurgé* ranged from established figures such as Roger Martin du Gard, Paul Claudel, and François Mauriac to lesser-known writers such as Guy Mazeline, Alphonse Sèche, and Henri Petit. Additional reviews of books by Maurras, Bernanos, Pierre Drieu La Rochelle, Victor Serge, Denis de Rougement, and Henri Poulaille engaged committed writers whose texts were openly informed by political and social issues of the period. A smaller set of reviews addressed foreign writers such as Virginia Woolf, Thomas Mann, Rainer Maria Rilke, Aldous Huxley, and G.-F. Ramuz.

In the first issue of *L'Insurgé* (January 13, 1937), Blanchot showed that by early 1937 he had come to see Blum as the latest in a succession of post-World War I leaders—Briand and Poincaré were the others mentioned— whose policies had strengthened perception from abroad of a mediocre and inept France, a perception at odds with what the majority of French still saw as a proud and strong nation. Yet for better or worse, Blanchot continued in "Réquistoire contre la France" (Grievance against France), Blum *was* France. Whatever he chose to do or not do, all the French were responsible: "And this is just. Others, by a possibly absurd vote, elected Blum. But we are all putting up with him. It is therefore just that, until a change of guard occurs, Blum remain the symbol and the spokesman of the abject France to which we belong" (3). Negative affect was a key element in the portrait of "la France abjecte" Blanchot saw as the political and social condition of a nation headed for ruin. Recognizing the extent of this abjection was thus a prerequisite for the new and vital France modeled by a nationalist impulse adapted from what was happening elsewhere in Europe. As in Blanchot's texts in *Le Rempart* in 1933, Germany under Hitler remained integral to Blanchot's nationalist vision. Yet its exemplarity was not to be misconstrued. Rather than a model regime to be emulated, Germany was a threat to the future and thus—for Blanchot—a prod forcing France to mobilize in its defense.

In "Notre première ennemie, la France" (Our first enemy, France), in *L'Insurgé* 4 (February 3, 1937), Blanchot chided those who feared Hitler without acknowledging the validity of his warnings about the Soviet Union. He was no less harsh with those who saw the validity of those warnings but failed to recognize the threat Hitler embodied: "We believe that it is because Germanism is in the right against France that France has never been more threatened by it. France defends peace by methods that Germany rightly judges as ridiculous and by alliances that it rightly judges as suspect. France attracts war to the extent that it is separated from itself. It is thus not in reconciling itself casually with the Reich but in achieving true reconciliation with itself that France can still be saved" (1). Along similar lines, "Ce qu'ils appellent patriotisme" (What they call patriotism) in the eighth issue of *L'Insurgé* (March 3, 1937) intensified Blanchot's critique of moderation all along the political spectrum "from the communists to those known as conservatives by way of the baseness of the radicals" (4). The column headline "Libéréz la France" (Liberate France) likewise advocated violence as a corrective to "moderate" policies. For Blanchot, such a purge was imminent and desirable: "If anything can save them, if anything can save this country, it is that the violence of the catastrophe will make the French aware of their degradation and will give them disgust with what they are" ("Ce qu'ils appellent patriotisme," 4).

Blanchot's initial contributions to *L'Insurgé* were prophetic and chilling. Their invocation of a new order and their dismissal of political moderation came as close as anything Blanchot ever wrote at the time to endorsing the values of a native French fascism. Looking to Germany as a model for how France might save itself was likewise to risk promoting a sense of nation based on the moral and physical violence commonly associated with fascist regimes. After the fact, the idea of adapting German tactics in order to promote a revitalized French nation can be seen as playing into the hands of those who later defended Vichy against the perceived ineptitude of republican rule. Some fifty years later, the politics of the nonconformists remained open to question. Speaking at a colloquium in 1983, François Walter (pen name Pierre Gérôme), a founder of the antifascist Comité de Vigilance des Intellectuels Anti-fascistes (CVIA), confessed that he still found it hard to sort out what in the writings of *Combat* was ideology, tactics, or verbosity: "It was nonetheless quite clear . . . that it was a matter of adapting and of proposing to France a recipe that had succeeded elsewhere. It is also clear that this proposal of a French-style fascism was not well received and that the doctrinal testing that was to found it was untenable."[10] Walter's remarks were more generous than one might have expected. Yet they did little to diminish the conformity of the dissident nationalism in Blanchot's articles in *Combat* and *L'Insurgé* with values of the Vichy regime to follow.

It is significant that full formulation of the dissident nationalism in the texts Blanchot wrote for *L'Insurgé* coincided with his initial attempts to theorize literature. "De la révolution à la littérature" (From revolution to literature) was Blanchot's first contribution to the "Lectures de *L'Insurgé*" column, published in the first issue of the weekly, and it was less of a critical exercise—no specific book was listed under review—than a statement of purpose for the cultural program that Blanchot and his collaborators hoped to develop on the new weekly. In retrospect, it can also be seen as an initial draft of the theorizing of literature and culture elaborated by Blanchot over the following months in *L'Insurgé* and, over a longer duration of seven years, in dozens of texts he wrote for *Le Journal de Débats* during the Occupation. Finally, "De la révolution à la littérature" can be seen as bearing a number of affinities with Blanchot's 1942 pamphlet "Comment la littérature est-elle possible?" (How is literature possible?) and, over the next two decades, with *L'Espace littéraire* (*The Space of Literature*) and *Le Livre à venir* (The book of the future). In January 1937, however, the attempt to assert the specificity of literature still resonated with the harsh tone of dissident reactionary nationalism.

Blanchot first sought to remove his conception of literature from what he termed the predictable ravings of ideologues on the right as well as the left: "Even without experiencing these fanatics who, in newspapers on the left—but there are also some on the right—judge works with as much hatred as they judge men, we would not impose this minor humiliation of claiming to something that might resemble impartiality" (1). To this end, he questioned whether—"at a time when revolution is to be wished for"—there were not some relevant affinities between the notions of revolution and literature: "At first glance, it seems that in raising this question, literature is made to run a mortal danger. Literature does not easily tolerate being drawn away from itself, even to be confronted by its object" (1). For Blanchot, this danger was mortal only from the perspective of a mentality that made it subservient to partisan conceptions of political revolution with which it contended at a perpetual disadvantage. Against such ideological conceptions, Blanchot asserted literature's capacity to enact a revolution in which the potential threat of a fallen world was a precondition for the genesis of the work of art.

What made literature revolutionary was its oppositional force: "What also counts is the force of resistance the author has set against his work by the facilities and freedoms he has refused unto it, the instincts he has mastered, the rigor by which he has submitted himself to it" (1). In sum, the revolutionary potential of literature resulted less from militancy in the name of a party, cause, or program than from a violence whose action was obscure and unpredictable: "But the violence—sometimes hidden—in which [literary works] remain, the tension in which they constrain us, the act of liberation they force us to desire by the perfection in which they carry us are such that they act, in an unknown moment, on a world they have not known" (1). "De la révolution à la littérature" announced Blanchot's desire to theorize literature through politics, but it was as yet unclear to what extent this redirection was an evolved position because the specificity of literature as Blanchot sought to assert it was still dependent on drawing out the nature of its affinities with revolution. In sum, because literature was taken as a counterterm to revolution, "De la révolution à la littérature" seemed still to privilege politics—associated by Blanchot with reactionary nationalist revolution— over literature. At the same time, Blanchot questioned this privilege when he set literature apart—"a certain indifference to vain things" ("une certaine indifférence aux choses vaines")—from the short-term events associated with politics. Through 1937, the trajectory from revolution to literature remained incomplete and open to further consideration.

How Was Literature Possible?

"De la révolution à la littérature" shows the extent to which Blanchot's theorizing of literature in the late 1930s was shaped by assumptions concerning politics and revolution. It should be repeated that Blanchot was not at the time merely a young intellectual with a passing interest in the politics of interwar France and Europe. "De la révolution à la littérature" cannot be dismissed as a minor aberration or curiosity. Nor does it suffice to trivialize it or Blanchot's other interwar writings as primitive formulations located somehow before and thus apart or at a distance from his subsequent theorizing of literature. Not only do the articles in *Combat* and *L'Insurgé* illustrate the inadequacy of restricting Blanchot's theory of literature to postwar collections such as *La Part du feu, L'Espace littéraire,* and *Le Livre à venir;* they also show this inadequacy as an effect of critical approaches to Blanchot as novelist, theorist, and critic with which the 1930s texts would appear to clash.

Topical concerns invariably deflect Blanchot's early articulation of politics and literature toward recent debate surrounding Martin Heidegger and Paul de Man. These concerns should caution us against misconstruing Blanchot's writings of the 1930s as transgressive texts whose revelation might be used—too quickly—to overturn received opinions about his place in literary modernity. It is thus precipitous to maintain with Jeffrey Mehlman that echoes of a wartime text by Blanchot in Jacques Derrida's "Like the Sound of the Sea Deep within a Shell" implicate Derrida in an attempt to repress the protofascist pasts encoded in wartime writings by de Man and Blanchot and to conclude that "the motif on the encoded farewell to a fascist past not quite acknowledged, that is, seems to threaten deconstruction from more than one quarter."[11] The text referred to above by Mehlman is "De l'insolence considéréé comme l'un des beaux-arts" (On insolence as a fine art), a review by Blanchot of Henry de Montherlant's *Solstice de juin* published in *Le Journal de Débats* on January 6, 1942, and reprinted in *Faux pas*. Mehlman takes evident care to trace the echoes and intertexts "of a piece" he finds in Montherlant, de Man, Blanchot, and Derrida. It is thus all the more surprising that he fails to include the first of the two sentences Blanchot quoted from Montherlant. Had he done so, he might have seen that Blanchot had already performed on Montherlant an ironic decoding of the very association of play with oblivion and disclosure that Mehlman sought, in turn, to impose on Blanchot nearly a half-century later. If Mehlman wanted to apply to Blanchot the tactic Blanchot had applied to Montherlant, he needed to do more than juxtapose a belated allusion. Here is the full quotation from Montherlant with which Blanchot ended his review of *Solstice de juin* in *Faux pas:* "To the writers who for some months have given too much importance to the present, I predict—for this portion of their work—the most total oblivion. The newspapers, the journals of today, when I open them, I hear rolling over them the indifference of the future, as one hears the sound of the sea in certain seashells one puts to one's ear."[12]

Mehlman's genealogy of deconstruction's repressed politics lent itself especially to appropriation by those who sought to attack deconstruction on moral grounds. It did this by locating in a denied fascism the origin of a displaced discourse that Mehlman claimed to decode in the intertexts of deconstruction's political prehistory. This is the moment for me to state that, regarding Blanchot, my misgivings concern the case Mehlman has made in support of his allegations rather than the issues these allegations raise. In 1979, Mehlman accused Blanchot of having agreed to work with Pierre Drieu La Rochelle in 1942 to restore the *Nouvelle Revue Française* to its prewar status as France's most prestigious literary monthly. Here is how Blanchot responded in a letter addressed to Mehlman, dated November 26, 1979: "You suggested that I was the representative of Drieu at the *NRF*, the collaborator of a notorious [*insigne*] collaborator. But what happened was precisely the opposite."[13] The disclaimer on Blanchot's part was clear and strong. Yet, for the record, Mehlman's claims were corroborated in Pascal Fouché's account of the "petite histoire" of the *NRF* under German censorship: "En avril 1942 Maurice Blanchot est venu assister Drieu en assurant le sécrétariat général de la revue; cela a d'allieurs provoqué un violent article de *L'Appel* qui y voit déjà l'éviction de Drieu" ("In April 1942 Maurice Blanchot came to assist Drieu in providing for the general administration of the review; moreover, this provoked a violent article in *L'Appel* that already sees Drieu's eviction").[14]

As the theorizing of literature undertaken by Blanchot in "De la révolution à la littérature" evolved over the next decade, echoes of the earlier conception in that article were reinscribed in wartime and postwar texts. A first substantial reinscription occurred in "Comment la littérature est-elle possible?," a pamphlet from 1942 in which Blanchot disparaged ideologues on the left and the right who judged men and their works ("oeuvres") with the same hatred. But because "De la révolution à la littérature" anticipated Blanchot's wartime theorizing by some four to five years, I want to return briefly to a text of his from the mid-1930s in order to explore what literature had become for Blanchot in the interim. From 1942 *back* to 1936 and with Jean Paulhan *before* Blanchot, I want to retrace what is at stake in evolving conceptions of literature and terror. In order to see this evolution in its full force, it is necessary to set Paulhan momentarily *before* Blanchot, in the spring of 1925.

When Jean Paulhan became editor of the *Nouvelle Revue Française* in 1925, the monthly was a leading exponent of the literary modernity propounded by André Gide and the review's other founders some sixteen years earlier. During his term as editor from the spring of 1925 until the fall of France in June 1940, Paulhan extended the review's prestige by promoting a young literary generation that included Henri Michaux, Francis Ponge, André Malraux, and Jean-Paul Sartre. The limits imposed on the monthly by Gide's *moeurs littéraires* became all the more evident as Paulhan's attempts to mediate between "high" literary culture and politics were attacked from both left and right. In 1925—a year after the publication of the *Manifeste du surréalisme* and three years after the death of Marcel Proust—the *NRF* embodied an all-encompassing modernity whose ability to assimilate disparate practices was characterized alternately as complacent, ahistorical, conservative, and predictably upper middle class. A decade later, its ties to a turn-of-the-century modernism growing out of postsymbolist aesthetics and the circle surrounding Gide made it into an elegant anachronism.

To his credit, Paulhan tried to keep the monthly involved with the heated politics of French culture in the 1930s. The December 1932 issue of the *NRF* contained a polemical insert ("Cahier de revendications") in a series of statements by a generation of intellectuals in their mid to late twenties. Recruited for Paulhan by Denis de Rougement, the contributors included Georges Izard and Emmanuel Mounier of the *Esprit* group, French Communist party members Paul Nizan and Henri Lefebvre, and Blanchot's future director at *Combat* and *L'Insurgé*, Thierry Maulnier. The position statements expressed a shared discontent that outstripped clear differences of party and ideology. Moreover, they invoked militancy and violence as appropriate responses to an alienation that was spiritual as well as social. Four years later, many in France were to see the election of the Popular Front as a move beyond alienation. For others such as Blanchot, this move was not the right one. Returning to the Blanchot/Paulhan convergence, we need to reconstruct context and chronology in order to show the extent to which Paulhan's initial remarks on literary terror responded to an interwar nonconformism whose instability allowed it to serve the ends of the French right.

Paulhan's *Les Fleurs de Tarbes ou la terreur dans les lettres* (The flowers of Tarbes; or, terror in literature) first appeared as a series of essays in the *NRF* between June and October 1936. It was reprinted five years later by Gallimard under the Occupation and expanded to book form. From the start, Paulhan set his concerns for literature and rhetoric against the strong associations of the term of "terror" in his title. This invocation of the 1793–94 revolutionary period pointed to a secondary discourse of connotation whose force increased over the five years between the two versions of the essays.

An opening portrait in *Les Fleurs de Tarbes* described terror as a condition of crisis arising from uncertainty over the health of literature. The trope of health and sickness linked a traditional mistrust of eloquence to the values of conservative groups such as Action Française for whom the parliamentary politics of the Third Republic threatened the spiritual and political health of the nation. The trope of health also asserted a continuum between politics and culture as debated during the Popular Front on the left and—especially—on the right.

For Paulhan, the object of the terrorist's mistrust was language in its capacity to deform the purity of thought and emotion: "Of Language, and thus of literature. Because one does not go without the other. It is not only in books, but in conversation as well that perfection upsets. 'Too eloquent to be sincere,' we used to think. 'Too well put to be true.'"[15] The flowers in Paulhan's title were those of rhetoric as they appeared in an allegory toward the start of the book. A woman walking through the city park of Tarbes with a bouquet in her hands was stopped by a groundskeeper who informed her that it was forbidden to pick flowers in the park. The woman answered that she had carried the flowers into the park from outside. A short time later, a new sign at the entrance stated that henceforth it was forbidden to enter the park carrying flowers.

What can be done to and with literature once the flowers of rhetoric have been banished? Against practical conceptions in guides to rhetoric that had flourished in France since at least the seventeenth century, the terrorist attitude turned eloquence into a suspect virtue that threatened a purity of thought and emotion. Under sway of the terrorist attitude, the eloquence of nineteenth-century figures such as Victor Hugo, Charles Augustin Sainte-Beuve, Paul Verlaine, and Arthur Rimbaud was deemed nothing more or other than artifice. At the source of this suspicion was a wider mistrust—Paulhan coined the term *misologie*, which translates loosely as "hatred of words"—linked to a myth of the power of language. As Paulhan concluded, everything depended on a belief that the idea was distinct from and superior to the word.

The implied extension of terror from literature to politics was overdetermined by historical circumstances surrounding the later version of *Les Fleurs*. In 1941, it was difficult not to read references to France under Vichy in what Paulhan described as a preservation of order gained at the cost of rejecting method, knowledge, and technique: "Whence it occurs that citizens see themselves called to account rather than their works: the chair is forgotten for the cabinetmaker, the remedy for the doctor. Meanwhile, qualities of skill, intelligence, and know-how become suspect, as if they were hiding some lack of commitment" (47). Comparisons between the 1936 and 1941 versions show that this definition was added to the latter. As in Paulhan's allegory of the city park in Tarbes, prohibitions against the flowers of rhetoric suggested that the realm ("garden"?) of letters was far from Edenic. What Paulhan detected in the terrorist's apparent claims to reason was the remains of a perverse Cartesian method: "Thus dividing the difficulty into as many particles as are needed to resolve it, requiring evidence from each particle, and taking nothing for granted that has not been verified, accepting ultimately that there is nothing in such materials that our attention, once applied, cannot seize and understand. Such is the foundation on which Terror builds its war machine [engin de guerre]" (65).

The third section of *Les Fleurs* began with an abrupt turnaround when Paulhan stated that because terror projected meaning onto—and often against—intention attributed to the author, it was necessarily an effect of reading and interpretation. As a result, Paulhan confessed that his approach could not help but be terrorist in its own right: "We are ourselves what we were pursuing. We are personally involved" (105). What motivated this apparent turnaround was Paulhan's desire to convert the potential terrorist within all readers into the proponent of a new rhetoric based on communication. Paulhan had to make his conversion exemplary by allowing the terrorist attitude to assert itself as a common form of critical suspicion. By admitting to his own involvement, Paulhan hoped to gain credibility for the conversion he sought to promote.[16] Once disabused of his or her mistrust, Paulhan's reader would presumably pass through the terrorist attitude as a moment or phase of critical doubt within a dialectic leading to the new synthesis Paulhan formulated as his rhetoric of communication. In place of the prohibitions against rhetoric alluded to in Paulhan's allegory, one might hope one day to find a sign stating that henceforth it would be forbidden *not* to carry flowers into the garden.

In his response to *Les Fleurs*, Blanchot asserted that because the force of language remained integral to Paulhan's rhetoric of communication, the terrorist attitude remained constant: uncontained and untranscended. Paulhan may have exposed the false distinction between thought and language, but he failed to address the full implications of his own position. In order to overcome the terrorist attitude, Paulhan needed both to acknowledge its inevitability and to refute its claims to sufficiency. As Blanchot asked pointedly, "The book that has just been approached, is it really the right one to read?"[17] To what other book, then, might *Les Fleurs de Tarbes* serve as preface or introduction? Here is how Blanchot sketched the implications of Paulhan's argument: "If the writer makes proper use of images, units of rhyme— in other words, of the renewed means of rhetoric—he can rediscover the impersonal and innocent language that he seeks, the only one allowing him to be what he is and to have contact with the pure newness [nouveauté vierge] of things" (99). When Paulhan wrote about *re*discovering a *nouveauté vierge,* his assertion of a privileged origin extended the very terrorist attitude he had earlier sought to overcome!

Blanchot concluded that Paulhan's attempt to transcend terror failed because terror *was* literature or, at least, its essence. To question terror was, in effect, to question literature. Even if the progression from terror to communication desired by Paulhan never occurred, literature was nonetheless a reality about which one still needed to talk:

> It is a fact, literature exists. It continues to be, despite the internal absurdity that inhabits it, divides it, and makes it nothing short of inconceivable. There is in the heart of every writer a demon who pushes him to murder literary forms and to become aware of his dignity as a writer to the degree that he breaks with language and literature: in a word, to question tacitly what he is and what he does. How, in these conditions, can literature exist? How can the writer who distinguishes himself from others by the very fact that he challenges the validity of language and whose effort ought to be to prevent the formation of a written work [oeuvre] finally create a literary product [ouvrage]? How is literature possible? (97)

Blanchot saw terror as a permanent condition of risk integral to any serious questioning of what literature was and might be. Literature was possible only in view of two inescapable illusions. The first was that of those who struggled against convention by reinventing it; the second, of those who claimed to renounce literature in the name of something such as religion or metaphysics. Where Paulhan exposed the first illusion and fell victim to the second, Blanchot saw literature defined anew in and by every act of writing: "It is a matter of revealing to the writer that he gives birth to art only by a futile and blind struggle against it, that the work he thinks he has torn away from common and vulgar language exists because of the vulgarization of pure language, by an overload of impurity and debasement" (99).

"Comment la littérature est-elle possible?" asserted instability as an essential condition of literature. This conception differed from what Blanchot had argued in "De la révolution à la littérature" by displacing the violence and radicality of political revolution onto the concept of literature itself.

How, then, did *Les Fleurs de Tarbes* mediate the theorizing of literature as it evolved in "De la révolution à la littérature" and "Comment la littérature est-elle possible?"? Setting *Les Fleurs* between the Blanchot texts of 1937 and 1942 emphasizes how the latter displaced the explicit articulation of literature and revolution in the former by excising Paulhan's interrogation of the terrorist attitude from his projected rhetoric of communication. "Comment la littérature est-elle possible?" offered a clear alternative to the conception of literature proposed by Paulhan. Yet Blanchot's position outstripped that taken by Paulhan only if we ignore the strong equivocation that problematized the progression toward the rhetoric of communication invoked at the end of *Les Fleurs*. Ultimately, terror was the only thing Paulhan asserted. Even though he sought to write in the name of a future rhetoric, the progression beyond terror remained idealized and indefinitely deferred.[18]

"Comment la littérature est-elle possible?" extended Blanchot's theorizing of literature by determining its force without proximity to revolution. Six years later in "La Littérature et le droit à la mort" ("Literature and the Right to Death"), Blanchot recast his postwar conception into terms with which he remains identified today. The essay began with a spare, almost aphoristic, reflection on the nature of writing. After allowing that it was certainly possible to write without asking why one did so, Blanchot asserted that literature began at the moment it became a question to be addressed "by language which has become literature."[19] Surprisingly, introspection and self-consciousness did not preclude revolution, even in the extreme instance of an encounter with death that came to dominate much of Blanchot's postwar theorizing: "Literature contemplates itself in revolution, it finds its justification in revolution, and if it has been called the Reign of Terror, this is because its ideal is indeed that moment in history, that moment when 'life endures death and maintains itself in it' in order to gain from death the possibility of speaking and the truth of speech. This is the 'question' that seeks to pose itself in literature, the 'question' that is its essence" (41).

From literature *back* to revolution? The inversion of terms in this passage suggested a return to the interwar problematic of the *Combat* and *L'Insurgé* articles, as supplemented by the wartime reference to the Terror. Yet when Blanchot cast Terror in 1948 as a moment during which life endured and maintained death, his description evoked the encounters with death recounted by the fictional narrator of his *L'Arrêt de mort*, published in the same year as "La Littérature et le droit à la mort." The reference was too strong to dismiss as inadvertent. It supported a thesis of doubling at work throughout Blanchot's postwar theorizing of literature. Yet simply to enu-merate allusions and parallels can lead one to conclude—too quickly—in favor of stability surrounding a signature, a work (*oeuvre*), and a career. To assert discontinuity and radical difference reduces the kind of understand-ing to be attained through a rethinking of the place of Blanchot's early texts on politics and literature within a corpus of writings that remains essential to literary modernity.

The alternative I propose in place of closure sets the doubling I have noted within a wider phenomenon of tendentious disclosure. The approach combines Freud's remarks on screen memory with the notion of truth as disclosure (*aletheia*) set forth in 1936 by Heidegger in "The Origin of the Work of Art." For Freud, a prime function of memories was to protect the ego from excessive or painful emotion. The operation was complex, both a matter of revealing the past while deleting from the image of its recall those elements that caused pain. In "The Origin," Heidegger asserted a similar in-terplay of revelation and censorship against a conception of truth based on a claim to certainty such as that upheld by Descartes in the *Discourse on Method*. In place of the latter conception, Heidegger held that truth oc-curred as disclosure or *aletheia*—as when, for example, a poet composed a poem. A material sense of language underlay Heidegger's conception of truth as *aletheia*. In "The Origin," Heidegger directed this sense toward liter-ary forms and, specifically, toward the interplay of absence and presence on which Blanchot was to ground his postwar reflections on the space of litera-ture. When, for example, Blanchot wrote in "Literature and the Right to Death" that literature sustained what it abolished in the very act of designat-ing it, he quoted from Mallarmé: "Je dis: une fleur! et . . . musicalement se lève, idée même et suave, l'absente de tous les bouquets" ("I say: a flower! and . . . musically arises, the idea itself and delicate").[20] This reference also described a dynamic of disclosure in which literature "hides, it does not give itself away" (48) ("S'esquive, elle ne se trahit pas"; *La Part du feu*, 318). The specificity of literature was its ability to replace the object designated by name with signification, so that what it asserted was "the very possibility of signifying, the empty power of bestowing meaning—a strange impersonal light" (48). The force of literature lay in its capacity to reconfigure presence and absence through language. Literature enacted the peculiar reality of lan-guage to negate the world while preserving it in the fiction of an imaginary point "where the world can be seen in its entirety" (57).

Literature as Blanchot conceived of it in the late 1940s constructed an imaginary world in language from a particular point of view set apart from the historical moment in which it occurred. Such isolation was often mistaken for a sign of deficiency and an inability to conduct serious work in the real world. Blanchot, however, associated this removal with difference over and above what convention might otherwise judge to the detriment of literature: "Spurned by history, literature plays a different game. If it is not really in the world, working to make the world, this is because its lack of being (of intelligible reality) causes it to refer to an existence that is still inhuman. Yes, it recognizes that this is so, that in its nature there is a strange slipping back and forth between being and not being, presence and absence, reality and nonreality" (57). What Blanchot had come to call literature's "different game" extended the logic of double negation in the *Combat* and *L'Insurgé* articles. It transposed onto literature the capacity to negate and change that Blanchot had ascribed a decade earlier to revolution in the name of a new French nation.

The example of Mallarmé (as well as that of Kafka) pointed to the capacity of literature to turn language into ambiguity at each moment and in each word. For Blanchot, this capacity resulted in an inability to determine with certainty that language was not always saying something different from what it seemed to be saying. Despite its isolation, language offered the alternative vision necessary to achieve change in the "real" world, even if this change invariably occurred "at the edge of the world and as if at the end of time" (57). Appearance enhanced the disclosure effect—"slipping back and forth between being and not being"—associated with language in literary usage while the "as if" construct promoted the vicissitude on which Blanchot grounded his postwar theorizing of literature. Yet because the "as if" construction displaced rather than negated, stable meaning was suspended and thus still always possible. In this sense, the instability and suspension that dispersed meaning also constructed it as dispersal. This was the aspect ("this amazing power") of negation that Blanchot equated with death and freedom, and that—through language—detached the work (*oeuvre*) from existence in order to recast it as significance: "Nothing can prevent this power . . . from continuing to assert itself as continually differing possibility, and nothing can stop it from perpetuating an irreducible *double meaning*, a choice whose terms are covered over with an ambiguity that makes them identical to one another even as it makes them opposite" (61; emphasis in the original).

Stepping beyond, Stepping Back

If history and revolution in "La Littérature et le droit à la mort" were dis-placed to "the edge of the world and as if at the end of time," they did not disappear. Blanchot's reflections on literature and revolution continued on an irregular basis some forty years after the Liberation and thus more than fifty years after the texts in *Le Rempart, Combat,* and *L'Insurgé.* Before trac-ing the postwar trajectory of these reflections, I want briefly to note a rele-vant passage from a text whose appearance nearly coincided with the 1936 version of *Les Fleurs de Tarbes* in the *Nouvelle Revue Française.* Less than three months after the Popular Front was elected, Blanchot called for mili-tant resistance against the Blum government in the form of terror as "a method of public safety":

> We are not among those who prefer to adopt the call for a peaceful, spiritual
> revolution, which is both senseless and cowardly. There must be a revolution,
> because a regime that holds everything and that has its roots elsewhere can-
> not be modified. It must be ended, demolished. This revolution must be vio-
> lent, because one cannot draw from a nation as deadened as our own the
> strength and passion suited to renewal by decent measures, but instead by
> bloody jolts, by a storm that will shake it up in order to awaken it. This is not
> at all peace of mind, but that is exactly what must be avoided. This is why ter-
> rorism seems to us at present a method of public safety.[21]

The stridency of this passage was hard to miss or explain away. Blanchot's words were harsh and the terms of violence he invoked ("by bloody jolts, by a storm that will shake it up") on a par with statements uttered in the same period by right-wing demagogues throughout Europe. Whatever Blanchot's subsequent trajectory toward progressive and even extremist positions on the French left over the following thirty years, the orientation of the articles that appeared under his name in *Combat* and *L'Insurgé* was irreducibly dis-sident and reactionary. However one might question or account for them over a longer duration, Blanchot's political writings of the Popular Front pe-riod clash with the postwar figure of the obscure man of letters. In so doing, they point to a most unsettling thesis: namely, that Blanchot's postwar theo-rizing of literary space followed a substantial interwar practice that placed literature openly alongside a corollary vision of politics at odds with what the postwar fiction and essays might lead one to expect. The interwar writ-ings continue to raise a number of issues for anyone wanting to situate Blan-chot's corpus within French literature and the wider cultures of modernity of the past sixty years. But because these issues engage questions of history and politics with which Blanchot's name was seldom associated on the basis of his postwar writings, they have elicited ongoing resistance—if not explicit dismissal—among readers unwilling to contend with the scandalous impact of what looks very much to be a politics of militant resistance on the interwar French right.

In order to avoid precipitous closure, I want to propose a working hypothesis as a way of aligning my remarks on Blanchot's postwar writings in the final section of this chapter. The hypothesis is in two parts and articulates attempts at a double movement—back and forth—in time. The attempts extend earlier references in narratives following the Liberation (*L'Arrêt de mort* and *La Folie du jour*) and continue up through more recent texts such as *L'écriture du désastre,Après coup*, and Blanchot's letter on Heidegger in *Le Nouvel Observateur* in 1988. First, disclosures over the past twenty years in the form of direct references to historical events in Blanchot's writings have expressed a deep ambivalence concerning attempts to contend with a complex and unresolved past related to the interwar and wartime periods. Second, the variety and extent of the recent disclosures have pointed increasingly to the wartime period as a gap or blank between seemingly incommensurate interwar and postwar practices. In more personal terms, they provide compelling evidence why attempts to impose a stable identity onto Blanchot have invariably collapsed into noncoincidence and heteronomy.

An alternative reading of Blanchot's career asserts that the concern with politics explicit in the interwar writings was reinscribed after 1945 in the fiction and essays associated first with literary space and, more recently, with passivity, patience, and the neutral. To put this somewhat differently, the thesis that the wartime period constituted a gap or break between interwar and postwar practices does not preclude the possibility that the latter continued to engage the concerns of the former, albeit indirectly and in a literary space only seemingly removed from the more explicit engagement of the earlier writings. In the astute formulation of Kevin Newmark, what is at stake for Blanchot in recent texts such as *L'écriture du désastre* (1980) is to think history "in a different way, thinking the historical element that would 'extend beyond' the history we now have, and that may not (yet) be available 'in the current sense of terms' like 'history' and 'the world.' "[22]

The apparent isolation of Blanchot's postwar writings within a hermetic space of literature is belied by a number of attempts to engage the interwar and wartime periods. Yet whether these attempts are cast as direct references or instead as oblique disclosures, it would be a mistake to attribute to them outright the status of definitive words on the subject. For to do so would be somehow to ground them uncritically on the openness and stability of a voice and a signature whose coherence had always been configured as obscure, even if the reasons for this obscurity turned out not to be what had been thought. *Le pas au-delà* (1973) extended a format of writing in fragments that Blanchot had explored in *L'attente l'oubli* (1962) and theorized at length seven years after that in *L'Entretien infini*. Like these earlier texts, *Le pas au-delà* (*The Step Not Beyond*) was cast as a hybrid practice between fiction and essay. Formal breaks between individual passages did not obscure a recurrent movement that configured fragmentary writing in terms of passivity, the neuter, and the eternal return. *Le pas au-delà* thus lent itself in form, tone, and concept to Nietzsche's *The Will to Power* and, even more directly, to the Derrida of "La Différance" and *La Dissémination*.

Fragmentary writing in *Le pas au-delà* enhanced the deferral of stable meaning associated with the model of disclosure in "The Origin of the Work of Art." Because individual fragments lent themselves to multiple determinations, they often resonated in a number of ways with the fragments surrounding them. Such open-ended interpretation derived from poetry and enhanced the ties between an aesthetics of interplay between presence and absence adapted from Mallarmé and Blanchot's postwar theorizing of literary space. A passage toward the start of *Le pas au-delà* asserted that once an event occurred in time, it rapidly fell away into the "terrifyingly ancient" where nothing was ever present. Two fragments later, Blanchot added that "if, in the 'terrifyingly ancient,' nothing was ever present and if, having barely produced itself, the event at once fell into it as the mark of irrevocability announced, it was because the event we thought we had lived was never in a relation of presence to us or to anything whatsoever."[23] The fragment is curious because while it might pass for an abstract statement unanchored in time, it could also be taken as a gesture of anticipation cast in a trope of prolepsis. From this perspective, the fragment could be seen to operate as a defensive ploy to destabilize the kind of historical specificity on which accountability and agency—of a Heidegger or a Blanchot, for example—might be grounded.

Like much of Blanchot's postwar writing, *Le pas au-delà* was an example of the conception of writing that it set forth. Much like Flaubert's reputed desire to write *Madame Bovary* as a book about nothing, *Le pas au-delà* seemed almost to disclose nothing in particular except itself.[24] Almost, but not absolutely. For the temporality of loss evoked in the passage quoted in the previous paragraph was linked to a dynamics of meaning asserted some fifteen pages later in the following fragment: "The past was written, the future will be read. This could be expressed in this form: what was written in the past will be read in the future, without any relation of presence being able to present itself *between* writing and reading" (30; emphasis in the original). As disclosure was equated increasingly with revelation, writing and reading were inscribed within a wider disclosure as deferral and dissimulation: "Writing is not destined to leave traces, but to erase, by traces, all traces, to disappear in the fragmentary space of writing, more definitively than one disappears in the tomb, or again, to destroy invisibly, without the uproar of destruction" (50). The process was ongoing, with a "perpetual separation of time, like a separation of place, belonging to neither time nor to place" that would define the point of writing (71).

The assertion in *Le pas au-delà* of belatedness as a perpetual separation of time supplemented an earlier conception of literary space exemplified by the writings of Mallarmé (and Kafka) with effects of language described by Derrida as *différance* and *espacement*. Still missing from the revised conception of literary space in *Le pas au-delà* was an explicit historical sense of this temporality. Yet although it provided nothing close to a clear referent, at least one fragment in *Le pas au-delà* disclosed a suggestive interplay of allusions: "Non-present, non-absent: it tempts us in the manner of that which we would no longer know how to meet, save in situations which we are no longer in: save—save at the limit, situations we call 'extreme,' assuming there are any" (6). The fragment was characteristically dense and convoluted. The two negations at the start recalled a similar formulation—"Ni vu, ni connu" ("Neither seen nor known")—in Paul Valéry's poem "Le Sylphe,"as well as a liminality consistent with Valéry's extension of symbolist aesthetics. A more ominous twist occurred as this liminality was directed from space toward time, from limits or borders—even if only figurative—toward extreme situations. This expression of "extreme situations" was highly suggestive of an existentialist idiom used by Sartre and others in reference to the urgency of choices to be made under duress. But even here, the assertion was qualified by a disclaimer ("assuming there are any") that set the initial assertion under erasure.

Published in 1980 and cast like *Le pas au-delà* as a series of fragments, *L'écriture du désastre* (*The Writing of the Disaster*) elaborated an even fuller disclosure of writing in conjunction with what Blanchot referred to as the experience of limits. A first limit was formal, as when Blanchot wrote that the disaster was a break with the star—broken down via etymology into *désastre*—that was equivalent to a break with "every form of totality."[25] Writing in fragments thus expressed an imperative of disruption and confusion so overwhelming that it imposed a passivity and a patience with which writing contended only belatedly in the form of a trace. A second limit was that of adequacy, taken both as a condition of the speaking or writing subject and as a capacity to act in accordance with will and/or desire. Passivity was a key term that identified the limited capabilities of the fragmented subject. Typically, this limit was expressed within individual fragments as a series of reversals:

> This is what is strange: passivity is never passive enough. It is in this respect that one can speak of an infinite passivity: perhaps only because passivity evades all formulations—yet it seems that there is in passivity something like a demand that would require it to fall always short of itself. There is in passivity not passivity, but its demand, movement of the past toward the insurpassable.
>
> Passivity, passion, past, *pas* (both negation and step—the trace or movement of an advance): this semantic play provides us with a slippage of meaning, but not with anything to which we could entrust ourselves, not with anything like an answer that would satisfy us. (16–17)

Passivity was the condition of the self reduced by disaster to a point that precluded even the possibility of resistance. Disaster annulled the "I" along with the question of the subject, not only because there was no "I" to undergo this experience, but because there was by necessity no possible experience of this annulment. While the disaster was moreover marked as "already" or "always already" outside history, it was, as Blanchot put it with a twist, "historically so" (40).

The same disjunction that isolated individual fragments and disrupted linear progression from one fragment to the next also enhanced the poignancy of certain statements. Historical references especially stood out because of their infrequency and because their status within the full series of fragments was difficult to ascertain. References to the Holocaust and to Auschwitz in at least three fragments added a temporal dimension as well as a strong affective charge to the images of the fragment, passivity, and the neutral by which Blanchot designated the wake of the disaster.

The first of the three fragments referred to the Holocaust as both date and *absolute* event in which the movement of meaning was utterly consumed. After the fact, the question raised in reference to the Holocaust was a question of representation: "How can it be preserved, even by thought? How can thought be made the keeper of the holocaust where all was lost, including guardian thought?" (47). A later fragment recounted the experience of a concentration camp survivor who was caught (saved?) as he tried to hang himself in shame and grief after having been forced to lead his family to the crematorium. To punish him for his attempted suicide, the SS required that he hold the heads of those to be shot so that the bullet could lodge more easily in their necks. When asked how he could bear to do this, he was supposed to have answered that he was interested in the behavior of people faced with death. Blanchot added that what remained to be recognized was that when confronted with the question of how he was able to bear being close to so much death, the man relied on the ultimate propriety he hoped to attain through the search for knowledge: "And how, in fact, can one accept not to know? We read books on Auschwitz. The wish of all, in the camps, the last wish: know what has happened, do not forget, and at the same time never will you know" (82). Readers of Blanchot recognized in this imperative an echo of earlier attempts to narrate the experience-limit of death. Notable as well was the extent to which the corollary imperative to remember was grounded in an explicit historical reference that elicited a high affective charge.

Passivity served in the wake of the disastrous violence at Auschwitz as a protective response against memories that might otherwise have been too painful to bear. The prisoner who supposedly responded that he wanted to observe the comportment of those faced with death asserted the precedence of forgetting over memory. Yet what would forgetting (*l'oubli*) be in the wake of the disaster, if not the effacement of that which was never inscribed, but which—even unwritten—left a trace that had to be obliterated? Forgetting occurred in this instance beyond the agency of the first-person subject and thus as something more or other than what simply opposed memory: "Inoperative forgetfulness, forever idled, which is nothing and does nothing (and which not even dying would reach): this is what, hiding itself from awareness and from unawareness too, does not leave us alone, nor does it disturb us, for we have covered it over with consciousness-unconsciousness" (85–86).

L'écriture du désastre represented an attempt to write the temporality of disaster both as general condition and effect of specific circumstances. Alternation between the general and the specific suggested that the intelligibility of individual events was inscribed within another history whose disastrous disclosure (as in the case of the Holocaust) determined the limit of what could be known. A long concluding fragment raised this question of intelligibility in terms of removal from the access and coherence afforded by direct invocation:

What about the *other* history, wherein nothing of the present ever happens, which no event or advent measures or articulates? Foreign to the succession of moments, which is linear even when it is hindered and as zigzagging as it is dialectical, the *other* history is the deployment of a plurality which is not that of the world or of numbers. It is a history in excess, a "secret," separate history, which presupposes the end of visible history, though it denies itself the very idea of beginning and of end. . . . The *other* history would be a feigned history, which is not to say that it is a mere nothing, but that it is always calling forth the void of a nonplace, the gap that is, and that separates itself from itself. It is unbelievable because any belief in it would have to overlook it. (138–39; emphasis in the original)

This "other history" was not simply the result of a deep temporality such as Fernand Braudel's long duration of centuries at a time. Nor was it a necessary fiction invented to escape the pressing urgency of events within shorter durations. Instead, it represented the necessary limit of experiences for which historical inquiry could claim to provide adequate account. This "other history" served as a general condition that set the limits of experience that could be known. At the same time, its occurrence in the form of disastrous disclosure showed that these limits were grounded in a violence that, invoked in the name of Auschwitz, conventional language could not convey in full.

Fragmentary form and historical reference in *Le pas au-delà* and *L'écriture du désastre* were marks of a movement in Blanchot's postwar writings toward disclosure of an uncertain past. Also notable was that the tone of these disclosures was moral rather than dissident, as in Blanchot's articles of the 1930s. Nowhere was this change in tone clearer than in a text from 1984, "Les Intellectuels en question," in which Blanchot analyzed the evolving role of the intellectual in twentieth-century France:

> From the Dreyfus affair to Hitler and Auschwitz, it has been confirmed that anti-Semitism (along with racism and xenophobia) has revealed the intellectual most strongly to himself; in other words, this is the form in which a concern for others has forced him to come out (or not come out) of his creative isolation. The categorical imperative, losing the ideal generality that Kant had given to it, has become that which Adorno has more or less set out as: *think and act in such a way that Auschwitz is never again repeated* [*Pense et agis de telle manière qu'Auschwitz ne se répète jamais*], which implies that Auschwitz should not become a concept and that an absolute was reached there in terms of which other rights and other duties must be judged.[26]

As in Blanchot's 1988 letter on Heidegger, the wartime period designated by reference to Auschwitz served as a marker of difference, both in the immediate jolt (*choc*) it imposed on consciousness and in its consequences for those who tried after the fact to contend with it. Recurrence of this jolt was an instance of aftereffect, both in the reference back to the initial shock at a temporal remove and as an extension of that past shock in the present. The name of Auschwitz enhanced the affect of Blanchot's remarks on the intellectual by condensing images and associations shared by witnesses, survivors, and their offspring—expressed or silent, living or dead—of the absolute difference on the basis of which judgment of "other rights and other duties" might yet occur. The full implications of this difference remained unclear. Blanchot seemed to engage the literary and moral issues raised in the wake of recent pasts. Yet his remarks equivocated, as if the confessional impulse to reveal were offset by a fear concerning the risks that this revelation entailed.

I began this chapter with Char on Blanchot. I want now to return to Blanchot, in "Les Intellectuels en question," on Char. After citing a passage in which Char evoked his intense suffering at reports of mass roundups of Jews, police brutality, and German raids against unsuspecting villages, Blanchot added: "This was written in 1943. . . . This improbable date remains suspended above our heads. Its return is always possible. It is what, I believe, forbids to intellectuals any hope of a disappearance that would remove them definitively from all questions" (28). From 1984 back to 1943, even this explicit gesture of disclosure—Blanchot introduced the passage by writing "Ce sera mon aveu personnel" ("This will be my personal confession")—remained partial and equivocal, as though Blanchot could not help but point to the blank he never quite filled in or let disappear. Whether or not the gesture was intentional, it detracted from the expectations raised by Blanchot's stated desire to disclose without irony or omission.

Disclosure bordered once again on the trope of simultaneous affirmation and denial known as apophasis. What Blanchot ostensibly sought to reveal was obscured in the very act of revelation. The effect may well have been inspired by a passage by Mallarmé, "Rien n'aura eu lieu que le lieu" ("Nothing will have taken place except the place"), revised by the shifting horizons of Heidegger's *aletheia*. It was all the more disconcerting because it seemed to preclude any responses other than those of silence and passivity associated with Blanchot's notorious obscurity. Yet even as apophasis undermined affirmation, meaning was channeled from the main text to its periphery. As with the postscript in Blanchot's 1988 letter on Heidegger in *Le Nouvel Observateur*, a marginal note in "Les Intellectuels en question" was of more than passing interest. The note began with a brief reference to Boris Sou-

varine and to *La Critique sociale,* a review of the 1930s in which Georges
Bataille published "The Notion of Expenditure" and "The Psychological
Structure of Fascism":

> Giving homage to Souvarine, I must, however, protest against the violent,
> unjust, and false criticisms that, in a preface to the reprinting of his review,
> he addresses to Georges Bataille, of whom he says that, fascinated by Hitler,
> he [Bataille] would, following the defeat [of France], not have failed to rally
> to the side of the occupiers, had he had the courage of his convictions. Sou-
> varine, who spent these somber years in America, acknowledges that only ru-
> mors rather than proofs support his accusations. As I have had the privilege,
> starting in 1940 (precisely at the end of this sinister year) of seeing Georges
> Bataille on an almost daily basis and to discuss with him all kinds of subjects,
> I can testify to his horror of Nazism as well as of the Pétain regime and its
> ideology (family, work, fatherland). [Bataille] came to regret the pages he
> had written on the "Psychological Structure of Fascism" (pages published
> precisely in *La Critique sociale*) and that might have lent themselves to equiv-
> ocation. Finally, he spoke to me often of Boris Souvarine, and always with
> great esteem and consideration. As, with the passing years, witnesses of the
> period become rare, I am unable to remain silent, while there is still time, so
> as to allow affirmations that I know to be uncontestably contrary to the truth
> to be taken as credible. (20)

The passage transmitted neither irony nor ambivalence. In fact, its tone
seemed all the more straightforward, all the more vocal and present, in light
of Blanchot's explicit invocation of personal experience. No marks of obscurity tempered the remarks critical of Souvarine and in defense of Bataille. In
fact, Blanchot openly acknowledged the urgency—"with the passing years
. . . while there is still time"—that obliged him to denounce statements he
knew to be contrary to the truth.

The progression from silence to testimony in the marginalia of "Les Intellectuels en question" further disrupted the myth of obscurity surrounding
the literary signature of the postwar Blanchot. The effect of disclosure was
enhanced not merely because Blanchot's statements broke with a pattern of
silence, but also because the gesture of breaking silence seemed motivated by
a need to set straight something that had been left unresolved. Whether or
not Blanchot's remarks sufficed to resolve the issues raised by Souvarine's allegations concerning Bataille, they were uncharacteristically personal. In
this sense, the note seemed to respond to an imperative or call (*une demande*) to bear witness on behalf of another who could no longer respond
in his own defense. The gesture bore marks of personal generosity grounded
on principles of justice. In addition, it carried the moral force embodied in
the witness who testified on the basis of personal experience.

None of these considerations, however, negated the strong affinities between Blanchot's defense of Bataille and the deep duplicity associated with the character of Clamence in *The Fall*. Like Clamence, the narrator of "Les Intellectuels en question" intervened as a generous apologist to speak on behalf of another who could no longer speak for himself. Like Clamence, the Blanchot who responded to Souvarine assumed an air of moral superiority grounded on a sense that he knew better or more than those whose claims he saw fit to dispute. My point here is neither to subvert nor to dismiss the authority Blanchot brought to his marginal remarks on Souvarine and Bataille. Yet to accept the passage without qualification—that is, as authoritative and unambiguous—is incommensurate with the complexity and ambivalence of other disclosures cast throughout Blanchot's postwar writings. Why, then, should this or any single disclosure be privileged over any other? With no clear way to read them systematically, individual disclosures remain eloquent within an isolation that precludes definitive interpretation.

The absence of a clear and stable protocol of interpretation suspends interpretation for yet another reason. The marginal remarks in "Les Intellectuels en question" were forceful not just in what they stated concerning Souvarine and Bataille, but also because they broke uncharacteristically with the silence of an obscure literary figure in order to speak out with such apparent clarity. Did breaking a long-term silence suffice to legitimize judgments directed toward another on the part of someone who had not yet set the record straight concerning his own past? With all due respect to the moral authority to which "Les Intellectuels en question" made claim, Blanchot's denunciation of Souvarine was too strong and his defense of Bataille too absolute for me to accept at face value. In light of unresolved questions concerning his early writings, Blanchot's defense of Bataille looked very much like a defensive gesture that displaced onto another the coming to terms with a certain past whose disclosure in personal terms remained partial and oblique.

Afterimage III

Although Blanchot's writings of the past twenty years point increasingly to the interwar and wartime periods, they leave a number of questions unresolved. Exactly who was the Blanchot who signed the articles in *Combat* and *L'Insurgé*? Who was "he" during and following Vichy in the wake of the early writings? These questions are not merely a play of pronoun and identity against signature. The wider issues they raise touch on literary history, but their implications also pertain to obscurity and effacement on a lived and personal basis. Little is known about Blanchot's politics during and immediately after Vichy. After the Liberation, he surfaced in 1946 on the editorial board of *Critique*, published three novels and a book of essays between 1948 and 1950, and even contributed to *Les Temps Modernes*. What happened in the interim to the 1930s politics of abjection? How did Blanchot emerge after the war as a committed writer in the Sartrean sense of the expression? My reading of "Literature and the Right to Death" and "Les Intellectuels en question" suggests that the theorizing associated with Blanchot's postwar essays through *L'Espace littéraire* is grounded on a displacement of his dissident writings of the mid-1930s. This displacement also helps to account for a blank of some fifteen years between the wartime articles published under Blanchot's signature in *Journal des Débats* and his involvement starting in 1958 in groups protesting French policies related to Algeria.

To what extent might one kind of militancy negate another? The ongoing silence surrounding Blanchot's interwar writings is all the more scandalous in light of what is known concerning his militancy during the crisis in France over the question of Algerian independence in the late 1950s. Michel Surya began his introduction to a dossier on the failed *Revue Internationale* project of the early 1960s by noting the interest in showing how Blanchot abstained from publishing or writing about politics from World War II to 1958.[27] Surya acknowledged the postwar blank he identified as worthy of study. Yet in so doing, he also deepened the silence surrounding Blanchot's early writings! The dossier in *Lignes* showed the extent to which, starting in 1958, Blanchot was once again taking a public stance on French politics. Of particular interest was the dissidence derived ostensibly from an anticolonialist stance on the left in support of concerted resistance to policies favoring a French Algeria. A letter from Blanchot to Sartre in 1960 stated the need to make the declaration in support of insubordination (also known as the Manifesto of the 121) the "start of something" (*Lignes*, 164). That something was to be *La Revue Internationale*, an ambitious venture to be directed by Dionys Mascolo, with contributing editors in Italy (Elio Vittorini, Italo Calvino), Germany (Günter Grass, Ingeborg Bachmann, Uwe Johnson), France (Leiris, Duras, Des Forêts, Barthes), Poland (L. Kolakowski), England (Iris Murdoch), and the United States (Richard Seaver). The project collapsed after producing a single issue in Italian under the title of *Gulliver*. Yet here, in the letter taken from the archives of the Einaudi publishing house, is how Blanchot expressed his ambitions for the new review to Sartre:

> I believe that if we want to represent as we must, without equivocation, the change whose presaging we all share, if we want to make it real and

deepen it in its moving presence, in its new truth, it will only be done starting with a different medium [à partir d'un organe nouveau] . . .

We all know that we are heading toward a crisis that will only make more manifest the critical situation that is ours (a crisis of which the military force would be only of minor aspect). In this perspective and also in a more distant perspective, I would be happy to work with you, as we have begun to do to such good ends with the Declaration, on the condition, of course, that this agreement be not only ours, but that of all the intellectuals who are fully conscious of what is at stake today. It is this consensus that a new review ought to represent.[28]

Visions of crisis and dissidence dominated Blanchot's involvement with the *Revue Internationale* project more than twenty years after the articles in *Combat* and *L'Insurgé*. In fact, the post-1958 writings contained enough traces of abject dissidence to question the common belief that Blanchot emerged from the war as though converted. It was almost as if the apparent progression from right to left were less meaningful than the force of commitment to an oppositional stance whose evolution remains to be recognized in its full trajectory.

Yet another twist—a suspension rather than a closure—takes the form of a brief text Blanchot wrote for a collection honoring Nelson Mandela in 1986. Reflecting on how to speak and write appropriately about the racial segregation in South Africa, Blanchot compared the doctrine of apartheid to the "wretched doctrine" of exclusion from and the right to life that the Nazis imposed on a part of humanity. Recurrence of this exclusion as apartheid in South Africa constituted a state of emergency with which it was necessary to contend. Blanchot concluded:

> I am not summoning up these hard facts merely so that they will not fade from memory, but also so that the memory of them makes us more aware of our responsibility. We are a party to the barbarousness, the suffering, and the countless murders to the extent that we greet these facts with a certain indifference and spend our days and nights untroubled. It is striking that the man unfortunately serving as the French prime minister scoffs at what he calls our concern for a clear conscience—his own is assuredly unaffected by what is happening down there, in another world. Moreover, the European community's inertia does discredit to the ideals and the civilization the community claims to represent. Let us realize, therefore, that we too are responsible and guilty when we do not voice an appeal, a denunciation, and a cry.[29]

Denunciation of "the man unfortunately serving as the French prime minister" echoed the tone of earlier ad hominem denunciations at removes of some thirty and fifty years, respectively. Moreover, while Blanchot invoked the seemingly abstract category of memory, his attitude toward French and European Community policies suggested that he was still looking for alternative means of opposing conditions he described as unbearable. Not even the moral ring of the title, "Our Responsibility," could hide a dissidence that remained constant despite the passage of time and change of context separating Blanchot's writings during the Popular Front from those of the Algerian crisis.

The implications of an ongoing dissidence need to be tempered with a sense of its evolution. Distinctions need to be made between different kinds of silence; that is, between silences of denial, of omission, and of piety. Further inquiry might specify the range of differences—ethical and historical as well as rhetorical and discursive—between what Heidegger refused to say after the war and what Blanchot has tried, even guardedly, to disclose. It is distressing that both men stopped short by refusing to fill in the blanks as though in a game whose stakes grew as its object was further removed with the passing of time. Will full disclosure ever occur? If so, how might it be recognized as such? I have argued that precipitous closure on these questions can offer no more than partial understanding. For now, detailed analyses of disclosure as it both reveals and hides might provide a preliminary sense of how what remains unsaid (and, by implication, unknown) determines what is and can be said. As Blanchot noted with a trace of irony when he invoked Vichy by way of 1943, that improbable date may yet return.

CHAPTER SIX

Modernity in a Cold Climate

To become good literary historians, we must remember that what we usually call literary history has little or nothing to do with literature and that what we call literary interpretation—provided only it is good interpretation—is in fact literary history. If we extend this notion beyond literature, it merely confirms that the bases for historical knowledge are not empirical facts but written texts, even if these texts masquerade in the guise of wars or revolutions.
Paul de Man, "Literary History and Literary Modernity"

The Ice Age

Aftereffect disrupts linear chronology through repetition and circularity. Yet it does this less as an instance of Nietzsche's eternal return of the same than as a variant of Freud's return of the repressed. In such terms and in light of recent controversies surrounding Vichy, Heidegger, and de Man, the belated return of the past is anything but inadvertent. Blanchot's writings of the 1930s have served as a test case within a broader genealogy of modernist practices in France since 1930. What, then, are the practical means of locating Blanchot within a revised conception of interwar modernity in France within which his early writings occur? How might the articles in *Le Rempart, Combat,* and *L'Insurgé* revise received accounts of Blanchot's place in France since 1930?

Reception is a first measure of assessment. In 1973, Roger Laporte discerned three distinct generations of Blanchot's readers.[1] The most recent came to his fiction via the *Nouveau Roman* and to his essays via concepts of writing, text, and meaning adapted variously from Derrida, Barthes, and Lacan. For these third-generation readers, Blanchot's fiction and essays devolved from a practice of dense writing beyond conventions of genres such as novel, *récit*, and criticism understood in a restrictive sense. This practice clashed with the values of a previous generation of readers for whom Blanchot's essays in the postwar *Nouvelle Revue Française* and *Critique* theorized the conceptions of literary space in shorter *récits* seemingly indebted to the postwar writings of Heidegger and a literary tradition of the fantastic. Allegory often entered interpretation through names and episodes that recalled passages from the Bible and classical mythology. Where *Thomas l'obscur* (new version, 1950) began with what seemed to be a death by drowning, the name of Henri Sorge, a character in *Le Très-haut* (1948) was purportedly adapted from the German term for worry or concern used by Heidegger. (Sorge is also the name of a character in Goethe's *Faust*.) The Orpheus myth and its variants appeared as a recurrent point of reference in a number of essays and narratives.[2] A first generation, that of Blanchot's readers of the 1930s, was more difficult to discern, for though it was known that Blanchot was writing in the 1930s, little was known of the early writings beyond rumors that they were political and conservative.

Laporte's three generations schematize the evolution of literary modernity in France over the past sixty years. In their wake, Blanchot's writings since 1973 supplement the existing corpus with a fourth generation of readers such as those addressed by the 1987 *Nouvel Observateur* portrait of Blanchot as an octogenarian recluse. Even if this fourth generation assimilated earlier readers, it is likely that the aftereffect surrounding Vichy and Heidegger has revised Blanchot's literary signature with difference at both ends, setting the postwar essays and fiction within a new configuration in which the early writings take on added force. In order to measure the potential impact of the early writings as a necessary supplement, it is instructive first to examine how Jean-Paul Aron, Tzvetan Todorov, and Paul de Man attempted to contend with an incomplete corpus that they took as fully constituted and that they sought to place in the genealogy of modernity in France since 1930.

When it appeared in 1984, Jean-Paul Aron's *Les Modernes* showed that a debate of major importance had developed over the previous decade as a hermeneutics of culture in postwar France. Debate at the time was focused on figures of the 1950s and 1960s (Sartre, Lévi-Strauss, Lacan, Barthes, and Foucault) whose careers had once disputed the notion that they might ever be assimilated within a received modernity. This resistance eroded after these figures of experimental postwar movements such as the *nouveau roman, nouvelle vague,* and *nouvelle critique* began to die. Where Lyotard had seen the relationship to modernity as integral to a postmodern condition of knowledge, Aron asserted something closer to a postmodernism of reaction.[3] *Les Modernes* could be read either as a polemical history of postwar French culture or, in more personal terms, as Aron's ad hominem complaint against a culture of "cold" modernity whose demise he was all too happy to chronicle. If it was not an official history, *Les Modernes* was certainly a collection of portraits among which those of Claude Lévi-Strauss and Maurice Blanchot formed a striking composite of the postwar intellectual in a zero-degree environment.

Aron began his portrait of Lévi-Strauss by evoking the appearance in 1949 of *The Elementary Structures of Kinship,* a text often credited with having launched structuralism in postwar France. For Aron, however, Lévi-Strauss was a dour academic whose "little doctoral thesis" ("petite thèse de doctorat d'état") was the product of a social scientist who had abandoned traditional fieldwork in favor of linguistic models. In *The Elementary Structures of Kinship,* Lévi-Strauss committed what Aron saw as the essential sin of postwar modernity when he displaced the immediacy of experience in favor of systems and models. Underlying this displacement was an untested faith in language as "hard" data that Aron did not share: "The immediacy, the everydayness of behaviors were sacrificed to the abstract mechanism which expresses them fundamentally. With Lévi-Strauss, the substitution of theory for the real occurred in France in one fell swoop" (*Les Modernes,* 40). By trying to subsume all social facts within models of symbolic exchange, Lévi-Strauss pursued what Aron saw as an impersonal and obstinate formalism that, in keeping with his preferred metaphor, left him cold.

Lévi-Strauss also culminated a tradition of the artist-intellectual whose origins Aron traced to the nineteenth century. Modernity as Aron reconstructed it was at least as much an attitude or style as a discrete historical phenomenon. In particular, his misgivings on the excessive importance of visibility were founded on a perception of culture going back to a generation of Young Turks (*jeunes loups*) of the mid-1800s who bore uncanny resemblance to their postwar counterparts a century later. Here is Aron's image of what he considers to be the prototype *moderne,* taken from a passage he found in Jules Simon's 1887 biography of Victor Cousin:

> I recall that with the approach of the 1848 revolution, the noise of political and social questions having somewhat drowned out what he used to make out of philosophical and religious questions, Victor Cousin trembled with fear of being forgotten: "Be seen," he used to say to me, "Be seen. I feel that we need to . . . " He used to say *we need* the way the king says *we want.* When he was Minister of Public Instruction (which was for only eight months), he filled *Le Moniteur* and the officious newspapers with his decrees, his memoranda, his public speeches, and his pet projects. Monsieur Damiron, who was, according to Cousin himself, wisest of the wise, chided him for it gently: "You are seen too often; you will tire the public." But Cousin answered him, "One must be seen." (Simon, *Victor Cousin,* cited in *Les Modernes,* 55)[4]

Aron tried so hard to denigrate Cousin as a self-centered politico intent on personal gain that he failed to consider Cousin's statement within the context of the university-level *professorat* between 1836 and 1848. Effort in this instance turned out to be the mark of failure, as the doubts Aron had hoped to cast on Cousin were deflected instead toward the intentions of the would-be critic.

Where Lévi-Strauss played the role of social scientist in Aron's "cold" culture of postwar France, Blanchot was more difficult to cast. In *Les Modernes,* he was first seen (in Cousin's sense of the verb *paraître*) as Georges Bataille's shadow or double on the advisory board of *Critique* and as author of two novels, *Thomas l'obscur* and *Aminadab* (not *Aminabad,* as Aron misspelled it, perhaps confusing the Blanchot title with Alain Resnais and Alain Robbe-Grillet's 1961 film, *Last Year at Marienbad* [*L'Année dernière à Marienbad*]). In short, Aron cast Blanchot as literary heir to Mallarmé and Heidegger, a resolute *moderne* whose writings he described as delayed-action firecrackers ("pétards à déflagration différée") that exploded twenty to thirty years after they were set:

> In 1946, the journal *Critique* takes control of the suicidal force which has been building in French culture since Mallarmé and which, like a macabre folklore, continues to pervert and poison our sensibilities in 1984. The double process leading in the 1960s to the laughable reign of talkers [*rhéteurs*] and the unrelenting decomposition of the literary function is set into motion at the Editions de Minuit a year after the armistice by a conservator of medals at the Bibliothèque Nationale . . . and by a strange, almost invisible man of letters who departs from the principles of Parisian life, having had so much success at preserving or controlling his anonymity that his enveloping presence, primordial role, and integral prestige seem ideally suited to the guidance which, from the start, he has addressed to what has ceased to be, or

to bring about what neither has nor will ever again have meaning. (*Les Modernes,* 22)

Curiously, the portrait of Blanchot in *Les Modernes* was directed less toward literature than toward politics and specifically toward his role as a prime mover behind the 1960 *Manifesto of the 121.* Aron's account of events surrounding the appearance of the *Manifesto* barely masked his contempt for what he described as the ineffectual attempts to rally support for a protest movement among the university community and a self-important intelligentsia in a Paris closed down for the summer holidays. Taking his cue from the 1960 convention of the Union Nationale des Etudiants de France (National Union of French Students), Blanchot was moved by those who were ready to face the consequences of their beliefs. Aron's account was sharp with irony: "One sees this invisible one, this phantom guru, this fragile *précieux,* this great federator of writing and death preoccupied with civil disobedience" (160). Unlike Aron's mean-spirited caricature of Lévi-Strauss as a spiteful academic "embittered as though he were somehow being denied his due respect" (39), Blanchot was made to look more like an opportunist whose foray into social protest—Aron tried to make ironic use of the term "intervention"—was nothing more than words.

For Aron, the *Manifesto of the 121* neither rallied support to the cause of conscientious objection nor mobilized popular sentiment to denounce France's resistance to Algerian independence. It served instead as a profession of faith reminiscent of the Dreyfus affair and a taste for public statements that Aron found typical of the *modernes:* "After 1945, at the height of the cold war, the rhythm of declarations picks up without weighing on the growing lists of protesters or, it must be said, exposing the latter to any major inconveniences" (160). After the fact, such protest took on mythic proportions. A signature on the *Manifesto* connoted a political liberalism and a corollary freedom of expression that Aron dismissed as empty display: "The spirit of the 121 henceforth blows on culture. I know impostors in 1984 who still hawk the legend of their subversive signature throughout Paris" (63).

Was this a diatribe against radical chic or a simple case of sour grapes? Aron's portrait of Blanchot appeared in France at a moment when American debate surrounding the place of theory in the study of literature and culture was heating up. Across the Atlantic, Aron repeatedly begged the question of how theory should relate to history. In so doing, he raised expectations that *Les Modernes* might set forth a critical rereading of modernity with a concern for adequate and accurate documentation. At most, however, Aron practiced rereading with a vengeance, evoking the *Manifesto* less in its historical or social specificity than as a product of a devalued generosity. Signing the *Manifesto* became a rite of passage by which the *modernes* entered into a heroic fraternity that, in fact, existed only on paper: a myth of self-promotion that was risk-free and increasingly removed from the true dissidence to which it aspired. By passing itself off as an outgrowth of the resistance movements and postwar Gaullism, the *clan* promoted its visibility by reducing action to words, much as Lévi-Strauss was earlier portrayed as reducing social life to linguistic models. The result, for Aron, was a predictable and hollow dissidence: "Are there people naïve enough to think that by calling for freedom to be reestablished in Poland, they are performing an exemplary act? Everybody gives his or her heart to Solidarity, everybody calls for the Russian evacuation of Afghanistan and the end of reigns of horror in Uruguay and Chile" (163).

Aron's hostility blinded him to the fact that much of Blanchot's writing of the past twenty years had engaged the problematic relations between personal experience and history. And despite Aron's insinuations to the contrary, Blanchot's reassessment was neither cold nor impersonal. In "Les Intellectuels en question," Blanchot had cited Lyotard's "Tombeau de l'intellectuel" ("Tomb of the Intellectual") as point of departure for his own reflections on the latest allegations of the so-called death of the intellectual.[5] For Blanchot, the negative image of the intellectual whom one chided for an inability to move from word to act derived from a misconstrued equation of action and commitment: "Intellectual, a name of bad repute which is easy to caricature and always ready to serve as an insult. Whoever remembers the Algerian War remembers having been a despised intellectual thereby, totally unready to defend oneself as such" ("Les Intellectuels," 4).

Rejecting the stance of the well-meaning liberal who claimed to speak for a universal subject, Blanchot described the function of the intellectual as inseparable from historical specificity. Taking his lead from Theodor Adorno, Blanchot qualified Kant's categorical imperative when he invoked the Holocaust and the period of the *Manifesto of the 121* to illustrate the irreducible historicity of the intellectual function:

> If I invoke the anticolonialist struggles, the role which the intellectuals played in it, and—as prime example—the initiative of the *Manifesto of the 121* on the right of insubordination during the Algerian War, I note that there, too, those who made their statement did not claim to be the prophets [*annonciators*] of a universal truth (insubordination for its own sake and in all cases),

but did nothing other than uphold decisions which had not been theirs, making themselves nonetheless responsible for them and thereby *identifying themselves* with those who had been obliged to do so. (27; emphasis in the original)

Nothing in this passage substantiated the irony and venom in Aron's portrait of Blanchot. To the contrary, the direct and unambiguous statements belied Aron's attempt to use Blanchot as an example to suggest that the social or political commitment of postwar *modernes* was mere posturing. In fact, Aron's account was so out of line with most accounts of the *Manifesto* that discredit pointed to its source rather than to its object. As in Aron's portrait of Lévi-Strauss, ad hominem the attack turned out to be self-defeating.

Second Thoughts

Tzvetan Todorov's role as theorist and critic has evolved from his efforts as editor of an anthology of Russian formalist writings published in 1965 and translated into French to a study in 1982 of cultural difference related to Spain's presence in sixteenth-century Mexico and the Caribbean.[6] In the interim, Todorov wrote prolifically on topics ranging from short forms of narration and the fantastic to the poetics of prose, theories of the symbol, and interpretation. A more self-conscious tone in Todorov's *Literature and Its Theorists* (1984) marked a reappraisal that was acknowledged in the book's subtitle as "a personal view of twentieth-century criticism." The change in tone was reinforced by the French title of the book, *Critique de la critique: un roman d'apprentissage* (translated literally as "Criticism of criticism: an apprenticeship novel"), which conveyed an exercise in metacriticism bordering on the confessional. As Todorov admitted at the start of a section on his former teacher Roland Barthes, personal acquaintance with many of the figures whom he studied in his book precluded any possible claim to impartiality on his part.

Blanchot appeared alongside Sartre and Barthes in a chapter of *Literature and Its Theorists* devoted to writer-critics (*critiques-écrivains*) for whom the act of writing criticism became a form of literature in itself. For Todorov, the category of writer-critic applied whether or not the writers in question also produced works of fiction. That Sartre was the author of *Nausea* as well as *What Is Literature?* and that *Roland Barthes by Roland Barthes* opened with a cautionary statement that it was to be read as though uttered by a character in a novel were less relevant than the "new relevance" given to the literary aspect in the critical writings by these authors and by Blanchot. Although he did not state it in so many words, what Todorov called "literary aspects" came close to fulfilling some functions of writing (*écriture*) in the sense of a morality of form that Barthes had given to the term thirty years earlier in *Writing Degree Zero.*

Todorov began by noting that the attraction exercised by the brilliance of Blanchot's critical work—"at once limpid and mysterious"—was close to paralyzing. As a result, attempts to approach these writings in a language other than their own were seemingly impeded by an unspoken taboo: "Paraphrase or silence: one or the other of these fates seems to befall all who try to comprehend Blanchot."[7] It is tempting to consider the nature of what Todorov referred to as an unspoken taboo, even if appearances spoke against relating it to the displacement of the interwar political writings. Todorov did, in fact, describe Blanchot at one point as "the spokesman for a certain anti-Semitism" (61), but the concerns he brought to bear were directed toward the postwar writings. Literature and philosophy rather than politics served as the primary elements in Todorov's account of Blanchot's criticism. History entered less in specific circumstances or contexts than in the guise of a Hegelian model of change through time in terms of which the modernity of art "for two centuries" derived from its failure to maintain a former ability "to convey the absolute." This loss led to what Todorov saw as a double transformation. Art approached its own essence at the very moment that it lost its sovereignty: "Now, the essence of art is, tautologically, art itself, or rather the very possibility of artistic creation, interrogation as to the place from which art arises" (57).

Todorov saw Blanchot's search for the origin of art as an extension of the Romantic doctrine that valorized the primacy of production and becoming. As art seemingly turned away from the world and came to assert nothing other than itself, it took on various expressions in a pantheon of literary immanence that included Friedrich Hölderlin, Joseph Joubert, Hugo Hofmannsthal, Rainer Maria Rilke, and Hermann Broch as well as Paul Valéry, James Joyce, Marcel Proust, Franz Kafka, and Samuel Beckett. All of these writers—Todorov described them as "abruptly linked" and "pathetically undifferentiated"—repeated that art was increasingly concerned with an inquiry into its origins and essence. But as art moved closer and closer to its essence and thus toward itself, new problems arose when, as Todorov noted, the essence of art was "tautologically, art itself, or rather the very possibility of artistic creation." The point was reductive and even somewhat hostile because it remained unclear to what degree the tautology to which Todorov referred was equated with the redundancy it implied.

Instead of extending this line of thought by pondering what might have motivated Todorov's account, I want to note his remarks linking what he called the Romantic doctrine of art to a nihilism adapted from Nietzsche and Sade, both of whom he invoked—somewhat abruptly—as "two of Blanchot's favorite authors" (61). What Todorov referred to as the "exorbitant privilege accorded to the present" expressed his doubts concerning the blindness of those for whom a rhetoric of crisis did little to undo or otherwise alter the intransitivity of discourse. If, in other words, the present moment always culminated the movement of history, history was always the present and thus always the moment in which history was abolished:

> The intransitivity of discourse, the literary work focused on its own origin, perhaps these are the characteristics of a specific literary production, during a given period, in Western Europe; they are characteristics of a culture to which Blanchot belongs. But why does Blanchot, fond as he is of declaring the necessity of recognizing the other, turn his gaze exclusively upon figures cast in his own image? . . . Why does he not notice that, while he was declaring the novel "an art of the future," under other skies, or even the same ones, the novel was about to undergo new and surprising transformations, placing it far from intransitive discourse as well as from a pure quest for its own origin? We can only say that Blanchot's own work bears witness, implicitly, to the acceptance of that ideal and no other, since his work itself becomes intransitive discourse, a question tirelessly pursued but never resolved; explicitly, it declares that we (but who are "we"? Westerners? Europeans? Parisians?) are the ultimate, unsurpassable moment of history. Even supposing that Blanchot's description of our time may be faithful, why must the present be the supreme moment? Is there not an inkling here of what child psychologists call the "egocentric illusion"? (58)

Like Aron, Todorov tried hard to make Blanchot representative of wider critical practices associated with a particular generation and sensibility. But where Aron had drawn the polemical edge of his portrait mainly from Blanchot's postwar stances on political and social issues, Todorov made Blanchot into a critic so blinded by self-absorption that he could see nothing beyond his immediate concerns. Centeredness in the guise of ethnocentrism was at least as illusory—and as dangerous—in its collective expression as at the level of the individual. Because the self in this instance was cultural as well as psychological, the concerns Todorov attributed to it extended from an assumed intransitivity of discourse to the alleged failure on Blanchot's part to recognize the otherness to which he referred.

Todorov's portrait of Blanchot also carried over to what he took for the supreme privilege of the present moment. As with the ethnocentric blindness in the passage just noted, an illusion of temporal immediacy grew from a doctrine of immanence Todorov attributed to modernist practices in the Romantic tradition. Blanchot was seen by Todorov as extending nontranscendence to a point where literature and criticism came together. Unlike other "immanentists," however, Blanchot did not locate meaning within the text. Nor did he find it somehow "out there" in the world. Meaning as Blanchot affirmed it was less of a presence than a movement of effacement and disappearance. For Todorov, this absence amounted to Blanchot's version of a nihilism derived from Nietzsche and, over a longer duration going back to Sade, from a tradition that valorized force at the expense of law. Todorov made no mention of Derrida, but his portrait of Blanchot was called "Force and Signification," recalling Derrida's 1963 essay in which he used Jean Rousset's *Forme et signification* as a point of departure to question the reduction of force to form among certain *nouveaux critiques* (new critics) of the period.[8]

The implied convergence of Blanchot and Derrida was problematic and its extent uncertain. Todorov explicitly located Blanchot within a nihilist tradition that transcended the framework of literature. Yet he never specified how this transcendence affected Blanchot's status as an "immanentist" and admitted as much when he wrote that this transcendence of literature was what especially disturbed him about Blanchot. The point is important because Todorov quickly aligned transcendence and nihilism with the atrocities of the recent past. After noting that Blanchot chose "this moment in history" to enlist literature and criticism in the destruction of universal values, Todorov added a lengthy justification:

> I will be told that I am introducing political considerations where only harmless matters are at stake, such as literature. But the transition has already been made in Blanchot's work. As we know, before the war Blanchot became the spokesman for a certain anti-Semitism. He changed his mind later on, and that is not what I am reproaching him for here. But it is in the postwar epoch that he would have us commit ourselves to the struggle against values. The revelation of the Nazi horrors did not shake his conviction, even though Blanchot speaks elsewhere with strength and gravity of the extermination camps: his immediate affective reactions have no effect on his principles. (61)

The passage was strongly worded and its tone accusatory. Like many of those who saw the writings of Nietzsche and Heidegger as dangerous because they were so easily appropriated by the National Socialists, Todorov took Blanchot's postwar statements (his references came almost exclusively from Blanchot's 1959 collection *Le Livre à venir*) as expressions of a nihilism whose ideological roots he associates with totalitarian regimes: "In our era, after World War II, knowing what we know about the Nazis and the Gulag, we are discovering to our horror just how far humanity can go when it rejects universal values and sets up the assertion of force in their stead" (61).

If such reasoning truly introduced political considerations into literary discussions that would, as Todorov suggests, otherwise be "harmless," a clear sense of what Todorov meant by politics was missing. At best, Todorov tried to argue for guilt by association when he set Blanchot within a nihilist tradition whose valorization of force was transposed under totalitarian regimes into overt acts of violence. Only a slippage of categories allowed Todorov to condemn Blanchot by association when he held that the revelation of horrors committed by the Nazis did not shake Blanchot's conviction and principles. The nature of those convictions and principles was identified only in general terms, however. A similar generality pertained when Todorov cited a passage from *L'Amitié* in order to argue that Blanchot showed a singular tolerance with respect to the 1917 October Revolution and the Soviet totalitarian regime that followed. Contrary to what Todorov implied, the political side of Blanchot's literary theory is not located in a nihilist tradition. Nor can it be characterized as that of a onetime ideologue turned obscurantist. Although Todorov showed that he was aware of the interwar writings, he chose not to confront them in a sustained way, and as a result he weakened his argument by transposing into philosophy the political discourse that might have substantiated his allegations.

The pages in *Literature and Its Theorists* were not Todorov's last words on Blanchot. Four years later, he included Blanchot in editorial remarks on a series of intellectual events that he saw as variations on the theme of Heideggerianism and the right. In the wake of debate on Heidegger sparked by the Farias book, Todorov noted similar disclosures related to de Man, Blanchot, and Jean Beaufret. (Beaufret [1907–1982] was one of Heidegger's major postwar exponents in France. Addressee of "Letter on Humanism," he came under suspicion in the last years of his life when it was alleged that he had supported revisionist claims denying the Nazi genocide of the Jews.) Todorov studied the four events less with a view toward judging or condemning than in order to assess what he saw at stake in the debates they promoted. He saw the unexpected defense of Heidegger as symptomatic of a greater malaise among intellectuals in France and North America. Todorov did not dismiss this defense; instead, he explored it systematically by enumerating what he took to be the four main strategies used by apologists who rushed "to defend Heidegger and his emulators."[9]

The four strategies listed by Todorov included denial of the facts, dissociation of an author from his or her works, nonexistence of truth and justice, and incoherence of doctrine. Blanchot's name appeared in conjunction with the first and fourth strategies. Against those who denied all evidence as irrelevant or ill conceived, Todorov noted that simply reading the documents in question would allow one to see that Blanchot was casting aspersions on the Jews by assimilating them to the Bolsheviks. Incoherence and discontinuity were likewise questionable excuses among those who claimed that a split within the work of a single writer could explain away what might otherwise be taken for compromising assertions. Todorov suggested that Blanchot's apparent reversal of ideas from the far right in 1937 to the far left in 1967 might be more continuous than one might have thought because both positions were incompatible with democratic values.

Defacement and Forgetting

Paul de Man's "Impersonality in the Criticism of Maurice Blanchot" appeared in French in the June 1966 issue of *Critique,* the monthly on whose editorial board Blanchot has served since 1946. Four years later, in 1971, the essay was translated into English as a chapter of *Blindness and Insight.* After the fact, de Man's remarks resonate today in the wake of the reassessment imposed since 1987 by debate over his own writings in wartime Belgium. This reassessment is even more pointed because a major issue raised in de Man's essay on Blanchot was that of the relations between literary history and literary modernity. How, then, did Paul de Man inscribe Blanchot in literary modernity? And what might a rereading of his 1966 essay on Blanchot reveal about the consequences of aftereffect on both figures in the interim? De Man located Blanchot within the succession of practices that kept alive the illusion of a fecund and productive modernity in postwar French literature. From the perspective of a somewhat longer duration, de Man portrayed Blanchot against figures like Sartre who asserted a literary vocation by trying to maintain a stable commitment while in contact with changing surface-currents of intellectual fashions: "When we will be able to observe the period with more detachment, the main proponents of contemporary French literature may well turn out to be figures that now seem shadowy in comparison with celebrities of the hour. And none is more likely to achieve future prominence than the little-publicized and difficult writer, Maurice Blanchot."[10]

The aftereffect at work when de Man's remarks are reread at a temporal remove of some twenty-five years borders on irony. Yet the intervening supplement of scandal surrounding de Man himself only added a new twist to what he had already seen in 1966 as Blanchot's recognition that self-reading was impossible and that all writers who handled language seriously had to contend with a necessary estrangement. The loss of control implied by this recognition transposed reading from an act founded on authorial intention to a mode of "listening" to the work that de Man adapted from Heidegger. This recognition also bore directly on the incommensurate experiences of author and reader-critic. Where the former largely concerned a role of estrangement, the latter held a potential for genuine interpretation if and when it allowed for what de Man called the "actualization in language of the potential language involved in reading" (66).

For de Man, such incommensurateness also raised problems concerning the role of forgetting in Blanchot's theorizing of literature. De Man implied that it was not enough simply to transpose estrangement so that what Blanchot called literary space became the space of impersonality. Forgetting was a necessary component leading to the invention of an authentic literary language. De Man acknowledged the Mallarméan dimension of this assertion, but he also noted the extent to which Blanchot drew out the fuller implications of Mallarmé's assertion: "Blanchot's recent work compels us to become aware of the full ambivalence of the power contained in the act of forgetting. It reveals the paradoxical presence of a kind of anti-memory at the very source of literary creation" (66–67). What was this anti-memory? How did de Man relate it to what he called the temporal destiny of fictional language in Blanchot?

Forgetting and anti-memory derived for de Man from a claim to absolute impersonality on the part of Mallarmé that fascinated Blanchot. In this sense, Blanchot's reading of Mallarmé repeated (accompanied) that claim by extending the experience of impersonality as an encounter with language and, through language, with death. Accompaniment here was understood less as a strict repetition than as a variation, playing out, or restaging that invariably broke with or differed from its model. In de Man's account, Blanchot's variation shared the Mallarméan experience of impersonality as grounded in an encounter with language as an alien entity at odds with subjective intent and practical application. Blanchot likewise followed Mallarmé in seeing language as both concrete natural entity and product of consciousness. Yet Mallarmé's attempt to found a poetics by making the semantic dimensions of language coincide with its material attributes was altogether different from what de Man took to be going on in Blanchot's writings.

De Man's remarks bore directly on forgetting and anti-memory by pointing to the Hegelian substructure in Mallarmé's poetics that led from the particular to the universal, from personal to historical recollection. They also showed how Blanchot's rejection of a dialectical poetics accounted for differences between the specific writing practices to which he granted privileged status and those favored by Mallarmé. De Man observed that Blanchot's writing seldom lingered "over the material qualities of things; without being abstract, his language is rarely a language of sensation. His preferred literary form is not, as for René Char with whom he is often compared, that of a poetry oriented toward material things, but rather the *récit*, a purely temporal type of narrative" (71). If Blanchot sometimes missed the mark in his readings of Mallarmé, it was because—according to de Man—his theorizing did not uphold the priority of material substance over consciousness asserted in Mallarmé's conception of poetry.

Nondialectical repetition as de Man found it in Blanchot's writings is best understood in conjunction with *ressassement*, the French term for resifting or harkening back. The term appears in *Le Ressassement éternel*, the title Blanchot gave to the publication in 1951 of two *récits*, "L'Idylle" and "Le Dernier Mot," written in the 1930s. (The same *récits* were reprinted in 1983 under the title of *Après coup*.) De Man invoked *ressassement* in relation to impersonality and the encounter of consciousness through language with the most general category of being. Because this encounter marked the reduction of the self to no one (*personne*) in particular, its repetition in the *récit* disclosed death by revealing and deferring it simultaneously. As in Beckett's postwar trilogy of novels, fiction mediated the experience of death by interposing a language that described it. The result suspended total abolition by transposing it into an unlimited series of *récits* whose structure de Man described as circular. The effects of this structure inverted linear chronology: "The prospective hypothesis, which determines a future, coincides with a historical, concrete reality that precedes it and that belongs to the past. The future is changed into a past, in the infinite regression Blanchot calls a *ressassement*, and that Mallarmé describes as the endless and meaningless noise of the sea after the storm has destroyed all sign of life, 'l'inférieur clapotis quelconque'" (75).

Circularity and nondialectical repetition set Blanchot's *récits* into a complex temporality. For if the *récits* wrote (rewrote?) the same experience of impersonality as an endless sequence of *ressassements*, these acts of writing and reading were nonetheless time-bound. Blanchot's writing repeated—in the sense of *ressasser*—variations of this interplay. But unlike the positive insight attributed to disclosure in Heidegger's later writings, it remained for Blanchot a negative process that confirmed a fundamental estrangement at the heart of all human experience: "The center always remains hidden and out of reach; we are separated from it by the very substance of time, and we never cease to know that this is the case" (76). Imperfect circularity precluded coincidence and imposed itself as a project or burden to be constructed and adhered to: "At most, the circularity proves the authenticity of our intent. The search toward circularity governs the development of consciousness and is also the guiding principle that shapes the poetic form" (77).

The circularity at work in Blanchot's criticism warranted close attention. When de Man set circularity in Blanchot apart from the "positive" disclosure of being in the later writings of Heidegger, he meant to show how Blanchot sought to free interpretation from empirical concerns. After—or beyond—Heideggerian disclosure, Blanchot asserted a revised self-interpretation on an act of reading that conceived of the literary work as autonomous. This assertion entailed a twofold movement: it was both a progression beyond disclosure in Heidegger and a repetition-return (*ressassement*) modeled on the experience of Mallarmé. For de Man, this double movement resulted from a necessary displacement: "The suppression of the subjective moment in Blanchot, asserted in the form of a categorical impossibility of all self-reading, is only a preparatory step in his hermeneutic of the self. In this way, he frees himself of the insidious presence of inauthentic concerns" (77–78). De Man qualified the preceding point by stating that what attracted Blanchot to the Mallarméan experience of depersonalized reading was the obliqueness of experience and insight. Only by first eliminating from his work all elements derived from everyday experience and involvement with others could Blanchot turn toward the truly temporal dimensions of the text.

De Man's conclusion was suitably elliptical in that the projected turn to the truly temporal he identified in Blanchot's writings was also a return. Mallarmé was the best possible figure for Blanchot to invoke because the obliqueness of the Mallarméan experience always suspended full revelation. For de Man, then, the privilege granted to the oblique was a negative value in terms of which Blanchot equated explicit forms of insight with "other inessential matters that served to make everyday life unbearable—such as society, or what he calls history" (78). The distinction between essential and inessential matters was de Man's way of binding Blanchot's criticism to an equivalent of Mallarmé's distinction between primitive and essential languages. At the same time, however, it is difficult to accept de Man's decision to locate Blanchot's writings apart from "inessential" matters, especially when the latter are engaged at length in Blanchot's interwar writings. De Man's conclusion that a focus on the act of interpretation allowed Blanchot to reserve the revealed insight of interpretation for his narrative prose returned to the issues raised by Laporte and others of how best to read the fiction and the essays in conjunction with each other. De Man's insight can be faulted only in terms of fact. For while he did not account for the place of Blanchot's early political texts, his concluding remark that Blanchot preferred hidden truth to revealed insight prophesied some twenty-five years ago the supplement and revision that subsequent disclosure of Blanchot's early writings has imposed.

Confrontations

Whether they are taken individually or as a composite, the portraits of Blanchot by Aron, Todorov, and de Man extended ambiguity surrounding a name and a voice whose identity has remained complex and obscure. Each portrait had its peculiar insights and blind spots. Aron's "engaged" Blanchot of 1960 came across as a laughable contradiction: an aspiring *intellectuel* in the Sartrean mode of militancy who was seemingly unable to extricate himself from an almost metaphysical cult of the literary and a personal obscurity he had cultivated but no longer controlled. Aron saw through the ploy of obscurity to a point where he might well have raised the kinds of questions concerning the interplay between culture and politics in Blanchot's postwar writings that needed to be raised as well for the 1930s texts that he—like so many others—barely mentioned. But hostility toward Blanchot, Lévi-Strauss, and others whom Aron saw as responsible for a degraded postwar modernity kept his critical position dubious and the case he made to support his allegations little more than an untimely complaint.

Todorov directed his misgivings less toward the person or figure of Blanchot than toward wider attitudes related to otherness, intransitive writing, and history that he (Todorov) did not share. Yet Todorov's subsequent equation of immanentist and nihilist assumptions hardly legitimized his invocation of "political matters" when what he meant by politics was closer to an ethical concern he found lacking in a Blanchot whom he accused of remaining blind to the postwar revelations of Nazi horrors. References to a prewar Blanchot as "spokesman for a certain anti-Semitism" were likewise unelaborated except to note that Blanchot had "changed his mind later on" (61). De Man set his 1966 remarks on impersonality in Blanchot's criticism within a symbolist tradition in the wake of Mallarmé. All three critics sought to break the illusion of a unified corpus, but de Man alone engaged the long-term genealogy of Blanchot's theorizing within the terms of its explicit literary context. Where Aron and Todorov pointed each in his own way to slippages between Blanchot's practices of literature and politics, only de Man identified those slippages from within conceptions and practices of literature.

All three portraits asserted a gap or break related to received opinion concerning Blanchot. Differences from one portrait to the next invoked discontinuity and/or disparity as marks of a deeper separation whose exact nature was unclear. What remained constant by implication was a shared sense that current understanding was somehow incomplete and flawed. As with the case of Heidegger in France, it was uncertain when—if ever at all—access to "lost" or "forgotten" archival materials would disclose what current understanding identified only in negative terms of absence and obscurity. Until such disclosure occurred, a number of points remain to be clarified.

What Serge Klarsfeld, Robert Paxton, Pascal Ory, and Henry Rousso have done for Vichy remains to be done for France in the 1930s. Although the work of Denis Hollier, Alice Kaplan, and Jeffrey Mehlman has begun to do this, a sustained critical revision of received opinion concerning the political cultures of modernity in France since 1930 has yet to occur. It has not been my intention to cast my analyses ad hominem in order to discredit Blanchot or his contributions to contemporary French thought. As I argued in chapter 3, the transition from the topicality of the 1930s articles to the postwar theorizing of a more hermetic space of literature meant that the open engagement with history in the former dispersed rather than disappeared. In such terms, the texts in *La Revue Française, Le Rempart, Combat,* and *L'Insurgé* did not simply contextualize or prefigure the fuller corpus of Blanchot's writings to which they pointed. Context here does not imply losing sight of or otherwise "forgetting" the specificity of the text. To the contrary, context traces the marks of dispersed meaning within operations of disclosure such as those I have already explored in *L'écriture du désastre, Le pas au-delà, Après coup,* and Blanchot's letter on Heidegger published in *Le Nouvel Observateur* in 1988. Furthermore, context functions as a constant accompaniment, not simply parallel to the explicit theorizing in the wartime and postwar writings starting with "Comment la littérature est-elle possible?," but inscribed within this theorizing much like the "other" history—"a history in excess, a 'secret,' separate history"—invoked in *L'écriture du désastre.*

The resistance among critics to contend seriously with Blanchot's 1930s writings serves two functions. First, it rejects by omission what would appear to be a strongly ambiguous ("problematic") interplay of politics and culture at odds with more hermetic conceptions in the postwar writings. Silence and indirect disclosure thus operate as negative tropes, provisional erasures that embed assertion as hidden and secret.[11] From the perspective of the postwar theorizing associated with literary space, erasure bears on the absence of the early texts within Blanchot's corpus and on the incomplete sense of their trajectory related to processes of social formation. Denial oscillates between presence and absence as a variant of the trope of apophasis stages disclosure "under erasure" (*sous rature*). It asserts the existence of an essential flaw blocking attempts to account in full for a corpus whose obscurity is perhaps more determinate than one might think.

A second reason for analyzing Blanchot's writings of the 1930s in their specificity has to do with the cultural project of the interwar nonconformist right. I borrow the expression from studies on the Occupation and from practices legitimized under the Vichy regime to mobilize a national revolution leading to a renewed moral and intellectual order.[12] A similar renewal had animated attempts a decade earlier along the French right from Action Française and the nonconformists to the protofascists of *Je Suis Partout* who supplemented direct political action with cultural practices. For Herman Lebovics, the idea of a true France expressed an imperative that was upheld by both left and right from the time of the Dreyfus affair through the Occupation. Nevertheless, this claim to exclusivity was profoundly reactionary both in culture and politics because it sought to prescribe not just the way to participate in the culture of a country, but the natural organization that fit society: "The discourse of True France employs the essentialist, determinist language of a lost or hidden authenticity that, once uncovered, yields a single, immutable national identity. The idea of France it consecrates is profoundly static and ahistorical, indeed antihistorical, for despite all vicissitudes of history—monarchy, republic, empire—a vital core persists to infuse everything and everyone with the undying if seriously threatened national character."[13]

The paradigm of an essentialist cultural identity associated with True France reached its apotheosis under Vichy. Yet there is little doubt that attempts to sustain the conservative construct of an exclusive, unitary, and fundamentalist concept of French identity failed disastrously. Chief among the reasons for this failure was the irrelevance of an authoritarian paradigm increasingly at odds with a rival conception of True France as a republican ethos grounded in what Lebovics described aptly as its own "essentialism of democracy, social justice, and egalitarianism" (190). Rival conceptions of True France, even when transposed from explicit politics to culture, effectively turned national identity into a problem, not a solution (Lebovics, xiv). Moreover, the persistence of this rivalry during the Third Republic suggested the extent to which opposing conceptions of French national identity—exclusive, unitary, and fundamentalist on the right against democratic and egalitarian on the left—continued to evolve without attaining either stability or long-term advantage. At no time was this rivalry more intense or far-reaching than during the years of Blanchot's "early" articles in *La Revue Française, Le Rempart, Combat,* and *L'Insurgé.*

CHAPTER SEVEN

Afterthoughts and Gray Zones

To articulate the past historically does not mean to recognize it "the way it was" (Ranke). It means to seize hold of a memory as it flashes up at a moment of danger
Walter Benjamin, "Theses on the Philosophy of History"

To forget everything would be perhaps to forget forgetting.—Forgetting forgotten: each time I forget, I do nothing but forget that I am forgetting. To enter into this movement of redoubling, however, is not to forget twice; it is to forget in forgetting the depth of forgetting, to forget more profoundly by turning away from this depth that lacks any possibility of being gotten to the bottom of.—Then we must seek something else.—We must seek the same thing, arrive at an event that would not be forgetting, and that nonetheless would be determined only by forgetting's indetermination.
Maurice Blanchot, *L'Entretien infini*

Between History and Memory

Blanchot's early journalism supplements by disruption a received corpus whose trajectory needs to be considered as longer and more complex than has been acknowledged. The interwar writings also clash with a silence on the part of readers and critics either unable or unwilling to acknowledge the nature and extent of Blanchot's commitment to a right-wing militancy that he seemingly renounced by the end of the Occupation. This nonreception of the interwar writings extends a pattern of displacement and scandalous return that I have explored symptomatically in terms of an aftereffect phenomenon I have adapted from the vocabulary of psychoanalysis. In this final chapter I will explore some implications of the breaks and shifts I have come to identify in Blanchot's early writings as they relate to the ongoing study of France since 1930. In so doing, what might at first appear to be a move beyond or to the side of Blanchot is intended as a movement outward from (à partir de) his writings. A first consideration involves an interplay between history and memory I want to address through a montage of two intertexts. The first intertext is from *Jonah Who Will Be 25 in the Year 2000*, a feature film produced in 1976 by the Swiss director Alain Tanner, and the second is from a recent account of the work of a sixteenth-century Italian in China.

Intertext one: a memorable scene in Tanner's *Jonah* featured a sausage, a cleaver, a metronome, and Marco Perly, a sometime lycée teacher with a keen sense of pedagogy. After being introduced to his prospective students as "your new history teacher," Perly opened a suitcase from which he removed a length of sausage, a cutting block, a cleaver, and a metronome. Telling his students never to forget that his father was a butcher and that his mother sang light opera, Perly set the sausage on the block and flourished the cleaver before asking for a volunteer to cut the sausage in time with the metronome he set into motion. As a student cut the sausage, Perly began his lesson:

MARCO: So these are the pieces of history. What should we call them? Hours? Decades? Centuries? It's all the same and it never stops. The sausage is eaten with mashed potatoes. Is time a sausage? Darwin thought so, even though the stuffing changed from one end of the sausage to the other. Marx thought that some day everyone would stop eating sausage. Einstein and Max Planck tore the skin off the sausage which from then on lost its shape. What is sausage skin made of?

A GIRL: Pig's intestine.

MARCO: Very good. Now let's look at the sausage that hasn't been cut up yet. You can see the creases, folds. And that's what I want to talk to you about. What are time's folds made of?

In agricultural societies, men believed that time consisted simply of cycles, of seasons. Each winter solstice contained the same moment. An individual grew old of course, but that was simply because he wore himself out: he was the fuel which made the machine of the seasons go. Capitalism will supply the idea of time-as-highway. Highway of the sun, the highway of progress. The idea of progress was that the conquerors hadn't simply won the battle, but that they had been chosen and designated because they were superior beings. Their superiority would inevitably span the cycles and the seasons. It transformed them into corkscrews of which they, the conquerors, were the tip. And with that tip they opened the bottles of the lesser cultures, one after another. They drank until their thirst was quenched and tossed aside the bottles, assuring themselves that they would break. This was a new kind of violence. The arrow or the sword had previously killed, but what killed now was the verdict of history. The history of the conquerors, of course. With this new violence arose a new fear among the conquerors: the fear of the past, fear of the lesser beings in their broken bottles.

Ah! If only the past could one day overtake the conquerors, it would certainly show as little pity as they themselves had shown. During the nineteenth century, this fear of the past was transformed rationally into scientific law. Time then became a road without curves. The length of the road was a terrifying abstraction, but abstractions don't take revenge. From that point on, the thinkers of the nineteenth century opted for the fear of thought while eliminating the fear of the savage and his arrows. And their roads had boundaries. Absolutely regular. Millions of years divided into eras, into dates, into days, and into hours of work to punch in on the time-clock. Like sausage.[1]

The rhetorical force of Perly's demonstration derived from metaphors of machine and highway that he used to contrast different conceptions of duration and—for those who believed in progress—prophecy. The sausage, cleaver, and metronome served as props that Perly used to sensitize his students to the purposeful fashioning at work in the writing of history. To this end, these techniques and props enhanced the authority of historical narrative as an account of real events in a lived past with the combined authorities of form and rhetoric that were often seen in opposition to it. Perly's efforts to stage his historical account as a self-conscious performance endowed reality with a form that made it desirable by imposing on its processes the formal coherency that stories alone possessed.[2]

Perly also cast his lesson as a critique of the educational system by engaging his status as an individual—either civil servant or private agent for hire—authorized to transmit accounts deemed acceptable to produce and regulate knowledge of the past. This was, in fact, the authority against which Perly's lesson was meant to mobilize resistance. The "idea of progress" model from the perspective of the victor likewise staged a vision of history that equated power with necessity: "By conceiving history as a closed homogeneous, rectilinear, continuous course of events, the traditional historiographic gaze is a priori, formally, the gaze of 'those who have won it': it sees history as a closed continuity of 'progression' leading to the reign of those who rule today."[3] Ever the good dialectician, Perly set this top-down conception against a redemptive history from the perspective of the oppressed.

Finally, the "history as sausage" metaphor raised questions concerning available options for fashioning a historical narrative removed from the

Rankian goal of describing the past "as it really was." In such terms, the history lesson in *Jonah* did not merely enumerate multiple and conflicting conceptions of time; it also pointed to Perly's ambition to have his students see continuities between past and present in the immediacy of the current moment as well as the possibilities that these continuities held for change in the future. Adept in his role as pedagogue, Perly expressed this desire by provoking his students with reference to determinist biology:

> In an acorn are already present the creases which will give the oak its shape. What you are, each one of you, was already present in the chromosomes at the moment of my conception. Excuse me, your conception. I'm not a determinist, but in your first cell there was a message which you are now in the process of reading. There are things which make holes in time.
>
> And the holes line up perfectly. [He draws.] You can run a spit right through. Don't forget that my father is a butcher. Time bends so that the holes can coincide. And why is one never a prophet in one's own land? Because the prophets get only halfway through the holes, like this. [He pantomimes.]
>
> They exist between times. No one understood much about Diderot until an entire generation screamed "Monster" at Freud. That much time was needed to pass through the hole. The holes prophets make for looking into the future are the same through which historians later peer at the stuff of the past. Look at them leering through the holes dug by Jean-Jacques Rousseau in order to explain the eighteenth century to us. (42)

Perly provoked his students because he wanted them to do more than enact the message imposed on them by heredity. In fact, he wanted them to resist and overcome it. Reading the past was, then, not just a matter of decoding the genetic message in each of us. It was—or should be—active and disruptive because it should always strive to appropriate what was given in the present and, in particular, at those moments that made holes in time. Perly saw his role as a history teacher to prepare his students for those moments and, if necessary, show them how to make such holes on their own. This conception of history as visionary and transformative depended in large part on a capacity to recognize how the specific moment lined up the holes of time and what, in turn, this recognition made possible. For Perly, the progression from vision to action was liberating, even when its full expression was belated, as in the example of Diderot "seen" (that is, understood) through Freud.

Intertext two: some four hundred years before the history lesson in Tanner's *Jonah*, in 1596, Matteo Ricci wrote *Treatise on Mnemonic Arts* to teach the Chinese a system of mental constructs for storing human knowledge with a view toward access and retrieval. As described by Jonathan Spence, Ricci devised what he called his memory palace by assigning to every item to be stored an image and a position where the image would remain until it was recalled by an act of memory. Because the system worked only if the images stayed in their assigned places, it seemed desirable that the storage positions be real places so well known that they could never be forgotten. Ricci, however, questioned this prejudice toward the real when he argued that only by expanding the number of locations and the corresponding images they were capable of storing could memory be strengthened: "Therefore the Chinese should struggle with the difficult task of creating fictive places, or mixing the fictive with the real, fixing them permanently in their minds by constant practice and review so that at last the fictive spaces become 'as if real, and can never be erased.'"[4]

I have chosen the examples of Marco Perly and Matteo Ricci to address what I see as the crossovers between memory and history in questions raised over the past twenty years with regard to a recent past—surrounding Vichy, France in the 1930s, and the Holocaust—whose status remains contested. The evident differences of time and place between sixteenth-century China and post-1968 Europe (Tanner's *Jonah* was set in and around Geneva, along the French-Swiss border) are tempered by a number of parallels. In particular, the assertion of the fictive within the real that Ricci was reported by Spence as having prescribed underscored the extent to which memory in its collective expressions was always a construct. Were he to build his memory palace today, it is likely that Matteo Ricci would use a computer equipped with as much memory as possible. If so, he would be well advised to remember that all hard disks eventually crash and erase the files they have stored. Even more pointedly, because files can also be deleted by command at any time, erasure is always an alternate to storage.

This last point should not be taken lightly. For although Ricci counted on constant practice and review to ensure that memory would be permanent ("never be erased"), the conception of memory on which he built his palace seemed not to have accounted adequately for forgetting. Concerning the 1930s and Vichy, ongoing disclosures suggest that sustained inquiry will result not just in a sense of how France's recent past has been constructed and remembered, but also in an account of how and why this past might have been forgotten. In such terms, a necessary supplement to the interplay between history and memory points to the imperative—"Never forget"—invoked by Holocaust survivors as well as by Blanchot in *L'écriture du désastre* and echoed by Kundera in *The Book of Laughter and Forgetting* as the human struggle against forgetting. What, then, is at stake in this struggle in relation to the study of France since 1930?

Night and Day

Primo Levi tried at a number of points in *The Drowned and the Saved* to convey what he described as the intricate and stratified microcosm of life in the death camps. His attempts marked the ongoing resistance—internal as well as external—he encountered in contending with the force of a *Lager* phenomenon he considered of fundamental importance to the historian, the psychologist, and the sociologist. The specific aspect of life in the *Lager* he sought to convey occurred as an initial shock from which few prisoners recovered: "There is not a prisoner who does not remember . . . his amazement at the time: the first threats, the first insults, the first blows came not from the SS but from other prisoners, from 'colleagues,' from those mysterious personages who nevertheless wore the same striped tunic that they, the new arrivals, had just put on."[5] The "colleagues" in question, known as *Kapos,* were prisoner functionaries who had agreed to collaborate with camp authorities. Some did so because they believed it might prolong their lives, others to protect their fellow inmates.

Levi did not judge the motives of the *Kapos* and even asserted that many acted with the best of intentions. He did, however, note that whether or not they realized it, those who agreed to serve as *Kapos* divided the prisoner population against itself through a two-tiered system of rank and privilege. The system was, in fact, an illusion of convenience invented by the camp authorities for whom the *Kapos* intervened while remaining as susceptible as all other prisoners to the realities of incarceration. This initial breaking of solidarity among prisoners made the *Lager* experience all the more demeaning. Like Camus's Clamence in *The Fall,* the *Kapos* exercised a double profession within a gray band and zone that radiated from regimes based on terror and obsequiousness (Levi, 58). Complex and subtle, this zone marked a symbolic borderline where the roles of masters and servants simultaneously overlapped and diverged.

A figurative gray zone continues to surround the articles on politics and literature that appeared under Maurice Blanchot's name in *Le Rempart, Combat,* and *L'Insurgé* between 1932 and 1937. As in the *Lager* phenomenon Levi described in *The Drowned and the Saved,* ambiguity confuses those who seek to judge the early writings. A figurative zone is nonetheless discernible in a writing practice that, in the words of Roger Laporte, divides between postwar texts produced as an *écriture diurne* (daytime writing) and an earlier *écriture nocturne* (nighttime writing) for which Blanchot has been reluctant to account except in the most general terms. Laporte's model of two writings is taken from a keynote lecture he delivered in January 1993 at an international conference on Blanchot held at the Institut Français du Royaume-Uni in London. Later at the same conference, Laporte read a brief letter written by Blanchot in response to a question from Laporte concerning a paper scheduled to be read by Jeffrey Mehlman. The title of Mehlman's paper contained the name of Charles-Augustin Sainte-Beuve and the date March 10, 1942; "La Politique de Sainte-Beuve" (Sainte-Beuve's politics) had appeared in the March 10, 1942, issue of *Journal des Débats* as the title of an article that was signed with Blanchot's name.

Because the title of Mehlman's paper puzzled him, Laporte wrote to Blanchot, who claimed not to understand the reference. Laporte obtained a photocopy of the article and sent it to Blanchot, from whom he received a reply that Blanchot asked Laporte to read at the conference following the presentation of Mehlman's paper. Here is my translation of the letter in full, as distributed at the conference with Blanchot's permission on Friday, January 8, 1993:

December 24, 1992

My dear Roger Laporte,

Thank you for having sent this text to me (and for having located it). I had kept no memory whatsoever of it and doubted that it had ever been written.

I proceed directly to the worst. That in March 1942, Maurras is named (well, moreover, nothing calls for such a name), this is loathsome and inexcusable. I know for certain that it does not concern the evil-minded individual of that period, but the distant disciple of Auguste Comte who—thirty years earlier—refers, in imitation of his master, to the observation of social facts foreign to all dogmatism and near to science or a certain kind of science.

It remains that the name of Maurras is an indelible stain and the expression of dishonor. I never approached this man at any moment whatsoever and always at a distance from Action Française, even when Gide went out of curiosity to see him.

What more to say? This text, not simple and indeed tangled, has the merit of remaining outside time and in any case of bringing neither help nor hope to the regime that still ruled and was already crumbling.

Maurice Blanchot

P.S. It is suggested—you know censorship: the one designated here is not the still forceful individual, but the middling positivist condemned by the church.

Blanchot's letter corroborated what Laporte had suggested two nights earlier at the conference when he stated that Blanchot had seemingly forgotten the residual traces of his "nighttime" writing. Forgetting in this instance extended to a point where Blanchot's response when confronted with a wartime text bearing his name set denial ("I had kept no memory whatsoever of it and doubted that it had ever been written") against self-condemnation ("I proceed directly to the worst") along the very lines of terror and obsequiousness Levi had used in *The Drowned and the Saved* to describe the *Lager* experience. Yet if, as Mehlman and others at the London conference suggested, Blanchot judged himself harshly ("the name of Maurras is an indelible stain and the expression of dishonor"), the gesture also precluded closer examination of the article in question. Blanchot wrote in the letter that he had never approached Maurras, yet unless he took this expression in a narrow sense of physical proximity, he seemingly forgot the name and work of Maurras he had invoked in the early ("nighttime") writings such as the review of Curtius's *Essai sur la France* published under his name in *La Revue Française* in 1932.

It was also curious that Blanchot initially forgot his article when his subsequent recall of phases in the career of Maurras was so clear. That such forgetting seemed to border on selection if not suppression made it difficult to take Blanchot's letter to Laporte at face value. Somewhere between allegation and empathy, Blanchot's memory lapse concerning the 1942 text—"I had kept no memory whatsoever of it and doubted that it had ever been written"—recalled the words of Marguerite Duras, who, at the start of *The War: A Memoir,* recounted her discovery, some forty years later, of a diary kept in 1944:

> I found this diary in a couple of exercise books in the blue cupboards at Neauphle-le-Château.
> I have no recollection of having written it.
> I know I did. I know it was I who wrote it. I recognize my own handwriting and the details of the story. I can see the place, the Gare d'Orsay, and the serious comings and goings. But I can't see myself writing the diary. When would I have done so, in what year, at what times of day, in what house? I can't remember.[6]

Finally, it was suitably bizarre that Blanchot should have responded in advance to a paper he would not hear and that his response in French would be transmitted by an envoy who would hear the paper given in a language he would understand only in part. Though many at the conference, including Laporte and Mehlman, claimed to be moved by Blanchot's candor, few seemed ready to explore the early journalism in detail.

Attempts to articulate Blanchot's daytime and nighttime writings have consistently been hindered by his refusal of requests to allow the early texts to be reprinted. On the order of what Levi noted about the *Kapos,* uncertainty concerning Blanchot's early writings has divided his corpus from within, turning black and white . . . to gray. While such irresolution connotes duplicity and at least a hint of suspicion, resistance to closer scrutiny of the interwar and wartime texts remains high. Many readers still await a final word or statement from Blanchot that might save them from confronting an aspect of his writings they would prefer to dismiss or even "forget." Rumor has it that in 1986 Blanchot wrote a seven-page text on the early ("nighttime") texts for inclusion in a forthcoming study by Jean-Luc Nancy and Philippe Lacoue-Labarthe. Yet even if the rumors were true, such a text would resolve the matter of Blanchot's nighttime writings only in the narrow sense of "working through" (*Wiedergutmachung*) used in reference to the *Historikerstreit* in Germany. The real question raised by the early writings is, as the French say, "not there" ("la question n'est pas là") precisely because what matters is not simply what Blanchot may or may not disclose about what he did or did not do and write in the 1930s. Instead of looking to project accountability directly onto the figure of the individual, what needs to be resolved beyond the individual is the wider conception of culture and national identity within which the interwar writings were inscribed. To concentrate on the figure of Blanchot personalizes the issue by underscoring individual agency in ways that risk missing the wider implications of aftereffect of which Blanchot's writings are but one expression.

Memory in the Archive

Like Primo Levi in *The Drowned and the Saved,* Lawrence Langer concluded in *Holocaust Testimonies* that even when memory succeeded in identifying past traumas, they did not disappear. If, then, neither memory nor the passage of time healed those who had suffered unjustly, what might be gained by looking back at a complex and painful past? Debate over Vichy has raised this question in new forms by testing alternative approaches to interwar and wartime France within contexts of pathology and cure for which received accounts of the period have proven less and less adequate. Langer's analyses also showed that recall neither healed nor erased the "double profession" that afflicted fictional and real-life survivors from the children of the mid-century invoked by Camus's Clamence to those who recorded their experiences for the video cameras at the Fortunoff Archive at Yale. If recall could not mend the broken identities of those who had survived the traumas of the Holocaust and/or the *Lager*, of what good (*à quoi bon*) was it? Without dismissing memory outright, what adjustment or shift might it promote in the wake of an extended condition of trauma?

For Alice Kaplan, Vichy has evolved from an object of memory to a memory industry positing a new object and a new kind of labor:

> As memory retreats from its object, a new kind of work on the war is born. It can't approach its subject directly. It worries as much about what it doesn't as about what it does have to say. It speaks sometimes not about the war but in spite of it. It wants to know not what happened in that war, but how it was desired; how it was prepared in language, what use it is to speak of it now. Its critical idiom, its analytical tools were sharpened on the mass culture forms of the fifties and sixties. It knows that World War II itself is not just a memory, but a memory industry, with enormous political value. Bitburg, Gaza, Faurisson, Le Pen: by necessity it thinks of World War II not in terms of memory but of forgetting.[7]

What Kaplan referred to as the new memory industry was likely to elicit resistance among historians unwilling to adopt more self-conscious ("transferential") practices. In addition, there is reason to contend that what Kaplan called the "enormous political value" of the emergent memory industry has imposed scandal as a condition of response to the gaps and inconsistencies in received accounts of the Holocaust and Vichy that have become increasingly open to question. On its own, the impulse among historians to reexamine existing accounts of the past is neither exceptional nor suspect. Heightened attention to method reveals how inquiry occurs and changes. Because most practicing historians still consider these processes as internal to their profession, debate still tends to be grounded on conceptions of inquiry cast in an applied (problem-solving) mode.

Heightened self-consciousness concerning historical inquiry also implies that assumptions related to method cannot be detached from views on ends and objectives; that is, on how the past is to be used. Stephen Bann has noted the force of convention within a historical poetics that he described as "a set of rhetorical procedures which helped to account for the prodigious development of historical-mindedness ... as well as some of the difficulties which were experienced when the original codes were subjected to an ironic second view."[8] Earlier in *The Clothing of Clio,* Bann had studied how the evolution of historical-mindedness in nineteenth-century France and Britain included not only the specialized concerns of practicing historians but representations of the past accessible in museums, monuments, and exhibitions. It is in this more public dimension of memory—from professional groups and institutions to municipal and national sites of commemoration—where debate over the recent past is being staged. What Bann argued in *The Clothing of Clio* concerning nineteenth-century France and Britain holds true as well for the present.

The Memorial of the Deportation built in Paris about ten years ago is located at the eastern tip of the Île de la Cité, near the geographic center of the city. At the bottom of a staircase at the level of the Seine, the memorial evokes the restricted space of incarceration by means of narrow access, barred gates, and cell-like chambers whose walls list the names of those deported under the Vichy regime. The memorial is heightened by a grave honoring an unknown Jew, including an eternal flame like those found in all places of Jewish worship. The resemblance of this memorial to that of the unknown French soldier beneath the Arch of Triumph at the Place Charles de Gaulle, several miles west at the far end of the Champs-Elysées is uncanny in its overlaying of remembrance concerning a period that many in France would prefer to forget. A further irony involves the proximity of the deportation memorial to the Notre-Dame de Paris Cathedral. Is it simply a coincidence that the site chosen to remember the deportations under Vichy was located within clear view of one of the country's major cathedrals, whose name honored the cult of the Holy Mother with which France's national identity has long been associated on the nationalist right?

Irresolution continues to situate debate on Vichy within a wide public sphere. In 1992, the Comité du Vel d'Hiv pressed for official remembrance of the police roundup of Jews in Paris on July 16–17, 1942. The group took its name from the Vélodrome d'Hiver, a domed stadium where many of those arrested in the raids were held pending transfer to camps within and outside France. Remembrance in this instance was anything but joyous. The Vel d'Hiv group militated to have President François Mitterrand acknowledge that the persecution and deportation of Jews during the Occupation resulted from policies implemented by the Etat Français in conjunction with the German occupying forces. Mitterrand refused the group's requests by reasoning that the Etat Français and French Republic were not identical. Because the Resistance, the de Gaulle government, and the Fourth Republic had been founded on a refusal of the Etat Français, further acknowledgment of the illegitimate regime or recognition of its actions was unnecessary. Was this sophistry or patriotism? Mitterrand's refusal to meet the request from the Comité du Vel d'Hiv was seen by many as an open provocation. The perception was heightened four months later when Mitterrand ordered that an Armistice Day wreath be placed in his name on the tomb of Maréchal Philippe Pétain whom he claimed to be honoring as French military hero of World War I rather than as leader of the Etat Français.

In February 1993, Mitterrand finally signed a decree stating that victims of racist and anti-Semitic persecution in France between 1940 and 1944 would be remembered every year in ceremonies throughout the country on July 16. Commemorative monuments would be erected at the Vélodrome d'Hiver and plaques placed in every French *département*. Responding to the decree, Serge Klarsfeld praised what he saw as an explicit and solemn condemnation of Vichy's racist crimes and added that tolerance was "all the more necessary" in light of the shameful outbursts of racism, anti-Semitism, and xenophobia throughout Europe.[9]

In Los Angeles, the Museum of Tolerance opened in early 1993 with a mission to provide insight into the causes and history of social discord fueled by racial prejudice. Funded by the Simon Wiesenthal Center, the museum was conceived to educate the public about the varieties of racism and prejudice that have led to acts of atrocity in the modern United States of America, Cambodia, and Latin America. A significant part of the museum was devoted to the center's holdings of data on the Holocaust, with other exhibits devoted to the beating of Rodney King in 1991 and the riots a year later following the acquittal in California state court of four Los Angeles police officers charged with the beating.

That these two gestures of collective remembrance occurred within a week of each other was coincidental. Of different scales, in different places, and pointing to different pasts, the day of national remembrance in France and the Museum of Tolerance in Los Angeles nonetheless transposed coincidence into meaningfulness when I came across these two gestures as reported in the *New York Times* on February 5 and 10, 1993: the former was a news item and the latter a feature.

From Levi and Blanchot to the writing of history, a third gray zone extends to the basic concept of the archive as the sum of written materials such as deeds, records, proceedings, letters, and other texts taken as traces of a certain past. Archives can be public or private: that is, established either in conjunction with agencies, administrations, enterprises, and private entities charged with overseeing public services or by a nonpublic group or individual.[10] Never simply an inert or preconstituted mass of documents, the archive also presupposes the archivist represented by synecdoche as a hand that collects, classifies, and even conserves documents with a view toward future usage.[11]

The temporal difference conveyed by the prospect of future use (*usage éventuel*) underscores the assumption that the archive is neither transparent nor innocent, but always charged with a plurality of possible meanings. In this sense, the archive results not just from the archivist's passion, but from an excess of papers promoting an interplay of association and chance.[12] From too many papers to too many meanings, the archival process occurs as a figurative detective work of deciphering and interpretation whose yield is a "bit of truth" (Kaplan, "Working in the Archives," 115). Arlette Farge wrote along similar lines when she broke down the "bit of truth" yielded by archival work into multiple units she referred to as pieces of ethics (*des morceaux d'éthique*). This transition from truth to ethics echoed Michel Foucault's notion that although the archive itself did not speak the truth, there was invariably some truth (*de la vérité*) in what it said. To work in the archive was, then, not simply to recast a certain past as a "bit of truth." It also meant learning to read both what the archive disclosed and how it disclosed it: "The real [le réel] of the archive becomes not only the trace but also the arrangement of figures of reality; and the archive always maintains an infinite number of relations to the real"(Farge, 41). Working in the archive —perhaps also working the archive in the sense of making it work—reconstructs a "bit of truth" not simply by relating the past directly to the real, but by accepting that relation as one among a number of possible constructs. As a result, the interplay of "bit of truth" (Kaplan) and "piece of ethics" (Farge) underscores the extent to which the transition from archive to account points to the ethical grounding asserted by historical inquiry in a specific time and place.

More recently, Kaplan provided an apt example of such grounding when she described the ironies that surfaced during the Klaus Barbie trial in 1987.[13] A first irony divided the prosecution between witnesses who spoke on behalf of Resistance members whom Barbie was said to have tortured and others who spoke for prisoners allegedly deported under his orders. It was thus almost another crime in itself, Kaplan wrote, that the attempt to bring Barbie to trial should have muddled rather than clarified the basis on which judgment was to have occurred. The ironies in the case were not lost on Barbie's defense lawyer, Jacques Vergès, who argued that if his client were to be tried for crimes against humanity, it followed that France too ought to be charged with similar crimes committed in its name in Indochina and Algeria. Openly inflammatory, Vergès was audacious and the implications of his counterclaims dizzying.

Displacements of time and place—from the 1940s to the 1980s and from France and Germany to Bolivia (and back to France)—turned the proceedings at Lyon into a media spectacle that never attained the full accounting of events for the historical record. Kaplan rightly remarked that although the Barbie trial revived fragments of significant trauma, the catharsis and cure it produced were only partial. In sum, the mixed results of the Barbie trial restaged earlier corruptions of justice during the purge of writers and intellectuals following the Liberation and, fifty years earlier, at the first two Dreyfus trials.

Ambivalence surrounding Vichy remains too much a part of France's postwar identity to be overcome all at once. Beyond the short-term aftereffects of belatedness and scandal, what it has taken almost fifty years to disclose may require an equivalent period of additional analysis for which recent inquiry has set the agenda. The high visibility of recent debate surrounding the Holocaust has often bordered on excess. Geoffrey Hartman has rightly warned that we need to recognize the risk of an "information sickness" in the speed and quantity of data that impinge on and overwhelm us as individuals.[14] Yet if, like Hartman, we note the risk of a desensitizing trend that weakens the sense of reality by continually raising the threshold of personal response, this risk strikes me as necessary in light of the silence and repression that preceded it. Technology cannot be the culprit here when it forces us to contend, even belatedly, with ambivalence and irresolution that are all too easily displaced (hidden? forgotten?) in a postmodernity where historical specificity and affect are seemingly flattened. Or, as formulated by Fredric Jameson and others, the concept of the postmodern can best be understood paradoxically as an attempt to think historically in an age that has forgotten how to think historically.[15]

Closing Time

My readings in chapters 5 and 6 have sought to show the extent to which the binding of literature and politics in Blanchot's articles in *Le Rempart, Combat,* and *L'Insurgé* was at odds with the postwar conception of literary space from which history and politics were more or less elided. This elision is all the more significant because the interwar articles disclosed a political culture of the nonconformist right wing whose impact on wartime and postwar literature and philosophy in France remains undisclosed. Resistance to this political culture persists as a concern that silence is preferable to disclosure—even oppositional disclosure—that might be appropriated to legitimize prejudice grounded in national or ethnic difference.

Among historians of recent modernity, belatedness and irresolution obtain in the case of Blanchot to the long-term effects of a literary signature that remains divided from within. In more personal terms, they preclude understanding of how Blanchot seemingly evolved from a strong nationalist and anti-Popular Front stance in the mid-1930s texts he wrote for *Le Rempart, Combat,* and *L'Insurgé* to the position he took some twenty years later to protest French actions against self-rule in Algeria. The question of how to place Blanchot's interwar writings within his total corpus inevitably raises wider questions of how to temper the desire to assert a stable identity with the discontinuity imposed by the scandalous disclosure of internal difference. Discontinuity here is removed from the normative value often granted to stability, much as divided subjectivity is often seen as an effect or condition of language that is itself subject to ambivalence and plurality.

In *L'Entretien infini,* Blanchot addressed the imposition of discontinuity as an effect of writing when he asked how one might write in such a way that the continuity of writing allowed interruption as meaning—and rupture as form—to intervene fundamentally. The question went well beyond immediate effects of language and style. Blanchot invoked discontinuity as the mark or sign of an entirely different relation that challenged dialectics and ontology to raise a question that was "not one of being" (*The Infinite Conversation,* 10). Yet viewed from another perspective, whatever one might discern in Blanchot's writings—whatever "he" has written in *Le pas au-delà, L'écriture du désastre,* or elsewhere concerning Auschwitz or Heidegger—does not compensate for the sense of unresolved trauma from which, along the lines of what Levi and Langer concluded about surviving victims of the death camps, there was neither release nor redemption. As in clinical cases, identity that has undergone trauma can remain seemingly unified except for brief periods of scandalous breakdown, at which point identity either dissolves or reforms.

Freud argued in an essay written in 1917 that the withdrawal of affective attachment from a loved object following its death, abandonment, or disappearance occurred according to two patterns of grieving that he described in terms of mourning and melancholia. In the latter, the acceptance of irreparable loss resulted from a process of mourning (*Trauerarbeit*) during which the existence of the lost object was psychically prolonged while "each single one of the memories and expectations in which the libido [was] bound to the object [was] brought up and hyper-cathected."[16] The process was painful, but it was a means by which the ego worked through the impoverishment of the world resulting from the loss of the loved object. In melancholy, this loss was equated with loss in the ego by means of a narcissistic identification in which the loved object served as a mirror of the ego's sense of self and power. Melancholic response to loss occurred as a severe and often suicidal depression following a shattered fantasy of omnipotence. Associated by Freud with the primary narcissism and infancy, melancholy in the adult was regressive and all the more difficult to work through because it repressed the separateness of the lost object: "In mourning it is the world which has become poor and empty; in melancholia, it is the ego itself" (246).

Though Freud linked mourning and melancholy to divergent identity relations between the ego in its separateness—or lack of separateness—from the loved object, grief was in most instances a combination of the two. Yet if (as Adorno argued concerning Germany more than thirty years ago) the scope of identity were enlarged from singular to plural and from individual to collective, Freud's model could be seen as showing that what is referred to as incomplete mourning (*un deuil inachevé*) surrounding Vichy may, in fact, result from a collective identification dominated by melancholy. Especially because Freud cast melancholy as a more primitive mode of bereavement than mourning, what might be taken for incomplete mourning is perhaps not yet any kind of mourning at all.

Eric Santner has argued in his brilliant study of postwar German film that before Germans could begin to mourn for the victims of the Third Reich, they needed to shatter the specular relations they had maintained with Hitler and the Nazi myth of community: "In a word, a sense of self would first have to be reconstituted on the ruins of his narcissism."[17] In the case of Blanchot, the postwar texts may, in fact, extend an ongoing identification with France's wartime and interwar pasts whose mode of occurrence was closer to melancholy than to mourning. If melancholic grieving indeed motivated disclosure, it would account as well for fragmentary writing as a textual corollary of an unstable identity damaged by an early trauma from which full recovery—through a completed process of mourning—had not yet occurred.

In suggesting this I mean less to analyze or judge Blanchot the individual than to follow the lead of Tanner's Marco Perly, who wanted his students to look through the holes of time that lined up at a specific moment of insight.

The break with noncontextual approaches toward literature and philosophy in theorizing of culture over the past decade has shaken perceptions of difference concerning gender, race, religion, class, age, and ethnicity as they affect the historical agency of the individual. Whether deeply tainted (as in the documented French examples of Céline, Brasillach, and Drieu La Rochelle) or not, the attribution of individual agency remains grounded in grand narratives of culture and history whose coherence has become less and less compelling. It is this grounding and the periodizing of modernity to which it points that no longer hold.

Much as Rousso's *Vichy Syndrome* has succeeded in challenging received ideas by breaking down the postwar debate over the memory of Vichy into four phases, inquiry into France in the 1930s should disclose what has been left unseen and unsaid in earlier accounts. The larger project I have in mind involves source work on materials to which, for one reason or another, previous access was unavailable. To this work on and with sources such a project might add a critical ambition to demystify received opinions concerning taintedness and greatness, if not also the implication that taintedness was somehow always an offshoot of greatness. Debate in the wake of the Farias book has not meant that Heidegger's writings are no longer read. Instead, they are no longer read as they were read before; that is, contortedly and in order to avoid addressing aspects of his work that previous readers had (for whatever reason) not engaged. Critical revision as it has evolved surrounding Heidegger helps to clarify how analysis of Blanchot's journalism of the 1930s might—even belatedly—extend current debates over Vichy some fifty years after the fact.

Notes

Unless otherwise indicated, all translations from French and German sources are my own.

Introduction

1. Stephen Bann, "Analyzing the Discourse of History," in *The Inventions of History: Essays on the Representation of the Past*, 33. Along similar lines, Jean-Pierre Azéma has transposed Roland Barthes's distinction between *écrivains* and *écrivants* into *historiens* and *historiants*, defining the latter as "those who are not professional historians, but who have directed their works toward archives" (Jean-Pierre Azéma, "Vichy et la mémoire savante: quarante-cinq ans d'historiographie," in Jean-Pierre Azéma and François Bédarida, eds., *Vichy et les Français*, 23).

2. For a critical exposition of counterhistory related to apologetic-polemical ("revisionist") attempts to deny the Nazi genocide of the Jews, see Amos Funkelstein, "History, Counterhistory, and Narrative," in Saul Friedländer, ed., *Probing the Limits of Representation: Nazism and the "Final Solution,"* 66–81.

3. See Jean-François Lyotard, *The Postmodern Condition: A Report on Knowledge*.

4. Anton Kaes, *From Hitler to Heimat: The Return of History as Film*, ix.

5. Saul Friedländer, *Reflections of Nazism: An Essay on Kitsch and Death*, 19. The book was first published in French as *Reflets du nazisme* (Paris: Seuil, 1982).

6. Régine Robin, "The Intellectuals of the 1930s," 1.

7. Frantz Fanon, *The Wretched of the Earth*, 101.

8. Kwame Anthony Appiah, *In My Father's House: Africa in the Philosophy of Culture*, 6.

9. Gayatri Chakravorty Spivak, "Neocolonialism and the Secret Agent of Knowledge," 226.

10. See Nicholas B. Dirks, ed., *Colonialism and Culture*.

11. Robert Young, *White Mythologies: Writing History and the West*, 1.

12. Maxim Silverman, *Deconstructing the Nation: Immigration, Racism, and Citizenship in Modern France*, 34.

13. Tahar Ben Jelloun, *Hospitalité française: racisme et immigration maghrébine*, 14.

14. The most notable exceptions to such oversight are Michael Holland and Patrick Rousseau's listings of Blanchot's journalism of the 1930s in *Gramma* 3/4 and 5 (1976), and Jeffrey Mehlman, "Blanchot at *Combat:* Of Literature and Terror."

15. Michel Surya, "Présentation du projet de *Revue Internationale*," *Lignes* 11 (1990): 161; emphasis in the original. I am grateful to Nelly Halzen for pointing out that Surya had referred to Blanchot's early writings in the first edition of his *Georges Bataille, la mort à l'oeuvre* (Paris: Séguier, 1988). His silence in 1990 thus strikes me as all the more questionable.

16. Dominick LaCapra, *History and Criticism*, 123.

17. Eugen Weber, *My France: Politics, Culture, Myth*, 7.

18. Ibid., 10.

19. Alice Kaplan, *French Lessons: A Memoir*, 106.

20. Eric Conan and Daniel Lindenberg, "Que faire de Vichy?," 11.

21. Tony Judt, *Past Imperfect: French Intellectuals, 1944–1956*, 8.

22. Gayatri Chakravorty Spivak, "Introduction. Subaltern Studies: Deconstructing Historiography," 4.

23. Joan Wallach Scott, *Gender and the Politics of History*, 2.

24. Michel Foucault, "Nietzsche, Genealogy, History," 95.

25. Maurice Blanchot, "Les Intellectuels en question," 5.

26. The prime source remains Michael R. Marrus and Robert O. Paxton, *Vichy France and the Jews* (New York: Schocken, 1983). Current studies include André Kaspi, *Les Juifs pendant l'Occupation* (Paris: Seuil, 1991) and Susan Zuccotti, *The Holocaust, the French, and the Jews* (New York: Basic Books, 1993).

27. Quoted in Philippe Rochette, "L'Etat français, celui de Vichy, n'était pas la République," 8.

28. Primo Levi, *The Drowned and the Saved*, 24.

29. Conan and Lindenberg, "Que faire de Vichy?," 11.

One. Vichy as Paradigm of Contested Memory

1. Geoffrey H. Hartman, *Minor Prophecies: The Literary Essay in the Culture Wars*, 4.

2. See Sigmund Freud, *Project for a Scientific Psychology*, which dates from 1895. I had already considered *Nachträglichkeit* in relation to Blanchot's 1983 text *Après coup* (whose title translates freely into English as "afterblow" or even "aftershock") when I came across separate references to the term in Hans Kellner, *Language and Historical Representation: Getting the Story Crooked* (Madison: University of Wisconsin Press, 1989), 305, and Dominick LaCapra, *Soundings in Critical Theory* (Ithaca: Cornell University Press, 1989), 34–35.

3. James E. Young, *The Texture of Memory: Holocaust Memorials and Meaning*, xi.

4. Gregory L. Ulmer, "The Post-Age."

5. The openness to recent theoretical ferment that attracted so many literary scholars to the new historicism should not conceal the fact that its relation to literary theory remains unresolved and that, in the words of Stephen J. Greenblatt, it is more of a trajectory or practice than a doctrine. See Stephen J. Greenblatt, "Towards a Poetics of Culture," in *Learning to Curse: Essays in Early Modern Culture* (New York: Routledge, 1990), 146, as well as Greenblatt's introductory comments, especially on page 3.

6. Jean-François Lyotard, *The Postmodern Condition: A Report on Knowledge*, 79.

7. See Carlo Ginzburg, "Checking the Evidence: The Judge and the Historian," 91, and also my discussion later in this chapter of Michel de Certeau's reference to the trope of enthymeme.

8. Jean-François Lyotard, *Heidegger and "the jews,"* 27. Along the same lines, see Jean Laplanche, "Notes on Afterwardness," in *Seduction, Translation, Drives* (London: Institute of Contemporary Art, 1992), 217–23.

9. Jean-Marc Parisis, "Blanchot et ses voisins," 55; emphasis in the original.

10. François Poirié, *Emmanuel Lévinas*.

11. Diane Rubenstein, *What's Left? The Ecole Normale Supérieure and the Right*, 15.

12. Henry Rousso, *The Vichy Syndrome: History and Memory in France since 1944*.

13. Pierre Sorlin, *European Cinemas, European Societies: 1939–1990*, 78.

14. Henry Rousso, "Avant-propos à la deuxième édition," *Le Syndrome de Vichy de 1944 à nos jours* (Paris: Seuil "Points Histoire," 1990), 21–22. This foreword does not appear in Goldhammer's translation.

15. Rousso cites the Truffaut passage as it appears in Annette Insdorf's *Indelible Shadows: Film and the Holocaust* (New York: Vintage, 1983). I prefer Truffaut's own words, in *The Films of My Life*, 304. Anton Kaes, in *From Hitler to Heimat: The Return of History as Film*, describes a scene in Margaretha von Trotta's 1981 film *Marianne and Juliane* in which a female character based on the German terrorist Gudrun Ensslin is shown as a child watching footage of the concentration camp scenes in *Night and Fog*. The girl is so horrified by the images that she vomits. Kaes writes that many among the generation of Germans born at the end of World War II saw the atrocities of the Nazi regime as *an ineradicable stigma*. Accordingly, they believed that their

violent opposition to the Federal Republic "offered *belatedly* the resistance that their parents had failed to offer" (Kaes, 24, my emphasis).

16. For fuller discussions of these issues, see Serge Klarsfeld and Henry Rousso, "Histoire et justice" and Pierre Truche, "La Notion de crime contre l'humanité." Both texts appeared in the May 1992 issue of *Esprit*.

17. Habermas uses the expression in an article published in *Die Zeit* on May 24, 1985, and later translated by Thomas Levin as "Defusing the Past: A Politico-Cultural Tract," 44. Susan Neiman provides a more personalized account in *Slow Fire: Jewish Notes from Berlin* (New York: Schocken, 1992), 14–16, before concluding in succession (305) that there has been no *Vergangenheitsverarbeitung*, that there has been one, and that it is obscene and worthless but better than nothing. My thanks to Kathleen Newman for pointing me to Neiman's book.

18. Charles S. Maier, *The Unmasterable Past: History, Holocaust, and German National Identity*, ix.

19. Theodor W. Adorno, "What Does Coming to Terms with the Past Mean?," 115.

20. Ernest Renan, "What Is a Nation?"

21. Young, *The Texture of Memory*, 21. The German term appeared in an earlier version of a chapter of Young's book, published as "The Counter-Monument: Memory against Itself in Germany Today," *Critical Inquiry* 18 (1992): 269.

22. Lawrence L. Langer, *Holocaust Testimonies: The Ruins of Memory*, 83.

23. Milan Kundera, *The Book of Laughter and Forgetting*, 159.

24. These categories and examples are taken from Marc Ferro, "Les Oublis de l'histoire." Ferro also describes an additional kind of forgetting related to those who are martyred at the hands of the enemy during times of war and crusade.

25. After *The Nasty Girl* won a major prize at the 1990 Berlin Film Festival, controversy over the film remained so intense that Verhoeven made a documentary about Rosmus, entitled *The Girl and the City: What Really Happened?* for German television.

26. Lest my example be seen as too topical, Sonja's experience echoes the following passage from a 1959 review by Fernand Braudel of Otto Brunner's *Neue Wege der Sozialgeschichte:* "All doors seem to me good when crossing the multiple threshold of history. Unfortunately, none of us can know them all. The historian first opens the door with which he is most familiar. But if he seeks to see as far as possible, he must necessarily find himself knocking at another door, and then another" [from Braudel, "On a Concept of Social History," in *On History*, trans. Sarah Matthews (Chicago: University of Chicago Press, 1980), 131].

27. Saul Friedländer, "The Road to Vichy," 32.

28. Lynn Hunt, "History as Gesture; or, The Scandal of History," 103.

29. Saul Friedländer, *Reflections of Nazism: An Essay on Kitsch and Death*, 18.

30. Saul Friedländer, "The End of Innovation? Contemporary Historical Consciousness and the 'End of History,'" 30.

31. Pierre Vidal-Naquet, "Theses on Revision," 304.

32. Pierre Nora, "Between Memory and History: *Les Lieux de mémoire*," 7.

33. Jean-François Lyotard, *The Differend: Phrases in Dispute*, 152.

34. Edmund Husserl, *The Phenomenology of Internal Time Consciousness*, 100.

35. Hayden White, *The Content of the Form: Narrative Discourse and Historical Representation*, 21.

36. Primo Levi, *The Drowned and the Saved*, 11.

37. Pierre Vidal-Naquet, "Le Défi de la Shoah à l'histoire," 71.

38. The passages by Blanchot are from *L'écriture du désastre* (*The Writing of the Disaster*).

39. Albert Camus, *The Fall*, 6.

40. Shoshana Felman, "The Betrayal of the Witness: Camus' *The Fall*," in Shoshana Felman

and Dori Laub, eds., *Testimony: Crises of Witnessing in Literature, Psychoanalysis, and History,* 182.

41. James E. Young, *Writing and Rewriting the Holocaust: Narrative and the Consequences of Interpretation,* 165.

42. See Friedländer's introductory remarks in Saul Friedländer, ed., *Probing the Limits of Representation: Nazism and the "Final Solution,"* especially 5–6.

Two. Revising Martin Heidegger

1. George Steiner, "Heidegger, Again," 36.

2. The set of mainstream objections to Heidegger are taken, respectively, from Allan Megill, *Prophets of Extremity: Nietzsche, Heidegger, Foucault, Derrida,* 108–9; Gerald L. Bruns, *Heidegger's Estrangements: Language, Truth, and Poetry in the Later Writings,* 2; and Anthony Gottlieb, "Heidegger for Fun and Profit," 22.

3. Karsten Harries, "Introduction," in Gunther Neske and Emil Kettering, eds., *Martin Heidegger and National Socialism: Questions and Answers,* xiv.

4. Richard Wolin, *The Politics of Being: The Political Thought of Martin Heidegger,* 113.

5. Theodor Adorno, *The Jargon of Authenticity.*

6. Christopher Fynsk, *Heidegger: Thought and Historicity,* 25.

7. Michael E. Zimmerman, *Heidegger's Confrontation with Modernity: Technology, Politics, Art,* xiv.

8. Emmanuel Lévinas, "Admiration and Disappointment: A Conversation with Philippe Nemo," 149.

9. Jürgen Habermas, "Work and Weltanschauung: The Heidegger Controversy from a German Perspective," *The New Conservatism: Cultural Criticism and the Historians' Debate,* 152.

10. Pierre Bourdieu, *The Political Ontology of Martin Heidegger,* 46; emphasis in the original.

11. The Farías book was first published in French. A German edition appeared in 1988 with a foreword by Habermas; an English translation was published in 1989 by Temple University Press.

12. See Avital Ronell's discussion of Lyotard's *Heidegger and "the jews"* in "The Differends of Man."

13. Jean-Michel Palmier, "Heidegger et le national-socialisme," 410.

14. Richard Wolin, "The French Heidegger Debate," 154.

15. After André Malraux rejected Sartre's text at the Editions Gallimard, presumably for inclusion in the *Nouvelle Revue Française,* Paul Nizan helped to place it in *Bifur,* no. 8 (1931), where Sartre is identified as a "young philosopher . . . at work on a volume of destructive philosophy" [cited in John Gerassi, *Jean-Paul Sartre: Hated Conscience of His Century* (Chicago: University of Chicago Press, 1989), 1:97]. See also Denis Hollier, "Plenty of Nothing: The Translation of Martin Heidegger's 'Was ist Metaphysik?' Appears in the Final Issue of the Avant-Garde Journal *Bifur,*" in Hollier, ed., *A New History of French Literature,* 894–900.

16. Sartre was among the first in France to recognize the potential importance of Heidegger's extension of and departure from Husserlian phenomenology. But even before the *Bifur* translation appeared, Heidegger and Ernst Cassirer had participated in a meeting of French and German philosophers held at Davos, Switzerland, in 1929. In February of the same year, Husserl came to the Sorbonne and gave the lectures on "Einleitung in die transzendentale Phänomenologie" (Introduction to transcendental phenomenology) that came to be known as *The Cartesian Meditations* and that Gabrielle Pfeiffer and Emmanuel Lévinas soon translated into French (Paris: Armand Colin, 1931). Proceedings of the Davos talks have been published as Ernst Cassirer and Martin Heidegger, *Débat sur le kantisme et la philosophie,* Pierre Aubenque, ed. (Paris: Beauchesne, 1972). The "Letter on Humanism" first appeared in November 1945 in

response to a question by Jean Beaufret, Heidegger's strongest postwar advocate among the French. On the reception of German existentialism and phenomenology by the French, see the eyewitness accounts in Beaufret's *De l'existence à Heidegger* (Paris: Vrin, 1982) as well as Lévinas's *En découvrant l'existence avec Husserl et Heidegger* (Paris: Vrin, 1967). For more recent assessments, see the cogent remarks in Martin Jay, *Marxism and Totality: The Adventures of a Concept from Lukács to Habermas* (Berkeley: University of California Press, 1984), and Vincent Descombes, *Modern French Philosophy.*

17. Arnold I. Davidson, "Questioning Heidegger: Opening the Debate," 408.

18. Quotation from editorial preface to *Les Temps Modernes* 4 (January 1946). Eric Weil was among the first to identify a "Heidegger affair" in issue 22 (July 1947) of the same review. For a brief overview of three waves of postwar debate over Heidegger prior to the book by Farías, see Zimmerman, *Heidegger's Confrontation with Modernity,* 280–81. Zimmerman has written perceptively on debate in the wake of Farías in "L'Affaire Heidegger," *Times Literary Supplement* (October 7–13, 1988): 1115–17, and "The Thorn in Heidegger's Side: The Question of National Socialism," *Philosophical Forum* 20 (1989): 326–65.

19. This German book by Ott was published in 1989 in Frankfurt by Campus; the English edition, translated by Allen Blunden, was published by Basic Books in 1993. In English, see the extensive references to secondary sources in German cited by Davidson, "Questioning Heidegger," 408 n. 2; George Steiner, *Heidegger* (New York: Penguin, 1982); and Karsten Harries, "Heidegger as a Political Thinker."

20. François Fédier, *Heidegger: Anatomie d'un scandale,* 30.

21. Herman Rapaport, "Literature and the Hermeneutics of Detection."

22. Thomas Sheehan, "Heidegger and the Nazis" and Paul Gottfried, "Heidegger on Trial" are convincing indictments of the tendentiousness with which Farías relied on existing sources and documentation.

23. My biographic sketch relies in large part on Elisabeth Young-Bruehl, *Hannah Arendt: For the Love of the World.*

24. The German version of the piece was published in 1969; Heidegger was born in September 1889. My references in the text are to the English translation that appeared two years later: Hannah Arendt, "Heidegger at Eighty," *New York Review of Books* (October 1971), reprinted in Neske and Kettering, eds., *Martin Heidegger and National Socialism.*

25. Rüdiger Bubner, *Modern German Philosophy,* 6–7.

26. Richard Rorty, "Taking Philosophy Seriously," 32. Rorty's title echoes the following passage from a discussion of Heidegger's politics by Karsten Harries in which the notion of seriousness takes on a markedly different emphasis: "The more seriously we take Heidegger, the more weight we must give to the path he has cleared, the more carefully we must consider where he is leading us and by what authority" ("Heidegger as a Political Thinker," 307).

27. Christopher Norris, *What's Wrong with Postmodernism: Critical Theory and the Ends of Philosophy,* 222.

28. Luc Ferry and Alain Renaut, *Heidegger and Modernity,* 53–54. I have changed some of the phrasing of Franklin Philip's translation.

29. Philippe Lacoue-Labarthe, *Heidegger, Art, and Politics,* 15. There are two French versions of this text, both entitled *La Fiction du politique: Heidegger, l'art et le nazisme.* The first appeared in February 1987 as a limited edition printed by the University of Strasbourg Press. A revised version (Paris: Christian Bourgois, 1988) included a postscript written after Lacoue-Labarthe read the Farías book while teaching at the University of California at Berkeley. Page citations are from the translation by Chris Turner.

30. Chris Turner's translation of "l'essence du politique moderne" as "the essence of modern politics" understates the differences between *le politique* and *la politique.* If, as Lacoue-Labarthe and Jean-Luc Nancy had argued in *Rejouer le politique,* the former term referred to

"the essence of things political," then "l'essence du politique" was really closer to the more Heideggerian convolution of "the essence of the essence of things political."

31. Hayden White, *The Content of the Form: Narrative Discourse and Historical Representation*, 4.

32. Geoffrey H. Hartman, *Minor Prophecies: The Literary Essay in the Culture Wars*, 10.

Three. White Out

1. The books by Derrida were published by Editions de Galilée. *De l'esprit* has been translated into English as *Of Spirit: Heidegger and the Question*. See also Herman Rapaport, *Heidegger and Derrida: Reflections in Time and Language* (Lincoln: University of Nebraska Press, 1989).

2. Jacques Derrida, "Heidegger, l'enfer des philosophes," 70; my translation.

3. Karl Löwith, *Mein Leben in Deutschland vor und nach 1933: ein Bericht*.

4. Jacques Derrida, "The Time of a Thesis: Punctuations," in Alan Montefiore, ed., *Philosophy in France Today* (New York: Cambridge University Press, 1983), 41; my emphasis.

5. Jacques Derrida, "Like the Sound of the Sea Deep within a Shell: Paul de Man's War," 130.

6. Maurice Blanchot, "Michel Foucault as I Imagine Him," 83. Blanchot's text appeared first as *Michel Foucault tel que je l'imagine*.

7. See, for example, Blanchot's "The Thought from Outside," in *Foucault/Blanchot*, 61–109. The text appeared originally as "La Pensée du dehors," *Critique* 229 (1966): 523–46.

8. The 1951 and 1983 versions were printed by Editions de Minuit. References to the text will cite Paul Auster's translation, *Vicious Circles: Two Fictions and "After the Fact."*

9. Maurice Blanchot, *Death Sentence*, 81.

10. The novel was written in the 1930s and published in France by Gallimard in 1948. Pierre Madaule's *Une Tâche sérieuse?* (Paris: Gallimard, 1973) is an attempt to contend with the deletion of the afterword in 1971.

11. The article first appeared in *MLN* in 1980. A French version in *Tel Quel* 92 (1982) prompted a number of responses, including one from Mathieu Bénézet, "Maurice Blanchot, Céline, et *Tel Quel*," *La Quinzaine Littéraire* 374 (July 1–15, 1982).

12. Kristin Ross, "Two Versions of the Everyday."

13. See, in particular, Mikhail Bakhtin, *Problems in Dostoevsky's Poetics*, 232–36. The loophole technique is evident throughout Beckett's postwar trilogy, especially in *Molloy*. The pertinent difference here involves a trope of irony that Beckett—following Dostoyevsky—uses primarily for comic effects that Blanchot seldom, if ever, executes.

14. Roland Barthes, "The Reality Effect."

15. G. W. F. Hegel, *The Phenomenology of Mind*, 806.

16. Perry Anderson, *A Zone of Engagement*, 283.

17. Vincent Descombes, *Modern French Philosophy*, 27. See also Elisabeth Roudinesco, *Jacques Lacan & Co.: A History of Psychoanalysis in France, 1925–1985*, trans. Jeffrey Mehlman (Chicago: University of Chicago Press, 1990), 134–47.

18. Alexandre Kojève, *Introduction to the Reading of Hegel*, 435; also cited in Descombes, *Modern French Philosophy*, 27.

19. Hegel, *The Phenomenology of Mind*, 807; German terms are taken from G. W. F. Hegel, "Phänomenologie des Geistes," *Gesammelte Werke*, 9:1–526.

20. Hendrik de Man, "An Age of Doom," cited in Peter Dodge, *Hendrik de Man: Socialist Critic of Marxism*, 346.

21. Maurice Blanchot, *La Communauté inavouable*, 40. This and subsequent English translations of this text are my own.

Four. From Reaction to Militancy

1. See, for example, Thomas Sheehan's review of book-length studies by Richard Wolin and Ernst Nolte, "A Normal Nazi," *New York Review of Books* (January 14, 1993): 30–35.

2. Allan Stoekl, *Politics, Writing, Mutilation: The Cases of Bataille, Blanchot, Roussel, Leiris, and Ponge*, xii.

3. Fredric Jameson, *The Political Unconscious: Narrative as a Socially Symbolic Act*, 23.

4. Jean-Louis Loubet del Bayle, *Les Non-conformistes de années 30*, 458–59.

5. Jeffrey Mehlman, "Blanchot at *Combat*," 9.

6. Eric J. Hobsbawm, *Nations and Nationalism since 1780: Programme, Myth, Reality*, 10.

7. Ernst Robert Curtius, *Essai sur la France*, 11–12. These sentences do not appear in Olive Wyon's English translation, and I have taken them from Jacques Benoist-Méchin's French translation. The original German title of the Curtius book, published in Berlin in 1930, was *Einführung in die französische Kultur*. Future quotations will refer to Wyon's translation.

8. Maurice Blanchot, "La Culture française vue par un Allemand," 363.

9. Zeev Sternhell, "The Political Culture of Nationalism," 22.

10. See also Loubet del Bayle's wider discussion of "La Jeune Droite" and its evolution, in *Les Non-conformistes des années 30*, 39–77.

11. The elements of nationalism and race that Blanchot invokes in reference to Germany warrant further study in terms of subsequent appropriations in France. For a start, Blanchot's positions in *Le Rempart* should be compared to those taken by Georges Bataille in his 1933 essay "The Psychological Structure of Fascism," in *Visions of Excess: Selected Writings, 1927–1939*, 137–60.

12. Fritz Stern, "The Burden of Success: Reflections on German Jewry," in *Dreams and Delusions: The Drama of German History*, 97–98.

13. Philippe Lacoue-Labarthe and Jean-Luc Nancy, "Ouverture," in *Rejouer le politique*, 15.

14. Nancy Fraser, *Unruly Practices: Power, Discourse, and Gender in Contemporary Social Theory*, 77, 91.

Five. Under Erasure

1. René Char, "Note à propos d'une deuxième lecture de 'La Perversion essentielle,' in *Le 14 juillet* 1959." Char appears to have mistaken the date of Blanchot's text. All other references I have come across list "La Perversion essentielle" in *Le 14 juillet* 3 (June 1958). See the reprint in *Gramma* 3–4 (1976): 19–27; quotations from this essay are my translations of the *Gramma* text.

2. Zeev Sternhell, *Neither Right nor Left: Fascist Ideology in France*, 244.

3. Alice Kaplan, "The Late Show," in *Reproductions of Banality: Fascism, Literature, and French Intellectual Life*, 162. In addition to the book with Brasillach, Bardèche has written studies of Proust, Flaubert, and, recently, Céline.

4. Géraldi Leroy and Anne Roche, *Les Ecrivains et le Front Populaire*, 62.

5. Jean-Louis Loubet del Bayle, *Les Non-conformistes des années 30*, 67.

6. See also Mehlman's more tendentious discussion of the ties between *Combat* and the Cercle Proudhon, in "Blanchot at *Combat*: Of Literature and Terror," 8–9.

7. Eugen Weber, *Action Française: Royalism and Reaction in Twentieth-Century France*, 510.

8. For an overview of marketing strategies related to interwar cultural weeklies all along the political spectrum, see Claude Estier, *Les Hebdomadaires de gauche*.

9. Dominique Bertin, quoted in Leroy and Roche, *Les Ecrivains et le Front Populaire*, 73.

10. "Témoignage de M. François Walter," in Anne Roche and Christian Tartung, eds., *Des Années trente: groupes et ruptures* (Paris: Editions du Centre National de la Recherche Scientifique, 1986), 71.

11. Jeffrey Mehlman, "Prosopopeia Revisited," 141.

12. Maurice Blanchot, *Faux pas*, 352. Mehlman's remarks on Blanchot are part of his attempt to link deconstruction to collaboration. He has been quoted as claiming that sufficient grounds exist for viewing "the *whole* of deconstruction as a vast amnesty project for the politics of collaboration during World War II" [cited in David Lehman, "Deconstructing de Man's Life," *Newsweek* (February 15, 1988): 63]. For a dissenting response to Mehlman, see Ian Balfour, "'Difficult Reading': De Man's Itineraries," in Werner Hamacher, Neil Hertz, and Thomas Keenan, eds., *Responses: On Paul de Man's Wartime Journalism* (Lincoln: University of Nebraska Press, 1989), 13–44.

13. Jeffrey Mehlman, "Blanchot at *Combat:* Of Literature and Terror," 117.

14. Pascal Fouché, *L'Edition française sous l'Occupation, 1940–1944*, 2:80. Letters from Jean Paulhan to Pierre Drieu La Rochelle also suggest that Blanchot was involved with the *NRF* under Drieu's direction as late as the spring of 1942. See especially the letters of June 9 and 10, 1942, in Jean Paulhan, *Choix de lettres, II (1937–1945)*, 280.

15. Jean Paulhan, *Les Fleurs de Tarbes ou la terreur dans les lettres*, 23. This edition, published by Gallimard "Idées" in 1973 and edited by Jean-Claude Zylberstein, amends the 1941 text with a number of appendices.

16. For a fuller analysis of Paulhan's notions of rhetoric and communication, see the contributions by Silvio Yeschua, Michel Beaujour, and Frédéric Grover to Jacques Bersani, ed., *Jean Paulhan le souterrain* (Paris: UGE, 1976).

17. Maurice Blanchot, "Comment la littérature est-elle possible?" in *Faux pas*, 97. The essay was first published as a pamphlet in 1942. Texts carrying the same title appeared in late fall 1941 in *Journal des Débats*.

18. See Michael Syrotinski, "How Is Literature Possible?"

19. Maurice Blanchot, "Literature and the Right to Death," in *The Gaze of Orpheus and Other Literary Essays*, 21. Future quotations in the text are also from this translation. The essay in French is "La Littérature et le droit à la mort," in *La Part du feu*. 291–331. Early versions appeared in *Critique* 18 and 20 (November 1947 and January 1948).

20. The passage is taken from Mallarmé's "Crise de vers" in "Variations sur un sujet," in the Pléiade edition of the *Oeuvres complètes*, ed. Henri Mondor and G. Jean-Aubry (Paris: Gallimard, 1945), 368.

21. Maurice Blanchot, "Le Terrorisme, méthode de salut public," reprinted in *Gramma* 5 (1976): 61.

22. Kevin Newmark, "Resisting, Responding: Maurice Blanchot and the Promise of Writing," in *Beyond Symbolism: Textual History and the Future of Reading*, 178n. See also Andrzej Warminski's remarks on Blanchot's rewriting of Hegel's negative "in a different place, to the side," in "Epilogue. Dreadful Reading: Blanchot on Hegel," in *Readings in Interpretation* (Minneapolis: University of Minnesota Press, 1987), 185.

23. Maurice Blanchot, *The Step Not Beyond*, 15. Subsequent quotations of this text are also taken from Lynnette Nelson's translation.

24. When Timothy Clark wrote that Blanchot made language double upon itself, he inadvertently showed how close Blanchot was in 1973 to Roland Barthes, who had argued several years earlier that "to write" was an intransitive verb (Clark, *Derrida, Heidegger, Blanchot: Sources of Derrida's Notion and Practice of Literature*, 66).

25. Maurice Blanchot, *The Writing of the Disaster*, 75. Subsequent quotations of this text are taken from Ann Smock's translation.

26. Maurice Blanchot, "Les Intellectuels en question," 25; emphasis in the original.

27. Michel Surya, "Présentation du projet de *Revue Internationale*," 163.

28. Letter from Blanchot to Jean-Paul Sartre, December 2, 1960; cited in *Lignes* 11 (1990): 219–20.

29. Maurice Blanchot, "Our Responsibility," 250.

Six. Modernity in a Cold Climate

1. Roger Laporte and Bernard Noël, *Deux Lectures de Maurice Blanchot.*

2. See Walter A. Strauss, *Descent and Return: The Orphic Theme in Modern Literature* (Cambridge: Harvard University Press, 1971); and Jeffrey Mehlman, "Orphée scripteur: Blanchot, Rilke, Derrida."

3. Hal Foster, "Postmodernism: A Preface," xii.

4. The French verb *paraître* used by Simon appears throughout my translation in the passive mode, "to be seen."

5. See Jean-François Lyotard, "Tombeau de l'intellectuel," in *Tombeau de l'intellectuel et autres papiers* (Paris: Galilée, 1984). The text first appeared in *Le Monde* (October 8, 1983). An English translation appears as "Tomb of the Intellectual," in Jean-François Lyotard, *Political Writings*, trans. Bill Readings and Kevin Paul (Minneapolis: University of Minnesota Press, 1993), 3–7.

6. The texts are *Théorie de la littérature* (Paris: Seuil, 1965) and *La Conquête de l'Amérique* (Paris: Seuil, 1982), the latter translated into English by Richard Howard as *The Conquest of America: The Question of the Other* (New York: Harper & Row, 1984). Among his most recent books are *Nous et les autres: réflexion française sur la diversité humaine* (Paris: Seuil, 1989), translated as *On Human Diversity: Nationalism, Racism, and Exoticism in French Thought* (Cambridge: Harvard University Press, 1993), and *Les morales de l'histoire* (Paris: Editions Grasset & Fasquelle, 1991), translated as *The Morals of History* (Minneapolis: University of Minnesota Press, 1995).

7. Tzvetan Todorov, "Critics as Writers: Sartre, Blanchot, Barthes," in *Literature and Its Theorists: A Personal View of Twentieth-Century Criticism*, 55. Subsequent quotations of this work are also taken from Catherine Porter's translation.

8. See Jacques Derrida, "Force and Signification." The essay was first published in *Critique* 193–94 (June–July 1963). The full title of Rousset's book is *Forme et signification: Essais sur les structures littéraires de Corneille à Claudel* (Paris: José Corti, 1962).

9. Tzvetan Todorov, "NB," 676. Todorov stated that the authors he mentioned often used several of the practices in combination.

10. Paul de Man, "Impersonality in the Criticism of Maurice Blanchot," 61. The original French title was "Circularité de l'interprétation dans la critique de Maurice Blanchot" (Circularity of interpretation in the criticism of Maurice Blanchot).

11. See David Spurr, *The Rhetoric of Empire: Colonial Discourse in Journalism, Travel Writing, and Imperial Administration*, especially chapter 6 "Negation."

12. Jean-Pierre Azéma, "Vichy," 197.

13. Herman Lebovics, *True France: The Wars over Cultural Identity, 1900–1945,* 9.

Seven. Afterthoughts and Gray Zones

1. John Berger and Alain Tanner, *Jonah Who Will Be 25 in the Year 2000,* 38–40. See also Robin Bates, "Holes in the Sausage of History: May '68 as Absent Center in Three European Films."

2. Hayden White, *The Content of Form: Narrative Discourse and Historical Representation,* 20.

3. Slavoj Zizek, *The Sublime Object of Ideology,* 138.

4. Jonathan D. Spence, *The Memory Palace of Matteo Ricci,* 2.

5. Primo Levi, *The Drowned and the Saved,* 20.

6. Marguerite Duras, *The War: A Memoir,* 3. The complexity of recall is better conveyed by *La Douleur* (pain), the title Duras gave to the original version of the text in French.

7. Alice Kaplan, "Theweleit and Spiegelman: Of Men and Mice," 151.

8. Stephen Bann, *The Inventions of History,* 5.

9. Cited in Alan Riding, "France Will Remember Jews Sent to Nazi Camps by Vichy."

10. I take this definition from Michel Dreyfus, "Du côté des Archives," in *L'histoire en France* (Paris: La Découverte, 1990), 113–15.

11. Arlette Farge, *Le Goût de l'archive*, 9.

12. Alice Kaplan, "Working in the Archives," 103.

13. Alice Kaplan, "Introduction," in Alain Finkielkraut, *Remembering in Vain: The Klaus Barbie Trial and Crimes against Humanity*.

14. Geoffrey H. Hartman, "Public Memory and Modern Experience," 239.

15. Fredric Jameson, *Postmodernism, or the Cultural Logic of Late Capitalism* (Durham: Duke University Press, 1991).

16. Sigmund Freud, "Mourning and Melancholia," 245.

17. Eric Santner, *Stranded Objects: Mourning, Memory, and Film in Postwar Germany*, 4.

Works Cited

Adorno, Theodor W. *The Jargon of Authenticity.* Trans. Kurt Tarnowski and Frederic Will. Evanston: Northwestern University Press, 1973.

———. "What Does Coming to Terms with the Past Mean?" In Geoffrey H. Hartman, ed. *Bitburg in Moral and Political Perspective.* Bloomington: Indiana University Press, 1986. 114–29.

Anderson, Benedict. *Imagined Communities: Reflections on the Origin and Spread of Nationalism.* 2d ed. New York: Verso, 1991.

Anderson, Perry. *In the Tracks of Historical Materialism.* Chicago: University of Chicago Press, 1983.

———. *A Zone of Engagement.* New York: Verso, 1992.

Appiah, Kwame Anthony. *In My Father's House: Africa in the Philosophy of Culture.* New York: Oxford University Press, 1992.

Arendt, Hannah. "Heidegger at Eighty." In Günther Neske and Emil Kettering, eds. *Martin Heidegger and National Socialism: Questions and Answers.* New York: Paragon House, 1990. 207–17, 284–85.

Aron, Jean-Paul. *Les Modernes.* Paris: Gallimard, 1984.

Azéma, Jean-Pierre. "Vichy." In Michel Winock, ed. *Histoire de l'extrême droite en France.* Paris: Seuil, 1993. 191–213.

———, and François Bédarida, eds. *Vichy et les Français.* Paris: Fayard, 1992.

Bakhtin, Mikhail. *Problems of Dostoevsky's Poetics.* Trans. Caryl Emerson. Minneapolis: University of Minnesota Press, 1984.

Bann, Stephen. *The Clothing of Clio: A Study of the Representation of History in Nineteenth-Century Britain and France.* New York: Cambridge University Press, 1984.

———. *The Inventions of History: Essays on the Representation of the Past.* New York: St. Martin's Press, 1990.

Barthes, Roland. "The Discourse of History." In *The Rustle of Language.* Trans. Richard Howard. New York: Hill and Wang, 1986. 127–40.

———. "The Reality Effect." In *The Rustle of Language.* Trans. Richard Howard. New York: Hill and Wang, 1986. 141–48.

Bataille, Georges. *Visions of Excess: Selected Writings, 1927–1939.* Ed. Allan Stoekl. Minneapolis: University of Minnesota Press, 1985.

———. *Erotism: Death and Sensuality.* Trans. Mary Dalwood. San Francisco: City Lights, 1986.

Bates, Robin. "Holes in the Sausage of History: May '68 as Absent Center in Three European Films." *Cinema Journal* 24, no. 3 (Spring 1985): 24–42.

Bauman, Zygmunt. *Modernity and the Holocaust.* Ithaca: Cornell University Press, 1991.

Ben Jelloun, Tahar. *Hospitalité française: racisme et immigration maghrébine.* Paris: Seuil, 1984.

Berger, John, and Alain Tanner. *Jonah Who Will Be 25 in the Year 2000.* Trans. Michael Palmer. Berkeley: North Atlantic Books, 1987.

Bhabha, Homi K., ed. *Nation and Narration.* New York: Routledge, 1990.

Blanchot, Maurice. "La Culture française vue par un Allemand." *La Revue Française* 10 (March 27, 1932): 363–65.

———. "Comment la littérature est-elle possible?" Paris: José Corti, 1942.

———. *Faux pas*. Paris: Gallimard, 1943.

———. *L'Arrêt de mort*. Paris: Gallimard, 1948. *Death Sentence*. Trans. Lydia Davis. Barrytown, N.Y.: Station Hill Press, 1978.

———. *La Part du feu*. Paris: Gallimard, 1949.

———. *Lautréamont et Sade*. Paris: Minuit, 1949.

———. *Thomas l'obscur*. Paris: Gallimard, 1950. *Thomas the Obscure*. Trans. Thomas Lamberton. Barrytown, N.Y.: Station Hill Press, 1988.

———. *Le Ressassement éternel*. Paris: Minuit, 1951. In *Vicious Circles: Two Fictions and "After the Fact."* Trans. Paul Auster. Barrytown, N.Y.: Station Hill Press, 1985.

———. *L'Espace littéraire*. Paris: Gallimard, 1955. *The Space of Literature*. Trans. Ann Smock. Lincoln: University of Nebraska Press, 1982.

———. *Le Livre à venir*. Paris: Gallimard, 1959.

———. *L'attente l'oubli*. Paris: Gallimard, 1962.

———. *L'Entretien infini*. Paris: Gallimard, 1969. *The Infinite Conversation*. Trans. Susan Hanson. Minneapolis: University of Minnesota Press, 1992.

———. *L'Amitié*. Paris: Gallimard, 1971.

———. *La Folie du jour*. Montpellier: Fata Morgana, 1973. *The Madness of the Day*. Trans. Lydia Davis. Barrytown, N.Y.: Station Hill Press, 1985.

———. *Le pas au-delà*. Paris: Gallimard, 1973. *The Step Not Beyond*. Trans. Lynnette Nelson. Albany, N.Y.: State University of New York Press, 1992.

———. *L'écriture du désastre*. Paris: Gallimard, 1980. *The Writing of the Disaster*. Trans. Ann Smock. Lincoln: University of Nebraska Press, 1986.

———. *The Gaze of Orpheus and Other Literary Essays*. Trans. Lydia Davis. Barrytown, N.Y.: Station Hill Press, 1981.

———. *The Sirens' Song*. Gabriel Josipovici, ed. Trans. Sacha Rabinovitch. Bloomington: Indiana University Press, 1982.

———. *La Communauté inavouable*. Paris: Minuit, 1983. *The Unavowable Community*. Trans. José Pierre. Barrytown, N.Y.: Station Hill Press, 1988.

———. *Après coup précédé par "Le Ressassement éternel."* Paris: Minuit, 1983. *Vicious Circles: Two Fictions and "After the Fact."* Trans. Paul Auster. Barrytown, N.Y.: Station Hill Press, 1985.

———. "Les Intellectuels en question." *Le Débat* 29 (1984): 3–28.

———. *Michel Foucault tel que je l'imagine*. Montpellier: Fata Morgana, 1986. "Michel Foucault as I Imagine Him." In *Foucault/Blanchot*. Trans. Jeffrey Mehlman and Brian Massumi. New York: Zone Books, 1987. 61–109.

———. "Our Responsibility." Trans. Franklin Philip. In Jacques Derrida and Mustapha Tlili, eds. *For Nelson Mandela*. New York: Seaver Books, 1987. 247–51.

———. "Penser l'apocalypse." *Le Nouvel Observateur* (January 22–28, 1988): 43–45. "Thinking the Apocalypse." Trans. Paula Wissing. *Critical Inquiry* 15 (1989): 475–80.

Bourdieu, Pierre. *The Political Ontology of Martin Heidegger*. Trans. Peter Collier. Stanford: Stanford University Press, 1991.

Bruns, Gerald L. *Heidegger's Estrangements: Language, Truth, and Poetry in the Later Writings*. New Haven: Yale University Press, 1989.

Bubner, Rüdiger. *Modern German Philosophy*. Trans. Eric Matthews. New York: Cambridge University Press, 1981.

Camus, Albert. *The Fall*. Trans. Justin O'Brien. New York: Vintage, 1956.

Char, René. "Note à propos d'une deuxième lecture de 'La Perversion essentielle,' in *Le 14 juillet 1959.*" In *Oeuvres complètes.* Paris: Gallimard "Bibliothèque de la Pléiade," 1982. 744.

Clark, Timothy. *Derrida, Heidegger, Blanchot: Sources of Derrida's Notion and Practice of Literature.* New York: Cambridge University Press, 1992.

Conan, Eric, and Daniel Lindenberg. "Que faire de Vichy?" *Esprit* (May 1992): 5–15.

Curtius, Ernst Robert. *Einführung in die französische Kultur.* Berlin: Deutsche Verlagsanstalt, 1930. 2d ed. Bern: Francke, 1975. *Essai sur la France.* Trans. Jacques Benoist-Méchin. Paris: Grasset, 1932. *The Civilization of France.* Trans. Olive Wyon. New York: St. Martin's Press, 1932.

David, Catherine. "Heidegger et la pensée nazie." *Le Nouvel Observateur* (January 22–28, 1988): 41–42.

Davidson, Arnold I. "Questioning Heidegger: Opening the Debate." *Critical Inquiry* 15 (1989): 407–26.

de Man, Hendrik. *Après Coup: Mémoires.* Brussels and Paris: La Toison d'Or, 1941.

de Man, Paul. "Impersonality in the Criticism of Maurice Blanchot." In *Blindness and Insight: Essays in the Rhetoric of Contemporary Criticism.* 2d ed., revised. Minneapolis: University of Minnesota Press, 1983. 60–78.

———. "Literary History and Literary Modernity." In *Blindness and Insight: Essays in the Rhetoric of Contemporary Criticism.* 2d ed., revised. Minneapolis: University of Minnesota Press, 1983. 142–65.

———. *The Resistance to Theory.* Minneapolis: University of Minnesota Press, 1986.

———. *Wartime Journalism, 1939–1943.* Werner Hamacher, Neil Hertz, Thomas Keenan, eds. Lincoln: University of Nebraska Press, 1988.

———. "Heidegger Reconsidered." In *Paul de Man: Critical Writings, 1953–1978.* Ed. Lindsay Waters. Minneapolis: University of Minnesota Press, 1989. 102–6.

Derrida, Jacques. "Force and Signification." In *Writing and Difference.* Trans. Alan Bass. Chicago: University of Chicago Press, 1978. 3–30.

———. "Heidegger, l'enfer des philosophes." *Le Nouvel Observateur* November 6–12, 1987): 70–74.

———. *Of Spirit: Heidegger and the Question.* Trans. Geoffrey Bennington and Rachel Bowlby. Chicago: University of Chicago Press, 1989.

———. "Like the Sound of the Sea Deep within a Shell: Paul de Man's War." Trans. Peggy Kamuf. In Werner Hamacher, Neil Hertz, and Thomas Keenan, eds. *Responses: On Paul de Man's Wartime Journalism.* Lincoln: University of Nebraska Press, 1989. 127–64.

———, and Mustapha Tlili, eds. *For Nelson Mandela.* New York: Seaver Books, 1987.

Descombes, Vincent. *Modern French Philosophy.* Trans. L. Scott-Fox and J. M. Harding. New York: Cambridge University Press, 1980.

Dioudonnat, Pierre-Marie. *"Je Suis Partout," 1930–1944: Les Maurrassiens devant la tentation fasciste.* Paris: La Table Ronde, 1973.

Dirks, Nicholas B., ed. *Colonialism and Culture.* (Ann Arbor: University of Michigan Press, 1992.

Dodge, Peter. *Hendrik de Man: Socialist Critic of Marxism.* Princeton: Princeton University Press, 1979.

Duras, Marguerite. *La Maladie de la mort.* Paris: Minuit, 1983. *The Malady of Death.* Trans. Barbara Bray. New York: Grove/Atlantic, 1988.

———. *The War: A Memoir.* Trans. Barbara Bray. New York: Pantheon, 1986.

Estier, Claude. *Les Hebdomadaires de gauche.* Paris: Armand Colin, 1962.

Fanon, Frantz. *The Wretched of the Earth.* Trans. Constance Farrington. New York: Grove Press, 1968.

Farge, Arlette. *Le Goût de l'archive.* Paris: Seuil, 1989.

Farías, Victor. *Heidegger et le nazisme.* Trans. Myriam Benarroch and Jean-Baptiste Grasset. Paris: Verdier, 1987. *Heidegger and Nazism.* Trans. Paul Burrell and Gabriel R. Ricci. Philadelphia: Temple University Press, 1989.

Fédier, François. *Heidegger: Anatomie d'un scandale.* Paris: Robert Laffont, 1988.

Felman, Shoshana, and Dori Laub, eds. *Testimony: Crises of Witnessing in Literature, Psychoanalysis, and History.* New York: Routledge, 1992.

Ferro, Marc. "Les Oublis de l'histoire." *Communications* 49 (1989): 57–66.

Ferry, Luc, and Alain Renaut. *Heidegger and Modernity.* Trans. Franklin Philip. Chicago: University of Chicago Press, 1990.

Foster, Hal. "Postmodernism: A Preface." In *The Anti-Aesthetic: Essays on Postmodern Culture.* Port Townsend, Wash.: Bay Press, 1983. ix–xvi.

Foucault, Michel. "La Pensée du dehors." *Critique* 229 (1966): 523–46.

———. "Nietzsche, Genealogy, History." In Paul Rabinow, ed. *The Foucault Reader.* New York: Pantheon, 1984. 76–100.

Fouché, Pascal. *L'Edition française sous l'Occupation, 1940–1944.* 2 vols. Paris: Bibliothèque de Littérature Contemporaine, 1987.

Fraser, Nancy. *Unruly Practices: Power, Discourse, and Gender in Contemporary Social Theory.* Minneapolis: University of Minnesota Press, 1989.

Freud, Sigmund. "Mourning and Melancholia." In James Strachey, ed. *The Standard Edition of the Complete Psychological Works of Sigmund Freud.* London: Hogarth Press, 1953–74. 14:243–58.

———. *Project for a Scientific Psychology.* In James Strachey, ed. *The Standard Edition of the Complete Psychological Works of Sigmund Freud.* London: Hogarth Press, 1953–74. 1:283–387.

Friedländer, Saul. "The Road to Vichy." *New Republic* 15 (December 1986): 26–33.

———. "The End of Innovation? Contemporary Historical Consciousness and the 'End of History.'" *SubStance* 62–63 (1990): 29–36.

———, ed. *Probing the Limits of Representation: Nazism and the "Final Solution."* Cambridge: Harvard University Press, 1992.

———. "Trauma, Transference and 'Working through' in Writing the History of the *Shoah.*" *History & Memory* 4, no. 1 (1992): 39–59.

———. *Reflections of Nazism: An Essay on Kitsch and Death.* Trans. Thomas Weyr. Bloomington: Indiana University Press, 1993.

Fynsk, Christopher. *Heidegger: Thought and Historicity.* Ithaca: Cornell University Press, 1986.

Gadamer, Hans-Georg. "Back from Syracuse?" *Critical Inquiry* 15 (1989): 427–30.

Ginzburg, Carlo. "Checking the Evidence: The Judge and the Historian." *Critical Inquiry* 18 (1991): 79–92.

Gottfried, Paul. "Heidegger on Trial." *Telos* 74 (Spring 1988): 147–51.

Gottlieb, Anthony. "Heidegger for Fun and Profit." *New York Times Book Review* (January 7, 1990): 1, 22, 24.

Habermas, Jürgen. "Defusing the Past: A Politico-Cultural Tract." Trans. Thomas Levin. In Geoffrey H. Hartman, ed. *Bitburg in Moral and Political Perspective.* Bloomington: Indiana University Press, 1986. 43–51.

———. *The New Conservatism: Cultural Criticism and the Historians' Debate.* Ed. and trans. Shierry Weber Nicholsen. Cambridge: MIT Press, 1989.

Harries, Karsten. "Heidegger as a Political Thinker." In Michael Murray, ed. *Heidegger and Modern Philosophy: Critical Essays.* New Haven: Yale University Press, 1978. 304–28.

———. "Introduction." In Günther Neske and Emil Kettering, eds. *Martin Heidegger and National Socialism: Questions and Answers.* New York: Paragon House, 1990. xi–xl.

Hartman, Geoffrey H., ed. *Bitburg in Moral and Political Perspective*. Bloomington: Indiana University Press, 1986.
———. *Minor Prophecies: The Literary Essay in the Culture Wars*. Cambridge: Harvard University Press, 1991.
———. "Public Memory and Modern Experience." *Yale Journal of Criticism* 6, no. 2 (Fall 1993): 239–47.
Hegel, G. W. F. *The Phenomenology of Mind*. Trans. J. B. Baillie. New York: Harper and Row, 1967.
———. *Gesammelte Werke*, vol. 9. Wolfgang Bonsiepen and Reinhard Weede, eds. Hamburg: Fellix Meiner, 1980.
Heidegger, Martin. *Holzwege*. Frankfurt am Main: Klostermann, 1950.
———. *Being and Time*. Trans. John Macquarrie and Edward Robinson. New York: Harper and Row, 1962.
———. "The Origin of the Work of Art." In *Poetry, Language, Thought*. Trans. Alfred Hofstadter. New York: Harper and Row, 1971. 15–87.
———. "The Rectorial Address." In Günther Neske and Emil Kettering, eds. *Martin Heidegger and National Socialism: Questions and Answers*. New York: Paragon House, 1990. 5–14.
———. "The Rectorate 1933/34: Facts and Thoughts." Günther Neske and Emil Kettering, eds. *Martin Heidegger and National Socialism: Questions and Answers*. New York: Paragon House, 1990. 15–32.
Hobsbawm, Eric J. *Nations and Nationalism since 1780: Programme, Myth, Reality*. New York: Cambridge University Press, 1991.
Holland, Michael, and Patrick Rousseau. "Bibliographie I." *Gramma* 3/4 (1976): 224–45.
———, and ———. "Bibliographie II." *Gramma* 5 (1976): 124–32.
Hollier, Denis, ed. *The College of Sociology*. Trans. Betsy Wing. Minneapolis: University of Minnesota Press, 1988.
———, ed. *A New History of French Literature*. Cambridge: Harvard University Press, 1989.
Hunt, Lynn. "History beyond Social Theory." In David Carroll, ed. *The States of "Theory": History, Art, and Critical Discourse*. New York: Columbia University Press, 1990. 95–111.
———. "History as Gesture; or, The Scandal of History." In Jonathan Arac and Barbara Johnson, eds. *Consequences of Theory*. Baltimore: Johns Hopkins University Press, 1991. 91–107.
Husserl, Edmund. *The Phenomenology of Internal Time Consciousness*. Trans. James S. Churchill. Bloomington: Indiana University Press, 1971.
Jameson, Fredric. *The Political Unconscious: Narrative as a Socially Symbolic Act*. Ithaca: Cornell University Press, 1981.
———. *Postmodernism, or the Cultural Logic of Late Capitalism*. Durham: Duke University Press, 1991.
Judt, Tony. *Past Imperfect: French Intellectuals, 1944–1956*. Berkeley: University of California Press, 1992.
Kaes, Anton. *From Hitler to Heimat: The Return of History as Film*. Cambridge: Harvard University Press, 1989.
Kaplan, Alice Yaeger. *Reproductions of Banality: Fascism, Literature, and French Intellectual Life*. Minneapolis: University of Minnesota Press, 1986.
———. "Theweleit and Spiegelman: Of Men and Mice." In Barbara Kruger and Phil Mariani, eds. *Remaking History*. Seattle: Bay Press, 1989. 151–72.
———. "Working in the Archives." *Yale French Studies* 77 (1990): 103–16.
———. "Introduction." In Alain Finkielkraut. *Remembering in Vain: The Klaus Barbie Trial and Crimes against Humanity*. Trans. Roxanne Lapidus and Sima Godfrey. New York: Columbia University Press, 1992. ix–xxxvi.
———. *French Lessons: A Memoir*. Chicago: University of Chicago Press, 1993.

Kojève, Alexandre. *Introduction to the Reading of Hegel.* Trans. James H. Nichols, Jr. New York: Basic Books, 1969.

Kundera, Milan. *The Book of Laughter and Forgetting.* Trans. Michael Henry Heim. New York: Penguin, 1981.

LaCapra, Dominick. *History and Criticism.* Ithaca: Cornell University Press, 1985.

———. "The Personal, the Political and the Textual: Paul de Man as Object of Transference." *History and Memory* 4, no. 1 (1992): 5–38.

Lacoue-Labarthe, Philippe. *Typography: Mimesis, Philosophy, Politics.* Christopher Fynsk, ed. Cambridge: Harvard University Press, 1989.

———. *Heidegger, Art, and Politics.* Trans. Chris Turner. Cambridge, Mass: Basil Blackwell, 1990.

———, and Jean-Luc Nancy. *Rejouer le politique.* Paris: Galilée, 1981.

Langer, Lawrence L. *Holocaust Testimonies: The Ruins of Memory.* New Haven: Yale University Press, 1991.

Laporte, Roger, and Bernard Noël. *Deux Lectures de Maurice Blanchot.* Montpellier: Fata Morgana, 1973.

Le Goff, Jacques. *Histoire et mémoire.* Paris: Gallimard, 1988.

Lebovics, Herman. *True France: The Wars over Cultural Identity, 1900–1945.* Ithaca: Cornell University Press, 1992.

Leroy, Géraldi, and Anne Roche. *Les Ecrivains et le Front Populaire.* Paris: Presses de la Fondation Nationale des Sciences Politiques, 1986.

Levi, Primo. *The Drowned and the Saved.* Trans. Raymond Rosenthal. New York: Vintage, 1989.

Lévinas, Emmanuel. *Sur Maurice Blanchot.* Montpellier: Fata Morgana, 1975.

———. "As If Consenting to Horror." Trans. Paula Wissing. *Critical Inquiry* 15 (1989): 485–88.

———. "Admiration and Disappointment: A Conversation with Philippe Nemo." In Günther Neske and Emil Kettering, eds. *Martin Heidegger and National Socialism: Questions and Answers.* New York: Paragon House, 1990. 149–53.

Loubet del Bayle, Jean-Louis. *Les Non-conformistes des années 30.* Paris: Seuil, 1969.

Löwith, Karl. *Mein Leben in Deutschland vor und nach 1933: ein Bericht.* Reinhart Kosellek, ed. Stuttgart: Metzler, 1986.

———. "Last Meeting with Heidegger." In Günther Neske and Emil Kettering, eds. *Martin Heidegger and National Socialism: Questions and Answers.* New York: Paragon House, 1990. 157–60.

Lyotard, Jean-François. *The Postmodern Condition: A Report on Knowledge.* Trans. Geoff Bennington and Brian Massumi. Minneapolis: University of Minnesota Press, 1984.

———. *The Differend: Phrases in Dispute.* Trans. Georges Van Den Abbeele. Minneapolis: University of Minnesota Press, 1988.

———. *Heidegger and "the jews."* Trans. Andreas Michel and Mark Roberts. Minneapolis: University of Minnesota Press, 1990.

Maier, Charles S. *The Unmasterable Past: History, Holocaust, and German National Identity.* Cambridge: Harvard University Press, 1988.

Megill, Allan. *Prophets of Extremity: Nietzsche, Heidegger, Foucault, Derrida.* Berkeley: University of California Press, 1985.

Mehlman, Jeffrey. "Orphée scripteur: Blanchot, Rilke, Derrida." *Poétique* 20 (1974): 458–82.

———. "Blanchot at *Combat:* Of Literature and Terror." In *Legacies: Of Anti-Semitism in France.* Minneapolis: University of Minnesota Press, 1983. 6–22, 114–19.

———. "Deconstruction, Literature, History: The Case of *L'Arrêt de mort.*" *Proceedings of the Northeastern University Center for Literary Studies* 2 (1984): 33–53.

———. "Prosopopeia Revisited." *Romanic Review* 81 (1990): 137–43.

Murray, Michael, ed. *Heidegger and Modern Philosophy.* New Haven: Yale University Press, 1978.

Nancy, Jean-Luc. "La Communauté désoeuvrée." *Aléa* 4 (1983): 11–49.

Neske, Günther, and Emil Kettering, eds. *Martin Heidegger and National Socialism: Questions and Answers.* Trans. Lisa Harries and Joachim Neugroschel. New York: Paragon House, 1990.

Newmark, Kevin. *Beyond Symbolism: Textual History and the Future of Reading.* Ithaca: Cornell University Press, 1991.

Niethammer, Lutz. *Posthistoire: Has History Come to an End?* Trans. Patrick Camiller. New York: Verso, 1992.

Nora, Pierre. "Between Memory and History: *Les Lieux de mémoire.*" *Representations* 26 (1989): 7–25.

Norris, Christopher. *What's Wrong with Postmodernism: Critical Theory and the Ends of Philosophy.* Baltimore: Johns Hopkins University Press, 1990.

Ott, Hugo. *Heidegger: A Political Life.* Trans. Allan Blunden. New York: Basic Books, 1993.

Palmier, Jean-Michel. "Heidegger et le national-socialisme." In Michel Haar, ed. *Cahier de l'Herne: Heidegger.* Paris: Livre de Poche, 1983. 409–47.

Parisis, Jean-Marc. "Blanchot et ses voisins." *Le Nouvel Observateur* (March 20–26, 1987): 55.

Paulhan, Jean. *Les Fleurs de Tarbes ou la terreur dans les lettres.* Ed. Jean-Claude Zylberstein. Paris: Gallimard "Idées," 1973.

———. *Choix de lettres, II (1937–1945).* Paris: Gallimard, 1992.

Paxton, Robert. *Vichy France: Old Guard and New Order, 1940–44.* New York: Norton, 1975. Original publication, New York: Knopf, 1972.

Poirié, François. *Emmanuel Lévinas.* Lyon: La Manufacture, 1987.

Rapaport, Herman. "Literature and the Hermeneutics of Detection." *L'Esprit Créateur* 26, no. 2 (Summer 1986): 48–59.

Renan, Ernest. "What Is a Nation?" In Homi K. Bhabha, ed. *Nation and Narration.* New York: Routledge, 1990. 8–22.

Riding, Alan. "France Will Remember Jews Sent to Nazi Camps by Vichy." *New York Times* (February 5, 1993): A6.

Robin, Régine. "The Intellectuals of the 1930s." *Annals of Scholarship* 8, no. 1 (1991): 1–8.

Rochette, Philippe. "L'Etat français, celui de Vichy, n'était pas la République." *Libération* (July 15, 1992): 8.

Ronell, Avital. "The Differends of Man." *Diacritics* 19, no. 3–4 (Fall-Winter 1989): 63–75.

Rorty, Richard. "Taking Philosophy Seriously." *New Republic* 11 (April 1988): 31–34.

Ross, Kristin. "Two Versions of the Everyday." *L'Esprit Créateur* 24, no. 3 (Fall 1984): 29–37.

Roth, Michael S. *Knowing and History: Appropriations of Hegel in Twentieth-Century France.* Ithaca: Cornell University Press, 1988.

Rousso, Henry. *The Vichy Syndrome: History and Memory in France since 1944.* Trans. Arthur Goldhammer. Cambridge: Harvard University Press, 1991.

Rubenstein, Diane. *What's Left? The Ecole Normale Supérieure and the Right.* Madison: University of Wisconsin Press, 1990.

Santner, Eric. *Stranded Objects: Mourning, Memory, and Film in Postwar Germany.* Ithaca: Cornell University Press, 1990.

Schneeberger, Guido. *Nachlese zu Heidegger.* Bern: Suhr, 1962.

Scott, Joan Wallach. *Gender and the Politics of History.* New York: Columbia University Press, 1988.

Shattuck, Roger. *The Innocent Eye: On Modern Literature and the Arts.* New York: Farrar, Straus & Giroux, 1984.

Shaviro, Steven. *Passion and Excess: Blanchot, Bataille, and Literary Theory.* Tallahassee: Florida State University Press, 1990.

———. "Complicity and Forgetting." *MLN* 105 (1990): 819–32.

Sheehan, Thomas. "Heidegger and the Nazis." *New York Review of Books* (June 16, 1988): 38–47.

Silverman, Maxim. *Deconstructing the Nation: Immigration, Racism, and Citizenship in Modern France.* New York: Routledge, 1992.

Sirinelli, Jean-François, ed. *Histoire des droites en France.* Paris: Gallimard, 1992.

Smock, Ann. "Disastrous Responsibility." *L'Esprit Créateur* 24, no. 3 (Fall 1984): 5–20.

Sorlin, Pierre. *European Cinemas, European Societies: 1939–1990.* New York: Routledge, 1991.

Spence, Jonathan D. *The Memory Palace of Matteo Ricci.* New York: Penguin, 1985.

"Der Spiegel Interview with Martin Heidegger." In Günther Neske and Emil Kettering, eds. *Martin Heidegger and National Socialism: Questions and Answers.* New York: Paragon House, 1990. 15–32.

Spivak, Gayatri Chakravorty. "Introduction. Subaltern Studies: Deconstructing Historiography." In Ranajit Guha and Gayatri Chakravorty Spivak, eds. *Selected Subaltern Studies.* New York: Oxford University Press, 1988. 3–34.

———. "Neocolonialism and the Secret Agent of Knowledge." *Oxford Literary Review* 13 (1991): 220–51.

Spurr, David. *The Rhetoric of Empire: Colonial Discourse in Journalism, Travel Writing, and Imperial Administration.* Durham: Duke University Press, 1993.

Steiner, George. "Heidegger, Again." *Salmagundi* 82–83 (1989): 31–55.

Stern, Fritz. *Dreams and Delusions: The Drama of German History.* New York: Knopf, 1987.

Sternhell, Zeev. *Neither Right nor Left: Fascist Ideology in France.* Trans. David Maisel. Berkeley: University of California Press, 1986.

———. "The Political Culture of Nationalism." In Robert Tombs, ed. *Nationhood and Nationalism in France: From Boulangism to the Great War, 1889–1918.* New York: Harper Collins, 1991. 22–38.

Stoekl, Allan. *Politics, Writing, Mutilation: The Cases of Bataille, Blanchot, Roussel, Leiris, and Ponge.* Minneapolis: University of Minnesota Press, 1985.

Surya, Michel. "Présentation du projet de *Revue Internationale.*" *Lignes* 11 (1990): 161–66.

———. *Georges Bataille, la mort à l'oeuvre.* Rev. ed. Paris: Gallimard, 1992.

Syrotinski, Michael. "How Is Literature Possible?" In Denis Hollier, ed. *A New History of French Literature.* Cambridge: Harvard University Press, 1989. 953–58.

"Témoignage de M. François Walter." In Anne Roche and Christian Tarting, eds. *Des Années Trente: groupes et ruptures.* Paris: Editions du Central National de la Recherche Scientifique, 1986. 69–72.

Todorov, Tzvetan. *Literature and Its Theorists: A Personal View of Twentieth-Century Criticism.* Trans. Catherine Porter. Ithaca: Cornell University Press, 1987.

———. "NB." *Times Literary Supplement* (June 17–23, 1988): 676, 685.

Tombs, Robert, ed. *Nationhood and Nationalism in France: From Boulangism to the Great War, 1889–1918.* New York: Harper Collins, 1991.

Touchard, André. *Tendances politique dans la vie française depuis 1789.* Paris: Hachette, 1960.

Truffaut, François. *The Films of My Life.* Trans. Leonard Mayhew. New York: Simon and Schuster, 1978.

Tucker, Robert. *The Fascist Ego: A Political Biography of Robert Brasillach.* Berkeley: University of California Press, 1975.

Ulmer, Gregory L. "The Post-Age." *Diacritics* 11, no. 3 (Fall 1981): 39–56.

Vidal-Naquet, Pierre. *Les Juifs, la mémoire et le présent.* Paris: Maspero, 1980.

———. "Le Défi de la Shoah à l'histoire." *Temps Modernes* 507 (October 1988): 71.

———. "Theses on Revision." In François Furet, ed. *Unanswered Questions: Nazi Germany and the Genocide of the Jews.* New York: Schocken, 1989. 304–19.

———. *Assassins of Memory: Essays on the Denial of the Holocaust.* Trans. Jeffrey Mehlman. New York: Columbia University Press, 1992.

Weber, Eugen. *Action Française: Royalism and Reaction in Twentieth-Century France.* Stanford: Stanford University Press, 1962.

———. *My France: Politics, Culture, Myth.* Cambridge: Harvard University Press, 1991.

Weil, Eric. "Le Cas Heidegger." *Temps modernes* 22 (July 1947): 128–38.

White, Hayden. *The Content of the Form: Narrative Discourse and Historical Representation.* Baltimore: Johns Hopkins University Press, 1987.

Wolin, Richard. "The French Heidegger Debate." *New German Critique* 45 (1988): 135–61.

———. *The Politics of Being: The Political Thought of Martin Heidegger.* New York: Columbia University Press, 1990.

———, ed. *The Heidegger Controversy: A Critical Reader.* Rev. ed. Cambridge: MIT Press, 1992.

Young, James E. *Writing and Rewriting the Holocaust: Narrative and the Consequences of Interpretation.* Bloomington: Indiana University Press, 1990.

———. *The Texture of Memory: Holocaust Memorials and Meaning.* New Haven: Yale University Press, 1993.

Young, Robert. *White Mythologies: Writing History and the West.* New York: Routledge, 1990.

Young-Bruehl, Elisabeth. *Hannah Arendt: For the Love of the World.* New Haven: Yale University Press, 1982.

Zimmerman, Michael E. *Heidegger's Confrontation with Modernity: Technology, Politics, Art.* Bloomington: Indiana University Press, 1990.

Zizek, Slavoj. *The Sublime Object of Ideology.* New York: Verso, 1990.

Index

Steven Ungar is professor of French and chair of the program in comparative literature at the University of Iowa. He is author of *Roland Barthes: The Professor of Desire* (1983) and the coeditor (with Betty McGraw) of *Signs in Culture: Roland Barthes Today* (1989); he is also an editor of *SubStance*. He has written widely on literature, philosophy, and history in twentieth-century France.